PEOPLE OF INDIA

# CHANDIGARH

VOLUME XVII

# PEOPLE OF INDIA

## NATIONAL SERIES

| | | |
|---|---|---|
| VOL. I | PEOPLE OF INDIA | AN INTRODUCTION |
| VOL. II | PEOPLE OF INDIA | THE SCHEDULED CASTES |
| VOL. III | PEOPLE OF INDIA | THE SCHEDULED TRIBES |
| VOL. IV | PEOPLE OF INDIA | ALL COMMUNITIES |
| VOL. V | PEOPLE OF INDIA | ALL COMMUNITIES |
| VOL. VI | PEOPLE OF INDIA | ALL COMMUNITIES |
| VOL. VII | PEOPLE OF INDIA | IDENTITY, ECOLOGY, SOCIAL ORGANIZATION, ECONOMY, DEVELOPMENT PROCESS AND LINKAGES: A QUANTITATIVE PROFILE |
| VOL. VIII | PEOPLE OF INDIA | COMMUNITIES, SEGMENTS, SYNONYMS SURNAMES AND TITLES |
| VOL. IX | PEOPLE OF INDA | LANGUAGES AND SCRIPTS |
| VOL. X | PEOPLE OF INDIA | THE BIOLOGICAL VARIATION IN INDIAN POPULATIONS |
| VOL. XI | PEOPLE OF INDIA | AN ANTHROPOLOGICAL ATLAS |

## STATE SERIES

| | |
|---|---|
| VOL. XII | ANDAMAN AND NICOBAR ISLANDS |
| VOL. XIII | ANDHRA PRADESH |
| VOL. XIV | ARUNACHAL PRADESH |
| VOL. XV | ASSAM |
| VOL. XVI | BIHAR |
| VOL. XVII | CHANDIGARH |
| VOL. XVIII | DADRA AND NAGAR HAVELI |
| VOL. XIX | DAMAN AND DIU |
| VOL. XX | DELHI |
| VOL. XXI | GOA |
| VOL. XXII | GUJARAT |
| VOL. XXIII | HARYANA |
| VOL. XXIV | HIMACHAL PRADESH |
| VOL. XXV | JAMMU AND KASHMIR |
| VOL. XXVI | KARNATAKA |
| VOL. XXVII | KERALA |
| VOL. XXVIII | LAKSHADWEEP |
| VOL. XXIX | MADHYA PRADESH |
| VOL. XXX | MAHARASHTRA |
| VOL. XXXI | MANIPUR |
| VOL. XXXII | MEGHALAYA |
| VOL. XXXIII | MIZORAM |
| VOL. XXXIV | NAGALAND |
| VOL. XXXV | ORISSA |
| VOL. XXXVI | PONDICHERRY |
| VOL. XXXVII | PUNJAB |
| VOL. XXXVIII | RAJASTHAN |
| VOL. XXXIX | SIKKIM |
| VOL. XL | TAMIL NADU |
| VOL. XLI | TRIPURA |
| VOL. XLII | UTTAR PRADESH |
| VOL. XLIII | WEST BENGAL |

PEOPLE OF INDIA

# CHANDIGARH

VOLUME XVII

*General Editor*
K.S. SINGH

*Editors*
V. BHALLA
SWARAN SINGH

ANTHROPOLOGICAL SURVEY OF INDIA

MANOHAR
1997

ISBN 81-7304-119-9

*Published on behalf of ASI by Ajay Kumar Jain*
*Manohar Publishers & Distributors, 2/6 Ansari Road, Daryaganj, New Delhi 110 002*

*Typeset by AJ Software Publishing Co. Pvt. Ltd, 305 Durga Chambers,*
*1333 D.B. Gupta Road, Karol Bagh, New Delhi 110 005*

*Printed at Rajkamal Electric Press, G.T. Karnal Road, Delhi 110009*

# CONTENTS

# A NOTE ON THE SERIES

There exists an information gap on a very large number of communities in India, and whatever information exists on them is scanty or needs to be updated. The Anthropological Survey of India (ASI) launched a project on the People of India on 2 October 1985. The objective of the project was to generate a brief, descriptive anthropological profile of all the communities of India, the impact on them of change and development processes, and the links that bring them together. This was in accordance with the objectives of the ASI, established in December 1945. The ASI has been pursuing bio-cultural research among different population groups from its eight regional centres. Its objectives have been redefined in the policy resolution, adopted in 1985, which commits this organization to the survey of the human surface of India.

The identification of the communities and their listing have had a long history which started from the early period of our history, with Manu. Regional lists of communities figured in Sanskrit works. Medieval chronicles contained a description of communities located in various parts of the country. Listings in the colonial period were undertaken on an extensive scale after 1806. The process gathered momentum in course of the censuses from 1881 to 1941. In our compilation of the lists of the communities of India under the 'People of India' project, we drew upon ethnographic surveys, the lists of Scheduled Castes and Scheduled Tribes, drawn up by the Government of India; the lists of backward classes prepared by the Backward Classes Commissions, set up by various state governments; and the list that exists in the Mandal Commission Report. We were able to put together about 6,748 communities at the start. This list was taken to the field, tested and checked, and finally 4,635 communities were identified and studied.

Unlike the surveys in the colonial period, which covered British India and a few princely states, our project covers the entire country, bringing within its ambit such parts that had not been ethnographically surveyed earlier or where the survey had been done in a perfunctory way. Each state and union territory was treated as a unit of study. It was decided to start with the investigation of the least-known communities, and then move on to a field study of the lesser-known and better-known ones. Investigators for the survey were identified for each area on the basis of their experience and expertise. Teams of investigators of the survey, as well as local scholars, were set up for each state and union territory to plan the surveys, seek the co-operation of local scholars, generate and evaluate findings, etc. Later, editorial boards consisting of local scholars—one or more of these were nominated as co-editors for each local volume—were set up for each state and union territory. We sought the co-operation of the state governments in implementing the project, and this we received in ample measure, particularly from the welfare and backward classes, departments of the state governments, local officers of the Census of India, tribal research institutes, university departments of anthropology, other departments of local universities, etc. Local scholars participated enthusiastically in our project as well as in the seminars held by us.

The progress in the investigation and coverage of communities, from 2 October 1985 to 31 March 1992, was steady and impressive. We were able to identify, locate and study 4,635 communities in all the states and union territories of India out of the 6,748 listed initially. As many as 600 scholars participated in this project, including 197 from 26 institutions. About 100 workshops and rounds of discussions were held in all the states and union territories, and in these about 3,000 scholars participated. The investigators spent 26,510 days in the field, which works out to 5.5 days per community studied in the various states and union territories of India. Our scholars interviewed a large number of people, out of whom we have recorded only the key informants, i.e. 24,951. This works out to about 5 'informed' informants per community. Of these informants, 4,981 were women. Our instruction to the investigators was to study a community at two or three places, and in at least two or three cultural regions into which the larger states of India were divided. Interviews were conducted in connection with the study of the communities in 3,581 villages, mostly multi-community villages, and in 1,011 towns and cities, spread over almost all the districts of India, i.e. 421 districts and 91 cultural regions. We were able, thus, to study, on an average, a community at about two places. It should be noted that most of the smaller communities could be studied only at one place since they are not located in more than one area.

A major achievement of this project was the preparation of cartographic maps showing the distribution of the communities and the location where they were studied. About 4,000 maps were prepared. Yet another achievement was the visual documentation of the people of India as part of the field operations. About 21,362 photographs were generated, most of them in black & white, and a substantial number in colour, by amateur photographers.

At an early stage of our project in March 1985 we decided to transfer the data to a computer. We were subsequently able to develop probably the first software in the country—and one of the first in the world—in ethnography, in close collaboration with the National Informatics Centre. From 28 May 1988, we started transferring the quantitative data collected in computer format to floppies. Simultaneously, the transfer of descriptive data (abstracts, etc.) on to the computer also started at almost all the regional centres. We succeeded in computerizing an enormous mass of data, and also in producing the first results of univariate analysis, by March 1990.

The descriptive material, running into 120 manuscript volumes, and the quantitative data contained in 157 diskettes, was released on 1 October 1990, by Sri Chimanbhai Mehta, Minister of State for Human Resource Development, in the presence of a distinguished audience in Delhi, for use by scholars at the Nehru Memorial Museum & Library, and at eight regional centres of the ASI.

The phase of more elaborate analysis started in July 1991, in collaboration with the Centre for Ecological Sciences, Indian Institute of Science, Bangalore. This resulted in a voluminous output of analysed data, which have been presented in a comprehensive matrix consisting of the four categories of populations—the constitutional, religious, occupational and locational. These sets of data, together with a map, were released by Shri Arjun Singh, the then Minister of Human Resource Development, on 24 December 1991. The last workshop on the People of India project was held at the Indian Institute of Social and Economic Change in Bangalore, where the preliminary results of the analysis, presented by the ASI, were discussed by distinguished scholars.

It should be noted that the study of communities has been conducted in 3,581 villages and 1,011 towns situated in 421 districts of the States and Union Territories of India. The information was collected from about 25,000 of the 'learned' informants by our scholars, 500 of them, over the period 1985 to 1992. Therefore, the observations relate to this limited time-frame and to the universe of the ethnographic project titled People of India. The percentages relate strictly to the responses made by the informants to the questionnaire contained in the schedule guideline and computer format, and to the queries made by the investigators at the places of investigation. The responses have been supplemented with the observations of the investigators, the secondary material has been checked and cross-checked at many levels with other sources of information by scholars, particularly local scholars.

We are presenting the material published under the People of India project in two parts which are interrelated. The first consists of the ten-volume national series, five of which contain an abstract on all communities across the length and breadth of the country. The data generated in this respect has been strengthened by the addition of information from census and other secondary sources. These volumes include two on the Scheduled Castes and Scheduled Tribes, prepared as part of the celebration of Dr. B.R. Ambedkar's birth centenary; three of all the communities of India, and two containing data on the languages and biological structures of Indian population. The remaining volumes contain description of the quantitative profile, communities and their segments, community-specific languages and the biological structure of Indian populations.

The second part comprises the state/union territory volumes based on a detailed write-up on each community of India. The contributors of the national volumes on the SC, ST and all communities are listed in the last volume, Volume VI. The Glossary given in Volume VI is common to all the national volumes. At the end of each account we have given references to the texts from which we have quoted, or references for further reading. This is only illustrative. An exhaustive Bibliography appears at the end of the national volumes, in Volume VI.

The Oxford University Press has been publishing the national volumes. A consortium of publishers has been set up to publish the material on states and union territories. Seven volumes each for the northern states, southern states and the islands, the central and western states are being published respectively by M/S Manohar Publishers & Distributors (New Delhi), M/S Affiliated East-West Press Private Limited (Madras) and M/S Popular Prakashan Pvt. Ltd. (Bombay). The eleven volumes on the north-eastern and eastern states are being published by M/S Seagull Books Private Limited (Calcutta), which has already published the introductory national volume.

I trust the series on the People of India, which is based on a comprehensive anthropological survey of the country, will be found useful by all sections of our people, including students, researchers, teachers, social activists, administrators and political leaders. I hope we have laid the groundwork for a comprehensive ethnography of the people of India which needs to be continually updated and built upon by successive generations of researchers and scholars.

K.S. SINGH

# FOREWORD

Chandigarh derives its name from the place where the temple of Chandi is situated, a few kilometres away. Chandigarh is an extension of the ethnographic scenario of north-west India, particularly of Punjab and its eco-cultural region, Malwa. However, Chandigarh has evolved its own identity during the recent past. The villages of the Union Territory where the People of India project was conducted still retain their identity in spite of the urban influences emanating from the adjacent city. The project covered for the first time all communities (42) of Chandigarh, particularly village dwellers.

The castes and scheduled castes in Chandigarh, which are generally part of the bio-cultural structure of the north-western populations, have been studied for their various biological traits. Colour blindness varies from 2.75 per cent to 10.00 per cent in the populations. G6PD deficiency is relatively high (5.20-9.62 per cent). The B gene preponderates (22.40-30.72 per cent) over the A (13.16-30.42 per cent), M gene shows a wide range of occurrence (52.00-88.23 per cent). The population of Chandigarh show high frequency of $R_1$ haplotype and a low incidence of r haplotype (15.10-25.00 per cent). $Ho^1$ gene occur in 18.50-27.10 per cent of population, $T6^B$ gene is reported from Chandigarh (0.00-1.39 per cent).

In the Union Territory nine different languages are spoken: Banjari, Hindi, Kangri, Marwari, Pahari, Pasto, Punjabi, Sansi and Urdu. A majority of the communities (24) speak Hindi and Punjabi (17), followed by Urdu (4). There are as many as sixteen communities who are linguistically heterogeneous, i.e. speaking more than one language. The heterolingual communities are mainly those who speak Hindi and Punjabi. The Sirkiband speak either Pahari or Punjabi, and the Bazigar speak either Pasto or Punjabi. The Sansi language spoken by the Sansi/Sansiya is an unclassified language. Pasto belongs to the Indo-Iranian subfamily. All other languages are Indo-Aryan.

According to the 1981 census, Hindi is spoken by the largest number of persons (249,721) followed by Punjabi (182,635 ). Urdu is spoken by 3,118 persons. Hindi, Punjabi, English and Urdu are languages that are commonly used for bilingual communication. Among the Hindi speakers, 73,914 persons are bilingual in Urdu. Among the Punjabi speakers, 60,258 persons are bilingual in Hindi. A large number, 58,069 persons are bilingual in English and 2,010 persons in Urdu.

Devanagari and Gurmukhi scripts are used in the Union Territory.

Like other parts of north-western India, there is a larger concentration of the scheduled castes in Chandigarh (9). The next cluster of communities represents the artisan groups, among whom the Sikligar and Tarkhan are typical. With growing demands many artisan groups from elsewhere, like the Lohar and Barhai, have gone into this area and have been working side by side the traditional artisans like the Sikligar, etc. Some of these groups and service castes are divided into Hindu and Muslim—and also Sikh—segments, with different stories of origin and relationship prevalent now.

The third category of communities is that of agriculturists. The Jats including the Jat Sikhs are dominant, followed by the Kamboj and Saini, all typical groups of north-western India. Yet another cluster of communities is engaged in business and trade such as the Bhaṭias, Soods and Banias.

As elsewhere, in this part almost all communities have reported diversification of occupation on a large scale, with the economic growth, and progress in agriculture, animal husbandry, poultry and small scale industries. There are also expanding opportunities for employment as labour, in government and private service and so on. For example, the Labana are no longer trading in salt but have settled down to cultivation and animal husbandry. The Noongars, again a community associated with extraction of salt have taken to selling vegetable and fruit and are engaged in labour. But the Chamars, the traditional leather workers, are also now engaged in cattle-rearing, agriculture and labour. The Chhimba, traditionally dyers of cloth, are now tailors. The Dhanuks described as hunters in ethnographic literature are now engaged in weaving, scavenging and other forms of labour. Gujjars have settled down to cultivation besides pursuing their traditional occupation in some form or the other. But there are many small communities like the Mirasis who continue with their traditional occupation.

With economic prosperity the levels of aspiration and the range of self perception among many communities have expanded. For example, the Kamboj and Soods not only now perceive their linkages stretching back in time but also spread over a large part of the country and even South Asia.

In this urban situation, a majority of the communities (30) identify themselves 'regionally' across the states, followed by those who identify themselves 'locally' where they feel they belong (26); some identify 'nationally' (15). For most of the communities whose members are mostly literate, ethnographic accounts (26) and historical accounts (19) exist. Twenty-five communities have migrated to their present habitat from neighbouring states.

Chandigarh shares with the rest of the north-west its food and food habits. Wheat is the staple cereal (41), along with rice (32). Maize is taken in winter (35). The cereals are supplemented with gram (36), *urad* (36), *moong* (34), *moth* (24) and *maswe* (35). Mustard oil (34) and groundnut oil (22) are used for cooking. Peas and beans (27) and roots and tubers (24) are eaten. The intake of vegetables is moderate (29). Most communities are returned as 'occasional' non-vegetarians (32) which is higher (76.97 per cent) than the national average of 37.20 per cent. Alcoholic drinks mainly procured from the market (34) are consumed by menfolk (37) on a scale higher than the national average (80.95 per cent against 37.20 per cent). The proportion of those consuming milk (40) and milk products (39) is very high. As an urban centre, with high purchasing power, Chandigarh records a higher level of consumption.

As in other parts of the north-west, internal divisions are reported among 39 communities in villages. These divisions regulate marriage and in some cases indicate status and descent. The communities invoke the norm of community endogamy (40) but intercommunity marriage is also reported (6). Consanguinity exists in a very low frequency though adult marriage is the practice (38), child marriage and *gaona* surprisingly has been reported among 3 communities. Mates are chosen by negotiation (39). Monogamy is the rule. Polyandry (fraternal) is reported among the Sikligar and Teli and non-fraternal polyandry in one community among them. Polygyny is reported for 3 communities.

The rule of residence is patrilocal (41). People tend to live in nuclear families (40) and vertically extended families (24). Male equigeniture is the rule of inheritance (31), and the eldest son succeeds to the position of authority (42) in family. The status of women is generally considered low (30) even though they play an important role in social functions (32), rituals (35), religious ceremonies (25) and economy (23).

In the urban centres, the population is mainly engaged in government service (22), self employment (15) and labour (21). A few are settled cultivators (6). Bonded labour exists among some communities such as the Penja, Lohar, Balmiki and Sikligar. Caste councils exercise social control (13) and the Panchayats implement welfare measures (23).

Most of the communities profess Hinduism (30) followed by Sikhism (15). The latter has a higher percentage (35.71 per cent against the national average of 2.30 per cent). Only 7 communities follow Islam. The 1991 Census shows a very steep rise in the Muslim population.

Folk/oral traditions (36) akin to those of Punjab and Haryana are reported from the villages of the Union Territory.

Chandigarh has the highest level of literacy. The administration has provided medical facilities, drinking water and employment, which are generally perceived as well distributed among all communities.

K.S. SINGH

# ACKNOWLEDGEMENTS

We thank our informants who extended co-operation to the field investigators. We express our thanks to the Administrator, Union Territory, Chandigarh, for his keen interest in the project and to his officers for extending all help to our investigators. We thank the Director, Census Operation, Union Territory of Chandigarh, for providing necessary library facilities to the research scholars during their fieldwork. We particularly thank Prof. V. Bhalla, and the fellows Mrs. Nupur Pathak, Miss Achala Sood, Miss Sushil Kumari and Miss Kulwinder Kaur, of the Department of Anthropology, Panjab University, and Dr. K.C. Kayastha and Virinder Singh of Department of Sociology, Panjab University Chandigarh who made their contributions to the project.

We express our sincere thanks to the Vice-Chancellor and Head of the Human Biology Department, Punjabi University, Patiala, for collaborating with the Anthropological Survey of India in organizing a workshop on the People of India: Chandigarh, from 21 to 23 August 1989 at Patiala. We acknowledge the photographs provided by Sh. Surinderjit Singh. We express our thanks to Dr. R. Malhotra, Anthropologist (P), Dr. A.K. Bhatia Asst. Anthropologist (P), Sh. A.R. Sankhyan, Research Associates (P) of North-Western Regional Centre of Anthropological Survey of India, Dehradun, for their contributions. Dr. V. Kaul and M.C. Bagchi of the same office contributed a note on Bio-anthropological information.

# INTRODUCTION

Chandigarh, the city beautiful, is situated at the foothills of the Shivalik hills. The name of the city is derived from the temple of Chandi (Chandi mandir) situated near the city. The city is a show piece of modern architecture and town planning. Dr. M.S. Randhava, who had a long spell as the Chief Commissioner and was one of the pioneers in the development of Chandigarh, states (1968): 'The Master Plan of Chandigarh is almost poetic and biological in form. The capital group is its commanding head, the commercial centre its heart, the industrial area its hand, the University, the Museum, the Medical Institute and Engineering College its brain, the road system involving the principle of 7 vs. its arteries and veins, the electricity system its nerves and the green spaces which stretch through from north to south its lungs.'

The city of Chandigarh was conceived by Prime Minister Jawaharlal Nehru as a modern capital of the Punjab. The erstwhile Punjab, before partition of the country, had Lahore as its capital. After the partition of the country, Jallandhar functioned as a temporary capital of Punjab, which was later shifted to Shimla. The need for a new place to serve as the capital of the Punjab was felt, as Shimla was found to be inconvenient due to its location in the heart of the Himalaya, and its extreme weather conditions.

The present site was chosen by the then chief minister of Punjab, Sardar Partap Singh Kairon, because of its natural south-west gradient which was considered ideal for efficient drainage and sewerage. The fertility of soil was considered necessary for development of green parks and meadows in addition to the scenic background of Shivalik hills and the abundance of availability of underground water. The climatic conditions, location away from the Grand Trunk Road and the distance from the international border, as also the flow of seasonal torrents on the east and the west, were other considerations for the selection of the present site. The city was planned in detail by Le Corbusier and construction was inaugurated by Jawaharlal Nehru on 2 April 1952.

Chandigarh is situated at 330 metres above sea level, next to Shivalik range of hills at $76^0$ E longitude and $33^0$ N latitude. The area is submontane and undulating. It is presently surrounded by the states of Punjab, Haryana and Himachal Pradesh. The satellite towns of Panchkula, in Haryana state, and Sahibzada Ajit Singh Nagar (Mohali) in Punjab state, have grown rapidly at the southern and eastern ends of the city. Since the reorganization of Punjab state on 1 November 1966 Chandigarh was made a Union Territory and has functioned as the joint capital of Punjab and Haryana.

The total area of the Union Territory of Chandigarh covers 114 sq. km. The city covers an area of 57.6 sq. km and is divided into 47 sectors and fringe settlements. The rural segment covers an area of 56.4 sq. km with 27 villages around. Sectors 1 to 30 were developed in the first phase of construction whereas the rest are being developed in the second phase. The whole area of about 3,642 hectares has been divided into sectors in such a way that each sector is 1.2 km long and 0.8 km wide in a rectangular grid plan. Each sector has been planned as a self-sufficient unit in its day-to-day needs, such as shopping-centres, schools, milk booths, post offices, local bus stops, rickshaw and scooter stands, a community centre, wide open parks and playgrounds and a dispensary. Houses do not open on to the main traffic roads. Complete segregation of fast traffic has been achieved by development of seven types of roads. Open green belts extend from the north to the south. Complete control on the land use and construction activity within the city and in an area of 16 km radius of the city is being strictly implemented.

The Union Territory of Chandigarh is often referred to as the 'city beautiful' as mentioned earlier and as 'city of roses'; it is a model of architectural grandeur displayed in its systematic lay-out and monumental buildings planned by Le Corbusier. The Secretariat, Vidhan Sabha (State Assembly), High Court and Open Hand (the symbol of the city) in the north, against the backdrop of the Shivaliks, are buildings of architectural excellence. Some other landmarks of tourist attraction are the City Centre (Sector 17), the Punjab University Campus, Art Gallery, Museum, National Gallery of Portraits, Rock Garden, Rose Garden and Sukhna Lake.

The climate of Chandigarh varies from extremes of cold and hot weather with the temperature ranging from 43.2$^{0}$C in summer in the month of June to 1.2$^{0}$C in winters in the month of December. The average annual rainfall in Chandigarh is 1115.0 mm, and is fairly well distributed due to proximity of Shimla hills. Maximum precipitation occurs in the months of July and August.

According to the Census of India (1981), the total population of Chandigarh was 4,51,610 individuals comprising 2,55,278 males and 1,96,332 females. It has one of the highest densities of population, i.e. 6,188 persons per square kilometre in the city and 630 in the rural areas. The sex ratio is 770 females per thousand males. The birth rate in 1981 was 45.8 and the death rate 44.4. The Scheduled Castes comprise of 14.09 per cent of the total population. There is no Scheduled Tribe in the Union Territory.

The Union Territory has two towns under its jurisdiction, namely Chandigarh and Manimajra. The area of Chandigarh has increased due to extension of city limits from 46.67 to 58.52 sq. km, during the decade of 1971-81 but the population rose from 2,32,940 to 4,22,841 registering an increase of 80 per cent in the decade. Though the rural area comprises

45.67 sq. km, which works out to 40 per cent, spread over 27 villages, it holds only 6.37 per cent of the population (i.e. 28,769).

Most of the residents of Chandigarh are generally educated and economically well-to-do. Chandigarh, though small, is a well developed education centre. In the Punjab University Campus, there is a Law Department, a Chemical Engineering Department, an evening college and 50 other departments. There are four polytechnics, one Engineering College, one Medical College, one College of Architecture, besides the Post Graduate Institute of Medical Education and Research (PGI), a premier institute of medical research and practice. There are 9 degree colleges, 34 higher secondary and secondary schools, 20 middle schools as well as Government-run model schools. It also has 24 primary schools.

As the Union Territory of Chandigarh enjoys the unique privilege of being the capital of two states, Punjab and Haryana, the civic administration is looked after by Chandigarh Administration which is directly controlled by the Government of India. The territory is well-connected with the rest of the country by road, rail and air. The city has a large industrial belt to its south-east, separated from the main city by a green belt. It has eight industries in the large and medium sectors and about 500 units in the small sector, employing 10,104 workers. The city is well served by electricity, road transport, sewerage and water supply. All of the 22 villages are electrified and provided with metalled roads.

Most of the urban population is either salaried employees or engaged in business or trade, whereas the rural population is engaged in agriculture. About 3,977.37 hectares of land is under cultivation and 41.51 per cent of this is irrigated by wells, tube-wells and *kuhals*. Wheat is the main crop. Other crops grown in this area include paddy, maize, pulses (gram, *masri*, *urd* and *moong*) and oil-seeds (groundnut, mustard, *toria*, *taramira* and sesame). The vegetable demand of the city is fulfilled by the rural area which grows cauliflower, cabbage, brinjal, carrot, radish, potato, tomato, onion, garlic, etc.

A list of 108 communities was originally prepared for Chandigarh. However, 42 communities were finally identified under 'People of India' project in Chandigarh. The township of Manimajra and villages of Attawa, Burail and Maloya were extensively covered for fieldwork. Most of the communities are either the original inhabitants of the villages or have migrated either from Punjab or Haryana. A total of 9 Scheduled Caste communities were studied in Chandigarh. Scheduled Caste communities with population of less than 100 and widely dispersed in the Union Territory were not studied.

Forty-two communities have thus been studied from the Union Territory of Chandigarh. They are the Ahluwalia, Balmiki, Bania, Barhai, Bazigar, Bharai, Bharbhunja, Bhatia, Bhatra, Brahman, Chamar, Chhimba, Christian,

Dhanak, Dhea, Dhobi, Gaderia, Gujjar, Jain, Jat, Jheewar, Julaha, Kamboh, Kayastha, Khatik, Kumhar (Hindu), Kumhar (Muslim), Labana, Lohar, Mazhabi, Mirasi, Nai, Noongar, Penja, Rajput, Saini, Sansi, Sikligar, Sud, Sunar, Teli (Hindu) and Teli (Muslim).

Chandigarh, being the capital of Punjab and Haryana, has attracted population from both the states and therefore the cultural impact of both is visible. However, since it was part of the Malwa region of the erstwhile Punjab State, the rural area is still completely dominated by Punjabi culture, whereas the city area, though dominated by cultures from Punjab, is also influenced by people who have settled from Haryana. Various cultural organizations like the Kerala Smajam, Tamil Sangam, Andhra Sanskrit-Sangam, Kannada Sangam, Maharashtra Mandal, Gujrati Mandal, Rajasthani Sabha, Durga Sarabjeen Sabha and Kashmiri Pandits Association, besides associations active in social sphere such as Rotarians and Lions are contributing to the development of socio-cultural life of Chandigarh. Sects like the Nirankari, Namdhari, Radha Swami, Sanatan Dharam and Arya Samaj have a good following in the Union Territory.

As already stated, most of the communities share their history, language, dress, food-habits, marriage customs, etc., with their counterparts in Punjab and Haryana. Though joint families still exist, the number of nuclear families is increasing. Customs and practices prevalent in Punjab, are in vogue but in a somewhat diluted form among the communities of Chandigarh. Caste restrictions and taboos as found in neighbouring states are either not visible or are not practised very rigidly, perhaps due to better education and economic status.

Most of the communities studied are either Hindu or Sikh or both, as per the details given in parenthesis: Hindu (21), Sikh (3), Muslim (6), Jain (1), Christian (1), and Hindu and Sikh (10).

The main Hindu festivals celebrated in Chandigarh are Diwali, Dussehra, Holi, Janamashtami, Makar Sankranti, Raksha Bandhan, Ram Navami, Shivratri and Basant Panchami, etc. Besides major Hindu festivals, the Sikhs celebrate Guru-purb or the birth anniversaries of the Gurus, but those of the first (Guru Nanak) and tenth (Guru Gobind Singh) are celebrated as festivals. Apart from Hindu and Sikh festivals, Muslim, Jain and Christian festivals are also celebrated here. Id-ul-Fitr and Id-ul-Zuha are the main festivals of Muslims, when they congregate at the beautifully built Masjid in Sector-20 in large numbers, to offer *namaz* (prayers). Christmas and Easter are the main festivals celebrated by Christians when their churches, particularly in Sector-18 and Sector-19 are tastefully decorated.

Punjabi and Hindi are the main languages spoken by the people in the Union Territory of Chandigarh, particularly in the rural areas. In Chandigarh, English is equally common. As per the Census report there are minority linguistic groups also who speak Kashmiri, Bengali, Marathi, Kannada, Tamil, Telugu and Malayalam. English and Hindi are the official languages of Chandigarh Administration. But Punjab and Haryana Government offices located in Chandigarh use Punjabi and Hindi respectively in official correspondence, besides English.

As already mentioned, each sector is a self-sufficient unit. Houses of varying sizes, ranging from as small as five *marla* to one *kanal* or bigger, can be found in each sector. Spacious bungalows particularly in the northern sectors, can be seen in one- to two-*kanal* plots of land. Smaller buildings with party-walls are quite common on smaller landholdings. Nowadays, Chandigarh Administration, under the aegis of the Chandigarh Housing Development Board, is giving preference to multi-storied flats in the second phase sectors.

In urban areas and most of the rural areas facilities of water, electricity and toilet are available within premises. In the rural area there are no large buildings. However, kachcha structures are increasingly being replaced by cement and concrete structures ranging from one to four rooms. Huts are also found in rural areas which cater to the requirement of poor people. As a bane of rapid urbanization and construction activity some slum colonies have also come up on the periphery of the city.

The effect of modern culture is visible in the city which is, perhaps, the trend setter in fashion for the northern states. The males wear Western dress and in addition the Sikhs wear turbans. The females wear *salwar-kameez* and *saree*. Changes in dress material and design are discernible as per the demands of changing fashion. The impact of Western attire is also evident on the younger generation of both sexes.

Food and dietary habits are also showing a gradual change, though these become distinct as one goes up the social/economic ladder. The lower and middle class still have their traditional types of food and eating practices. But the upper middle class and the rich are increasingly opting for a mixture of Western and traditional type of meals and eating habits, particularly the young ones. South Indian food and Chinese cuisine are becoming popular.

The regional ethos of the Punjabi and Haryanavi culture is visible in Chandigarh. Most people of Chandigarh city have come very recently for seeking employment or have settled here after retirement. Most parents prefer schooling in the medium of English and speak English, Punjabi and Hindi in their homes.

In the present study an attempt has been made to study the various communities of Chandigarh from its villages, because in the city most of the people seek marriage alliances with the people from their respective states. At one stage, the idea to study the communities of the Union Territory of Chandigarh for the present project was even dropped, because it appeared that there were no differences in the language, dress, food habits, material culture and occupations of the people of Punjab and the people of Chandigarh. However, as the communities from all the other states and Union Territories of India were under investigation, it was decided to study the communities of the Union Territory of Chandigarh separately.

In the urban milieu, they share schools, roads, places of worship or crematorium with the members of their, or other, religions. The member of one community can be either a Hindu, a Sikh or even a Muslim. The Hindus and Sikhs of the same community not only interdine but also intermarry. Hence they have the relationship of *roti* and *beti*, which is also practised in the neighbouring villages of the state of Punjab. The rate of literacy among the Scheduled Castes is very low, but some of them are educated and employed as they have been benefited by the job reservations. Some of the Scheduled Castes are nomadic. The Chandigarh Administration has taken special steps to help the Balmikis, who still work as *safaiwalas* by providing them with hand pulled *rehris* to carry garbage. People of Chandigarh city and its adjoining villages have in general been benefited by the various developmental programmes such as education, health, electricity, family welfare, employment opportunities and the latest agricultural technology related to the high-yielding seed varieties and fertilizers.

# AHLUWALIA

Aluajia, Kalal, Aluwala, Aluwalia and Aluwari are synonyms for Ahluwalia who are said to have originated from Ahlu, a village five *kos* (miles) east of Lahore. The real founder of the Ahluwalia *misl* was Sardar Jassa Singh Ahluwalia. Being a man of enterprise and possessing a knowledge of military tactics, Sardar Jassa Singh acquired a great reputation. His political talents, religious zeal and lofty aspirations combined made him one of the most powerful federal chiefs of the Punjab. He claimed descent from the Rajputs of Jaisalmer (though he reportedly belonged to the caste of Kalals or distillers) and became the founder of the Kapurthala reigning family, which to this day is known by the title of the Ahluwalias (Latif 1889).

The Kalal or Karal is a class of varying status and probably of composite origin. They claim Hindu Rajput ancestry and derive their name from Karauli, Rajasthan. They are divided into 52 clans or *gots* incuding the Tulsi and Pital (in Kapurthala). These Karals also styled themselves as Ahluwalia. Tulsi, Phul, Mali, Rekhi, Sad and Segat are the sections of the Ahluwalia. The Kalal are also Hindus, but they embraced Sikhism more frequently than the Karal. They are by profession distillers, and the word *kalal* appears to be derived from *kulal*, a potter. The Kalal *gots* are Bhagar, Bhamral, Bhandari, Bharwathia, Bhukal, Bimbat, Hatyar, Jajj, Janwathia, Ladhathia, Mammak, Paintal and Pall.

Ahluwalias of Chandigarh have migrated from Punjab and Haryana in search of jobs or for business. They are distributed in almost all the sectors in Chandigarh. They speak both Hindi and Punjabi within and outside the family. Devanagari or Gurmukhi script is used.

The male dress includes *kurta* (shirt), *pyjama*, trousures, etc. The women wear the *saree* or the *salwar, kameez* and *dupatta*.

Traditionally, the Ahluwalia are strictly vegetarian. But in Chandigarh, both men and women now occasionally take eggs and meat. The vegetarian food includes *masur dal*, onion and garlic. Traditionally, they are supposed to refrain from alcoholic drinks. But the men consume alcohol on special occasions like marriage. They take milk and milk products.

The Ahluwalias prefer wheat to rice. Their staple food is *dal* and *roti*. They take seasonal vegetables. Seasonal fruits are consumed by them moderately. The common cooking medium is mustard oil. *Ghee* (clarified butter) is also used by them. Roots and tubers are also consumed. The Hindu Ahluwalias commonly smoke cigarettes.

The Ahluwalias have two sub-castes, Kalal and Karal, according to occupation. This caste distinction was strictly prevalent in their community. Nowadays, the Kalal claim to be equal to Karals. Kalal are Sikh by religion and their occupation in the past was to distill alcohol. Karals on the other hand are mostly Hindus and claim that they are superior to the others. Since long Jaswalia was the traditional surname of the Kalal, but now Jaswalias claim themselves as Walias. Marriages between these two subcastes are being held nowadays since the Kalal have improved their economic condition considerably.

The Ahluwalia recognize their place as Kshatriyas in the *varna* system. They consider themselves next to the Brahman. The community's self-perception is high. During marriage, death or any other ceremony they offer uncooked rice, vegetables, or *puri* to the Brahmans who perform the religious ceremonies. Traditionally they would never accept water or cooked food from Sudras and Scheduled Caste people. Now such restrictions are breaking down.

There are seven *gots* amongst the Hindu Ahluwalias of Haryana, namely, Sullhan, Channy, Harsam, Sikan, Katiarjar, Bhurian, Kapil, etc., after the name of the villages. Earlier, there was no differentiation like Hindu and Sikh in the Ahluwalias. So the negotiation was also common amongst them. At present the Hindus accept brides from the Sikhs, but are reluctant to arrange marriages with Sikh grooms. The Ahluwalias are exogamous at the *got* level. Previously, the *gots* of both parents used to be avoided but at present only the *got* of the father is avoided. The preferred age of marriage for the boys is twenty-two, whereas for the girls it is eighteen years. The Ahluwalias arrange marriage by negotiation. The symbols for the married girls are *sindur* (vermilion) in the parting of their hair, *bindi*, finger-ring, ear-rings, nose-ring, toe-rings and glass bangles. Parents can give anything to their daughters according to their economic status. The bride stays with her in-laws after marriage. Rarely, in cases of extreme maladjustment, do they approach the court of law for their separation. Widow remarriage is now permissible.

Nuclear family is common. Earlier, they had joint families. Traditional inter-personal relationship like respect, love, avoidance, joking are prevalent in the family. Due to modernization, the avoidance relationship between the father- in-law and the daughter-in-law and between mother-in-law and the son-in-law is not so strict. All sons inherit the property of their father equally. If there are no sons, the daughter gets an equal share in the property. The status of women is considered low. They mostly attend to household jobs, but participate in economic activities too.

Post-delivery pollution is observed. After childbirth, the new-born baby and the mother are confined in seclusion to a room for five days. On the sixth day, the mother has a bath and comes out of her room. Ladies of the neighbourhood join to sing folksongs when sweets are distributed. This get-together is termed *chhatti*. The mother is not allowed to go to the kitchen till she completes purification, on the ninth or the eleventh day, when a Brahman is invited for the purification rites. They arrange puja and *havan* at home and also offer rice to a few members of the community. All this is more elaborate in case of male child. *Mundan* is observed only in the case of Hindu male child. For the selection of the dates for the *mundan*, the elder person of a family goes to the Brahman. Normally, the ceremony is arranged during Navaratara at the sixth year of age. The ceremony is performed at home or in a temple. The Brahman does puja and *havan* and *nai* (barber) cuts the hair of the child. A vegetarian lunch is offered to the relatives and neighbours. The marriage rituals are performed according to the Vedic tradition or *Anand Karaj*.

The Ahluwalias cremate their dead. Hindu Ahluwalias observe the pollution period up to the ninth day. During this period the sons or unmarried daughters do not wash their clothes with soap. They eat only boiled food with black *urad dal* without spices. Any consanguinal kin group can perform this ritual in the absence of sons and daughters. On the tenth day, they invite the Brahman and usually the elder son offers *pinda* (boiled rice with milk and *ghee*). The Brahman performs the *havan* and recites *mantras*. Traditionally, the barber shaves the heads of the sons in the morning. In Chandigarh most Ahluwalias maintain their traditional rites of death except the shaving of heads. On the thirteenth or the seventeenth day, they offer simple vegetarian food which includes *dal, roti,* rice and *sabzi* to the relatives. The ceremony is termed as *pagri*. The Brahman accepts uncooked rice and seasonal vegetables. Among the Sikh Ahluwalias, the pollution period is over on the fourth day, the *pagri* is offered and *akhandpath* is performed.

The Ahluwalias are basically an agricultural community. Every individual possesses land for cultivation. There is a gradual shift from agriculture to jobs in police, administrative and various government offices. Many of them have also joined the army. Approximately, one tenth of Ahluwalias are in the business. They usually worship according to the Hindu or Sikh religious system.

At present the Ahluwalias are sharing schools and religious places with other neighbouring groups. The boys and girls both attend school and many girls continue their studies after graduation. All the boys do not continue higher studies because many have to attend to the management of agriculture in their respective homes. They get medical facilities from the Government and have a favourable attitude towards family welfare. They have two or three children in each family. There is a widespread use of electricity for domestic purposes. Radio, television sets and refrigerators are used in almost all homes.

V. Bhalla,
Nupur Pathak

## BALMIKI

The word *balmiki* means 'born of the *barmi*' or 'serpent's hole'. The Balmiki are a section of Chuhras, deriving their name from Valmiki the seer and composer of the *Ramayana.* Other names for the group are Chuhra and Bhangi.

The story of saint Valmiki is well known. It is said that Valmiki, whose real name was Ratnakar, used to kill and rob passers by in the forest. One day, seven *rishis* (holy men) were passing through the forest, and as usual, Valmiki attacked them. The amazed *rishis* asked him why he was doing so. Valmiki replied that he had vowed to kill all those who would come in the forest. The *rishis* said, 'That is a sinful act that you do. Do you think your family members will share the sin that will come to you?' Valmiki said that most certainly they would, but prompted by the *rishis*, he went to ask them. Imagine his surprise when they said, 'The sin is your own, why should we be sharers in it?' The *rishis* had opened Valmiki's eyes and they told him to chant the name of Rama. Valmiki said, 'All my life, I have lived by killing. How can I say Rama now? All I can say is *mara.*' Valmiki went on saying it for twelve years. Since while chanting *mara*, it sounded like Rama, the purpose was accomplished. Valmiki's body withered and was covered by an anthill, yet he went on chanting. This was how the holy men found him when they returned after twelve years. Valmiki's sins were forgiven and he became a sage.

The Balmiki in Burail village have migrated from neighbouring Haryana and Punjab. According to the Census of India (1981) the total population of the Balmikis–Chuhra–Bhangi is 27,538 which includes 15,142 males and 12,396 females. The Balmiki has been recognized as a Scheduled Caste.

The language spoken within the family and kin group is Hindi and Punjabi. Devanagari and Gurmukhi scripts are used. Punjabi and Hindi are spoken with members of other communities. The usual dress of women comprises *salwar, kameez* and *dupatta.* Ornaments such as ear-rings, nose-rings, *payal*, bangles and necklaces are made of silver or gold depending upon the economic conditions of the family. Men wear *kurta, pyjama* and *dhoti.* Trousers are worn by the young. Necklaces made of *rudraksh* are worn by some men who wear orange robes and take *bhiksha* from house to house.

*Dal* and *roti* are the staple food. The Balmiki eat all types of pulses such as gram, *urad, moong, kulthi,* peas and beans, *masur, moth,* etc. They are non-vegetarian, and cook in mustard oil though occasionally coconut oil is also used. Roots and tubers are also consumed. Men consume alcoholic drinks regularly. Consumption of fruits such as mango, apple, orange, guava, grape, banana, etc., is moderate.

The Balmikis have been screened for six polymorphic systems, viz., A1, A2, BO, MN, Rh (D factor) blood group systems, ABO (H) secretion, P.T.C. tasting ability and colour-blindness. The results of ABO blood group system show that they have a high incidence of blood group A (38.09 per cent) followed by blood group B (33.33 per cent) and O (15.87 per cent) in that order. At the MN locus, they are characterized by a moderately high frequency of gene 'M' (0.6383). The incidence of Rh negative is very low (3.70 per cent). As to the ability to taste P.T.C., Balmikis show an exceedingly high incidence of tasters (90.38 per cent).

The community has various *gots* like Chachirak, Sohta, Malkhat, Parwal, Bohat and Lohat. The main function of the *gots* is to regulate marriage alliances. The Balmikis marry within their own community. They observe village exogamy. The age at marriage for the girls is between 16 and 18 years and that for boys is between 18 and 21 years. The married women use symbols like vermilion, bangles, *bindi*, finger-ring, toe-ring, ear-ring, etc. The dowry in the form of furniture, gold ornaments, clothes and other household materials is given at the time of marriage by the bride's parents to the bridegroom. Cash is also given. After marriage the girl stays at her husband's residence. In changes in marriage customs, the age at marriage has increased and child marriage has almost been abandoned. Divorce is permissible on grounds of maladjustment, impotency, cruelty, etc. After divorce, the husband has to pay compensation. Either husband or wife can seek divorce. Remarriage of widows or widowers is also permissible. A widow can marry the younger brother of her deceased husband and similarly a widower can marry his deceased wife's younger sister.

Both nuclear and vertically extended families occur. Nuclear families are becoming more common. Joking relationship is observed between *dewar* (husband's yonger brother) and *bhabi* (elder brother's wife): *jeeja* (sister's husband) and *sali* (wife's sister). All the sons inherit the property of their father equally. If there is no son, the daughters get equal shares. Succession is through the rule of primogeniture. The status of women is considered lower than men's. They play a role in the household activities and look after the animals. They collect fuel, bring potable water from common taps and do knitting at home. However, the women do participate in various rituals associated with births, marriage and death.

During childbirth, *chhatti* is celebrated and a feast is given to the neighbours and family members. *Mundan* (first ceremonial shaving of head) is observed and is usually performed at some sacred place. The ceremony of *mangani* (engagement) is held before marriage. *Sagan* and exchange of rings takes place during *mangani*. Marriage rituals are performed in the bride's residence according to the Hindu tradition. A feast is given by the girl's parents to the marriage party. Consummation of marriage takes place at the residence of the bridegroom. The Balmikis cremate their dead. The bones are disposed of at Hardwar in the river Ganges. They also perform the *shradh* ceremony or ancestor worship.

The Balmiki is a landless community. The main occupation is cleaning and keeping poultry and pigs. Some work as labourers while others hold jobs either in government offices or private commercial institutions.

Festivals of Holi, Diwali, Dussehra, Lohri, etc., are celebrated. Change of religion has taken place. But those who have embraced Sikhism are called the Mazhabi. Untouchability is still observed at the village level. People of 'higher' castes do not accept food or drink from the Balmikis but they accept food or drink from others. They share wells, crematoria, schools, religious places with other communities and also participate in traditional festivals. Formal education is given to both the boys and girls. However, the girls drop out from studies and serve in the house only. They usually study up to primary level; only a few read up to the secondary level. Boys continue up to college level.

Modern medical facilities are available. The attitude towards family planning is favourable but not strict. In most families there are more than three children. Drinking water is available within the locality, from wells and taps. Most Balmikis are self-employed either as sweepers, agricultural and industrial labourers, rickshaw-pullers, etc. Some keep pigs. The houses are provided with electricity. Fuel-wood, cow-dung cakes, coal, kerosene oil and cooking gas are used as fuel. Mid-day meal is given to children in *anganwadi* and primary schools. Facility of food and ration distribution through fair price shops is availed of.

V. Bhalla<br>Sushil Kumari

## BANIA (AGGARWAL)

The word Banya, or Bania, has its origin in Sanskrit *banijya* (trade). Bania is an occupational group engaged in business and trade. They are called Lala, Seth, Gupta, Vaish or Sahukar. Rose once described (1919: 59-60), the Bania as 'a poor creature ... looked down upon by the peasantry as a cowardly money-grabber ...; his position being that of a curiously mixed nature'. The situation has greatly changed since Rose wrote.

According to the Census of India (1911: 448), the Bania was the Hindu commercial class. There were distinct groups included in the term, of which Aggarwal was one—the distinction of Dassa and Bisa evidently signifies *dasa,* i.e. *dasi put* (son of a slave girl) and *vanshya* (belong to the family). *Dasa* got corrupted into *Dassa* (having 10) and *vanshya* was probably modified into the relative term Bisa (having 20). The Aggarwals are noted to have acquired 'Kshatriya characteristics of worshipping arms and a horse on Dussehra instead of Dewali like the purely trading classes (Marwaris and Bhatias of Bombay)'. According to Rose (1919: 60-1), 'The three territorial groups were the Aggarwal, Saralia, who are an offshoot of the Aggarwal and have the same *got*, and Jains who were converted in *sambat* 422.'

Rose also (1919), mentions divisions based on religious differences, such as Saraogi or Jain Maheshwari or Shaiva, Aggarwal-Vishnoi or Vaishnava. The Maheshwaris, derived their name from Mahesh or Shiva but are not Shaivas, for one of their members was converted to Jainism and founded the Tahtar *got* of the Oswal. The Shaiva groups formed two sub-castes.

The Aggarwals live in large numbers in the neighbouring states of Punjab and Haryana and there is at least one family in each village. They speak Punjabi, Hindi or Urdu. They use Gurmukhi or Devanagari script, while communicating with the members of their own community or with the outsiders. The men wear *pyjama, kurta* or very rarely *pagri,* i.e. turban. The women wear *salwar, kameez, dupatta* or *sari*. They are pure vegetarian and take cereals such as wheat and maize, and pulses such as gram, *urad, moong, moth* and *masur*. The cooking medium is either groundnut oil, mustard oil or *ghee*. They take milk and milk products, but alcoholic drinks are avoided. Fruits are taken particularly on special occasions and seasonally. They also smoke. The younger generation take non-vegetarian food outdoors.

The Banias are today divided into seventeen and a half *gots* such as Bansal, Garg, Singhal, Goyal, Mittal, Jindal, Kansal, Mansal, Mangla, Tayal, Tingal, Bindal, Dheran, Eran, Kuffal, Mudgil, Kuchla and Gand. They are endogamous but maintain exogamy at *gotra* and village levels. They observe hypergamy.

They place themselves in the Vaishya category.

Monogamy is the form of marriage. Marriage is arranged by negotiations. *Kanyadan* as a part of marriage rituals exists. Dowry in kind is allowed. Married women wear glass bangles, *sindur, bindi,* finger and ear-rings. They are patrilocal. Divorce (*talaq*) is permitted with judicial approval primarily due to maladjustment. However, divorce cases are very rare. *Punar vivah* (remarriage) is allowed . Those who practise *karewa* are called as Gatte Bania. There has been a marked rise in the age of marriage. Nowadays, symbols of marriage are not strictly maintained.

The Aggarwals have extended families but the nuclear families are on the increase. Conflicts in a family may be either due to disputes over property, check on the freedom of youngsters or challenge to the authority of the elders. Sons equally inherit their father's property and succession is through primogeniture. Women have low status and are confined to the home. There is post-delivery pollution period of seven days. Prayer is offered in the house. The post-delivery restrictions are observed for 40 days. Naming ceremony is performed after one year. When the male child is one, three or five years of age, *mundan* is performed by visiting *Matarani* or *Devi*. The marriage ritual of seven *pheras* is performed according to the Vedic rites at the residence of the bride. A feast (*roti*) is given by the parents of the girl to the *barat* (marriage party). *Suhagrat* (consummation of marriage) ceremony takes place at the bridegroom's residence.

Aggarwals cremate their dead. *Phul* (charred bones) are collected for immersion in the Ganges at Hardwar, on Monday, Wednesday or Friday. *Dasahi* is observed on the tenth day and the ladies wash their clothes. They offer a feast to the members of the community on the twelfth day after death. They worship their ancestors. Life-cycle rituals have in some cases been curtailed as they have become more expensive.

Aggarwals are engaged in business, trade, government and private services. Village Panchayats look after all affairs of common interest, including matters related to theft, marriage disputes or divorce. They are Hindus and worship all Hindu gods and goddesses specially Laxmi (goddess of wealth). The *pujari* (priest) is from another community; he is consulted on the various auspicious days in addition to the performance of various life-cycle rites. Aggarwals celebrate Holi, Diwali, Janamashtami, Lohri, Dussehra and visit various religious places such as Mansa Devi, Vaishno Devi, Jawalaji, etc. Women do embroidery work in their spare time. The *dholak* accompanies them while singing.

Traditionally they accept and exchange water and food with Jats, Rajputs and Sainis but avoided accepting food and drink from the Chamars, Ramdasia, Sansi, Muslims, Nais and Dhobis. They share *dharamsalas*, schools and crematoria with others. Patron-client relationships are absent. Modern intercommunity linkages are sustained through their participation as businessmen, scholars, white-collar job holders, teachers, administrators and doctors. Political leadership has emerged at the village level.

Formal education, health and medical care is considered important and attitudes towards family welfare are favourable. Hand-pump is the source of drinking water, kerosene or LPG is used as fuel. They avail themselves of nutrition programmes and ration-shop facilities. They help each other financially at the time of need.

Swaran Singh

# BARHAI

The Barhai, an occupational group of carpenters, are also known as Tarkhan. According to Ibbetson (1916: 312–13), the Lohar or blacksmith and the Khati or carpenter were undistinguishable, the same man doing both kinds of work; and in many, perhaps in most, parts of the Punjab the two intermarried. In Hoshiarpur, they formed a single caste called Lohar Tarkhan, and the son of a blacksmith would often take to carpentry and vice versa.

According to Rose (1919: 457), 'the Tarkhan better known as Barhai in the Hills, Barhi in the Jumna districts and Khati in the rest of the eastern plains was the carpenter of these provinces. Like the Lohar he is a true village menial mending all agricultural implements and household furniture and making them all except the cart, the persian wheel, and the sugarpress, without payment beyond his customary dues. The various synonyms of Barhai are Karigar, Bari, Badi, Tarkhan, Gharu, Khati, Karchob, Kharadi, Mistri (Mishtri), Arakash, Chatrera (or painter), Ramgarhia, Chattarsaz or umbrella-maker; Kamangar or lacquerer; and Suthar. The Tarkhan included a number of occupational groups which do not appear to form sub-castes, such as Ara-Kash or sawyers, the Kangi-Gharas or comb-maker in Sialkot; the Kharadi, a turner and the Raj, a mason: and the itinerant Lohars who comprised the Saiqalgirs or grinders and the Gadia (Gadhia) or cartmen.'

Barhai speak Punjabi and Hindi and use the Gurmukhi and Devanagari scripts. They are pure vegetarian and take *dal* and *roti* as their staple food. Groundnut oil is the cooking medium. Those who are Radhaswami do not take alcoholic drinks, whereas others take alcoholic drinks occasionally. They take milk and milk products. They form an endogamous community and observe exogamy at *gotra* and village level. The different *gotras* are Chinder, Khural, Rupal and Birdi. They recognize their position in the *varna* system and consider themselves Kshatriya. The age at marriage for boys is around twenty-five years and that of a girl is around twenty. Monogamy is practised. Parents arrange the marriage of their children by negotiation. Married women use *sindur,* glass bangles and nose, ear and finger rings as the symbols of marriage. Dowry is accepted . They are patrilocal. Divorce is very rare, but it is allowed with judicial approval depending on the age of husband and wife. The reason for divorce is usually maladjustment. Remarriage is allowed. Joint and nuclear family types are common. Sons inherit the property of their father equally. Succession is through the eldest son. The status of the women is low. They only attend to various household jobs.

Post-delivery pollution period varies from nine to eleven days. The post-natal restrictions on mother last for forty days. They observe the naming ceremony and consult either the Pandit or take *wak* from *Guru Granth Sahib* depending on their religion. On the first birthday of the male child, they invite their close relatives and offer a feast; this is termed '*chhati*'. The marriage ceremony is performed at the residence of the bride according to Hindu ritual, with seven *pheras*, or through the Sikh ritual of *anand karaj*. They cremate their dead. The bones of the dead are collected after three days and disposed of in the Ganges at Hardwar. The *dasai* is observed on the tenth day. On the seventeenth day in the case of women and eighteenth day in case of men, the prayers are offered either from the *Garuda Purana* or the *Guru Granth Sahib*. They also observe ancestor worship.

They are engaged in carpentry, metallurgy or masonry. They are covered under municipal committee and the members of the committee are elected by secret ballot. They follow both Hindu and Sikh religion and specially worship Guru Ram Rai and Mansadevi. Some of them belong to the Radhaswami sect. In case their *sukh* (wish) is fulfilled, they visit the Gurdwara and offer *ghee*. The sacred specialist is from other communities. They celebrate Lohri, Diwali, Dussehra, Baisakhi and Holi. Ladies do embroidery and weaving. The oral traditions and dances are similar to those found among other communities of Punjab.

They traditionally accept and exchange water and food with the Brahman, Bania, Rajput and the Jat. In matters of marriage they strictly follow the rule of community endogamy. The members of their community are in business, teaching and in the defence services.

Both boys and girls receive formal education; but due to poor economic condition and because of a host of other reasons the boys cannot continue their studies beyond secondary level and the girls beyond primary level. They make use of both indigenous and modern medicare and observe family planning methods. They get tap water for drinking purposes. Wood is used as fuel. Immunization facilities for child and mother are availed, as also financial help from banks.

Swaran Singh

# BAZIGAR

The name *bazigar* is derived from the Persian word *bazi* meaning to wager upon or acrobat. So Bazigar is an occupational name. They claim Rajput origin and bear Rajput clan names. The group is divided into three main clans, Rathore, Chauhan and Dheiya. These clans are exogamous and are further split into *gotras*. The three clans hold equal rank. According to them the name Bazigar got associated with them because of their unique occupation of making *bazi* or doing acrobatics. Denzil Ibbetson (1916) made the following remarks while writing about Nats and Bazigars. According to him, 'the Nat belonged to a "gypsy tribe" of Punjab. Bazigar was described as a tumbler and Nat as a rope dancer.'

Pandit Hari Krishan Kaul (Census of India, Punjab 1911) has stated that Bazigars were known as Badi and were akin to Nats. Only a few Bazigars (mostly resident of district Ambala) could state that Badi is a term sometimes used for the caste, while the large majority of caste members have shown ignorance about such a relationship. The Bazigars claim to be the direct descendants of Rathor Rajputs. They further believe that many castes have taken to acrobatic feats merely as a source of livelihood in recent years. They have not inherited the profession of acrobatic feats as a traditional occupation. The Bazigars of Punjab also refuse to accept that any others taking up the professions of playing music, rope dancing, acrobatic feasts, jugglery, snake charming, etc., can be called Bazigars. They state that Nat, Kalabaz, Madari, Bena, Kabutri, Sapela and Kanjar are merely functional groups and have no social relationship with the Bazigar. The Bazigars are today an endogamous group and do not have any intermarital or commensal relations with the above-mentioned functional groups. The Sikh Bazigar are of recent origin.

The Bazigars appear in the list of Scheduled Castes in Punjab, Rajasthan, Delhi and Himachal Pradesh. The population of the community in Chandigarh is 1,389 individuals, 712 males and 677 females (Census of India, 1981). The Bazigar commonly speak Punjabi with outsiders but they also converse in a dialect which is locally known as 'Pashto'. The term 'Pashto' is given to a dialect which is used for mutual conversation of a confidential nature. The traditional dress of women consists of loose skirt called *ghagri* and a short blouse called *choli*; the *dhotar* (a piece of cloth about three yards long) is worn as head cover. Males usually wear *kurta* and *chaddra* or *tamba,* wrapped around the waist. The head-dress is locally known as *pagri*. The ornaments worn by females are usually made of silver and of very rough craftsmanship. The different types of ornaments include the ring or *challe* and the *honkli*. The

Bazigars are recognized as Scheduled Caste and are economically poor and mostly illiterate.

The main items of food comprises the meat of wild animals and camel's milk, which strengthen the muscles of the body. Use of *ghee* is not regular. They only boil all vegetables and pulses, though some put in a good amount of spices, salt and chillies. During summer *chapatis* are taken along with *lassi*. Mutton, chicken and pork are relished on certain occasions. They take alcoholic drinks on such occasions as birth, marriage, death, Panchayat meetings, as well as festivals. The Bazigars are very fond of hookah and smoking *bidis*. Women are also seen smoking *bidis*. A hookah is found in all Bazigar households. Cigarettes are not quite popular.

The Bazigars have three main clans, Rathor, Chauhan and Dheiya. The three rank equally and one group marries with the other two. Clans are split into *gotras,* known as *ailen,* named after some male ancestor. Some of the *ailen* are: (1) Rathore—Baljat, Namshot, Dhamchot, Chhot. (2) Chauhan—Barlia, Manulua, Macchal. (3) Dheiya—Khant, Jamshere-ke, Lala-key.

The functions of these *gotras* are to regulate marriage alliance and to indicate descent. The Bazigar group is strictly endogamous. In marriage they practise endogamy at the community level and exogamy at *gotra* or *ailen* level. A marriage within one's own *ailen* or *gotra*, in the mother's *gotra* and the *gotra* of father's mother is considered incestuous. The Bazigars treat cases of premarital or extra-marital relations with scorn. The offender is publicly disgraced by *chittron-ki-bochar* (shoe-beating). The age of marriage depends chiefly on the means of the family. Infant marriage is considered a means for saving the girl's juvenile chastity. In many cases, where marriage takes place at the age of eight or ten, consummation takes place only after the girl attains puberty. When two families agree to enter marriage alliance, the *nate, mangewa* ceremony takes place. The ceremony comprises announcement of bride-price in the presence of Panchayat and declaration of *nate* between the two families. The Panchayat has fixed the bride-price of Rs. 1,010 for economically poor Bazigars and Rs. 1,500 in the case of those who are economically better-off. The bride-price has to be paid to the girl's father by the boy's father before the marriage is solemnized.

After the marriage ceremony, clothes and household articles, given as *daj* (dowry), are displayed. Divorce is normally not allowed. Even in extreme cases of maladjustment, sickness, barrenness, the institution of marriage is respected. But sometimes second marriage takes place. Widow remarriage is allowed. Widower remarriage with the wife's younger sister may be allowed, if both the families agree for the same. Remarriage is known as *karewa* or *chaddar paona*.

The Bazigar family is patrilineal. After marriage the woman goes to stay with her husband. Both nuclear and extended family types are found. In the past, they had extended families known as *patti.* Avoidance relationship is observed between father-in-law and daughter-in-law, younger brother's wife and husband's elder brother, and between ladies and elder male community members. Joking relationship is observed among elder brother's wife and husband's younger brother; wife's younger sister and sister's husband; grandparents and grandchildren and wife's brother and sister's husband. Kin of both mother's and father's side have an important role to play, especially during marriage, child-birth and death. The son-in-law holds a very respectable position.

Women have traditionally a lower status than men. Inheritance is patrilineal. Women are confined to the household. They are economically dependent, though they do subsidiary jobs like stitching and knitting to increase the family income. They have a role in social functions, religious and ritual activities and in social control. No social or religious, ritual and festivity is complete without the active participation of womenfolk. Opinion is normally sought, especially of elder women, for settling a marriage or for purchase of a house or other property.

The life-cycle rituals are observed at the time of birth, *mundan* ceremony, marriage and death in the family. In the eighth month of pregnancy, *rit* is observed. The wife's parents send her a set of clothes and a *ser* (less than a kilogram) of jaggery. The husband and wife prostrate themselves before Jawalaji (the goddess of power). The *rit* is observed mostly in the case of first birth of a child in the family. Barrenness in the women is considered unnatural and unlucky. In the past, repeated abortions were attributed to evil influences of witchcraft or of evil spirits. The first delivery takes place at the husband's house. Prenatal restrictions are observed and the pregnant lady is not allowed to perform any strenuous household job. Post-delivery pollution is observed for forty days. *Poojan* is held and it marks the end of *chilla* (confinement) and the pollution period. The naming ceremony becomes a special occasion in the case of male child. *Mundan* is observed for both boys and girls, when the child is 60 days old or at the age of five years. *Kan bindhana* (piercing of ears) takes place in the case of both the sexes and both of them wear ear-rings. *Kan bindhana* is a ritual which takes place at the time of adolescence.

The marriage rituals are performed partially at the bridegroom's residence and partially at the bride's place. Bride-price, fixed by the Panchayat, is paid to the bride's father by the bridegroom's father. As per tradition the marriage ceremony consists of seven circumambulations of sacred fire (*phera*) under the auspices of the village Brahman hired for the occasion. Among the Sikh Bazigar the *phere* ceremony is performed according to the Sikh tradition of *anand karaj.* Dowry is given to the girl by her parents. A feast is arranged for the *barat* by the parents of the bride and the nuptial ceremony is held at the groom's residence.

Bazigars now cremate their dead. Earlier, the pollution period lasted for thirteen days but now it is observed only for three days. The *phul chugna* ceremony is performed three days after death. On the thirteenth day, *kaj* or *bara dolna* ceremony is performed, in the case of old persons, with great show, and great expenditure.

Bazigars had to forego their traditional occupation of acrobatics and take up the professions of grazing and breeding camels. Two reasons are adduced. First, it requires great energy and also dexterity. Secondly, the other sources of entertainment like *raaslilas, nautankis* and circus, etc., attract more village folk. Acrobatic feats are becoming a thing of the past, and many Bazigars have started working as agricultural labourers either on *batai* or daily wages with landlords. Some have been able to possess small landholdings at cheap rates and have became independent cultivators.

The Bazigars have traditional Panchayats of their own which play an important role in regulating the affairs of the community. All the matters of importance relating to disputes within the family, performance of socio-religious rites (like settlement of marriage, selection of spouse), petty thefts etc., are dealt by *dera* Panchayat. In many cases the Panchayat also extends financial aid to the neighbours in the hour of crisis. In Panchayat, offices are hereditary. In the past, the entire *dera* was controlled by a *Sarpanch*, whose post was hereditary. If persons belonging to different *deras* (locations) are involved in any issue, inter-locality Panchayats are convened. These Panchayats at different levels do not have formally elected or appointed members. The *Sarpanches* and *Kharpanches* (who assist the *Sarpanch*) are elected on the spot by the members of the assembled community.

The Bazigars by and large follow Hindu rituals. Most of them practise the birth, tonsure, marriage and death ceremonies in accordance with the Sanatan Dharm rites. They revere Hindu Gods like Shiva, Brahma, Ram, Krishna, and Ganesh. On the other hand they are pronounced worshippers of the Devi cult. They vow offerings to Jawalaji, Kali, Chandi, Vaishno and Laxmi. Sikh Bazigars regularly pay homage to the *Guru Granth Sahib*. They also get the services of *granthis* during the socio-religious functions. *Gugga* is considered most important to be revered by the Bazigar. Bazigars also observe the *shradh*.

The Bazigars have a staunch belief in fate and luck. Sorcerers and *chelas* command a great influence in the community. The females are also apt in selling charms and beads to the barren women of other castes. Folksongs are sung on the occasion of marriage, birth and other happy occasions.

Bazigars receive traditional services from Nai, Dhobi, Lohar, Jheewar (water carriers), Bhangi and Brahman. They claim themselves to be Rathor Rajput by origin. They, however, do not enjoy the status of Rajput. They consider themselves to be 'higher' than the other Scheduled Castes of the area such as Chamar, Ramdasi, Mazhabi, Chuhra and Sansi. They will not eat or drink from the hands of these castes or smoke from their pipes. But they have definite associations with the Lohars, Dhobis and Tarkhans. They freely mix and invite each other on their rituals and festive occasions.

In their attitude towards development programmes, the community shows a positive response. Literacy and education are more preferable for boys than girls. Now some children have started studying in school and college. In health and medical care, mainly the indigenous medicare is used; they seldom visit hospitals, dispensaries and other medical institutions. Some of them are unaware of family planning programmes and have large families. They all use a common hand-pump. They listen to the radio and some of them have TV sets of their own. They live in kachcha houses and during natural calamities they have to suffer a lot. They have a small temple of their own. Kerosene oil, fuel-wood or cow-dung cakes are used as fuel. Electricity is lacking. Since they are illiterate they do not use banking facilities.

V. Bhalla
Sushil Kumari

# BHARAI

The Bharais are also called Sheikh. The word *bharai* has its origin in *pir-bhra* which means 'saint brothers'. It is also derived from *chauki bharna,* i.e. 'to keep a vigil'. Bharais go about beating a drum and begging in the name of Sakhi Sarwar and conduct parties of pilgrims to the shrine at Nigaha. They also receive the offering of the local shrine according to Ibbetson (1916: 229), but this has not been endorsed by the informants. According to Rose (1919) the Bharais, also known as Pirhaian had an ancestor Bukan Jat who was a devotee of Sakhi Sarwar who one day said to him *tujhe piri di*, 'the saint's mouth has fallen on thee', and hence the name.

About the origin of the community, Rose (1919 : 86) observed that the Bharais were 'an occupational group of spiritual brotherhood, which comprised men of many castes, Dogar, Habri, Rawat, Dum, Rajput, Mochi, Gujar, Tarkhan and last, but not least, Jat. The Jat Bharai were numerous. They claim descent from one Garba Jat, a Hindu attendant at Sakhi Sarwar's shrine, who was in a dream bidden by the saint to embrace Islam. On conversion he was called Sheikh Garba.'

Bharai identity operates at local and regional levels. They speak Punjabi and Hindi and those who are literate use Gurmukhi or Devanagari scripts. Males wear shirt, *dhoti* or trousers, and the female dress is *salwar, kameez* and *dupatta.* According to Rose (1919) 'The Bharai insignia are a drum (*dhol* ), beaten with a curiously shaped stick, like a short crook; a wallet (*khallar*) hung round the neck by a string. The stick and *khallar* are peculiar to the Bharai. The standard of the Pirhai is a fringe ( *jagadhri* ) of tassels on a long pole. These fringes are presented by women as thanks-offerings for the birth of sons and at weddings. They are supposed to be tied round the forehead of the saint as they would be tied on a bridegroom's forehead.' This practice continues to this day.

The Bharais were non-vegetarian. Rose (1919) studied the food habits of the Bharai as 'It is said that in many places Bharais eat only goat's flesh, and that leprosy would afflict him who eats any other kind of flesh. But this restriction is certainly not universal. Beef is avoided, because it is said, the Bharai have many Hindu votaries.' Vegetables are eaten today in moderate quantity and non-vegetarian food occasionally. Wheat, rice and maize are taken as cereals; gram, *moong, masur* and *moth* are eaten as pulses. Mustard oil is used as a cooking medium. Bharais consume tea and milk products. Alcoholic drinks are used occasionally by men only. They are changing from vegetarianism into non-vegetarianism, the use of pulses and vegetables has increased; but the consumption of fruit has decreased and they prefer *roti* to rice.

The Bharais are endogamous but observe exogamy at the village and *gotra* levels. *Gotras* are used to regulate their marriage alliances. Their own perception and the perception of other communities about them is low.

The Bharais are aware of the *varna* system. Parents arrange the marriage of their children by negotiation. Polygyny is the form of marriage. Married girls do not use any symbol of marriage. Dowry in kind and *mehar* is promised for future payment. Residence is patrilocal. Divorce due to barrenness, maladjustment, chronic sickness and cruelty is permissible. Widows, widowers and divorcees can remarry. The age of marriage has increased, and the incidence of divorce is on the increase. Nuclear and extended family types are common. Avoidance relationship between daughters-in-law and fathers-in-law is observed. The rule of inheritance is male equigeniture and succession is through the eldest son. Nuclear families are on the increase and the extended families are decreasing. Women have a role in animal husbandry, social functions and rituals, but their status is low.

Pre-delivery restrictions are observed. Post-delivery pollution and restrictions are observed by the mother. There is circumcision of males between five and nine years of age. *Aqiqa* ceremony is performed. Marriage rituals are performed at the bride's residence according to the Islamic tradition of *nikah*. Consent of the girl is obtained at the time of marriage and two advocates sign the marriage document. The amount of *mehar* is announced, and *roti* (feast) is arranged by the bride's parents. The nuptial ceremony is performed at the residence of the bridegroom. They observe pollution period and prayers are offered on the third, tenth, twentieth and fortieth day. There is no change in the observance of the rituals but they have become more expensive.

The Bharais are landless and their traditional occupation is to beat drums during festivals, weddings and other appropriate occasions. Some of them are also engaged as labourers. They have their traditional Panchayat. The *Lambardar or Pradhan* is elected by a voice vote for the lifetime; he is assisted by three to four *Lambardars* or *Pradhans* from the neighbouring states for arriving at any decision. They impose cash fines also. The matters related to divorce, marriage disputes, etc., are decided by them.

As they follow Islam, the Bharais offer *namaz* (prayer)and celebrate Id-ul-Fitr and Id-ul-Zuha as festivals. The *maulavi* (priest), from some other Muslim community, performs various rites associated with birth, marriage, and death and presides over congregations to disseminate religious teaching. Festivals are of socio-economic and religious significance for them. Ladies attend to knitting during their spare time. Men sing folksongs prevalent in the area. The *dhol* is the traditional musical instrument. Men participate in the *bhangra* (folk dance) on special occasions.

Bharais accept and exchange food and water with all the Muslim communities and other Hindu 'low' castes and also share burial ground with Muslim communities. On special occasions and festivals they play *dhol.* They visit their patron after every six months (*chhemahi*). Some members are in white-collar jobs. Political leadership has emerged at the village level.

Formal education is favoured but many of them cannot pursue studies due to poor economic conditions. They enjoy modern medicare facilities. They prefer three children and use family welfare methods other than sterilization. Piped water is available for drinking purposes. They are employed as labourers. Fire-wood and kerosene oil are used as fuel. Mid-day meal scheme for children and ICDS facilities are also available.

V. Bhalla
Achla Sood

# BHARBHUNJA

The Bharbhunjas are differentiated from the larger community of the Jheewars, Dhimars or Kashyap Rajputs only by occupation. The name is derived from *bhujna,* or *bhunana,* meaning parching, since they used to parch grain and maize as source of their livelihood. A community of this name was known in the Punjab, in various places in the districts of Amritsar, Gurdaspur, etc., to Chandigarh in the 1950s and 1960s. At present, the community considers the name 'Bharbhunja' derogatory; they now identify themselves as Kashyap Rajputs, which is synonymous with Mehre. The community perceives its distribution at regional and inter-regional levels, and its members are Hindu or Sikh.

Bharbhunjas have a major concentration in Attawa village, now a small township within the urban limits of Chandigarh. They speak both Hindi and Punjabi among themselves as well as with outsiders. Devanagari and Gurmukhi scripts are used. Some persons can communicate in English whereas the older people can read and write Urdu. The male dress is *kurta, pyjama* or trousers, while the female wear *kurta* and *salwar* with a *dupatta* or *chunni.* The older generation of Hindus wears a *safa,* mainly on ceremonial occasions. The common ornaments among women are the nose pin, ear-ring or pin or stud and a necklace. Some wear golden bangles as well.

The people are non-vegetarian, but not large consumers of egg, fish or meat. Members belonging to the Radhaswami sect, abstain from non-vegetarian food and liquor. Men consume country liquor purchased from the local market. Their staple food is wheat followed by rice; occasionally maize is eaten. They consume various types of pulses, viz., *urad, moong, masur, kulth, arhar,* gram, peas and beans, or *rajmah,* along with roots and tubers and various seasonal vegetables such as cauliflower and cabbage, carrot, raddish, turnip, lady finger, etc. Fruit intake is seasonal and moderate. Milk and milk products are consumed daily only by some; others usually take tea. *Kheer* and *halwa* (pudding), *puree, bhature, bhalle* (cakes of pulses) are taken on festive occasions. Food taboos are observed on fasts and during death pollution.

Except the religious division into Hindu and Sikh, there are no other broad divisions of the community. Bagal, Waddan, Dain, Mulle, Godre, Dateere, Tandon, Kaure, Tetri, Kainth, Dhinge, Bolleghan, are the major *gotras.* There is no internal hierarchy. The *gotras* only denote descent and are used for avoiding marriages among kin. They claim Kshatriya status but their social position in the regional *varna* hierarchy is very low and at par with the Sudras. The community is endogamous and Sikhs as well as Hindus often inter-marry. Exogamy at the clan and village level is followed. At Chandigarh, the concept of village exogamy is lost and marriage may also occur in the same ward or *mohalla*. In the pre-independence period, child marriage was practised and bride-price was accepted by the bride's parents. But at present, the former practice has been abandoned and dowry given in kind has replaced bride-price. Marriages are arranged through negotiation or through matrimonial advertisements in local newspapers. Monogamy is practised but bigamy is also socially approved if the first wife bears no male child. The symbols of marriage are *sindur*, glass bangles and nose and ear ornaments. The bride lives patrilocally. Widow remarriage may occur in case a young widow desires to re-marry. Junior levirate, followed earlier, is not liked by the young ones at present. A widower can re-marry his deceased wife's sister or any other girl. Divorce is socially allowed in certain cases of maladjustment and cruelty, but occurs only through judicial approval. The husband is liable to pay compensation and the children are the liability of the father. The divorcee may re-marry.

The family pattern is largely nuclear and vertically extended families hardly exist. This change is due to economic compulsions and limitation of space in houses. Avoidance and joking relationships are seen in specific cases and in this there is a regional pattern. The *bahuti* or *nuh* (son's wife) covers her face from her *saurah* (husband's father) in some families in which traditional norms are followed. But in many families avoidance relationship is practically non-existent. Joking is permitted between *jeeja* and *sali* (sister's husband and wife's younger sister) and *dewar* and *bhabi* (husband's younger brother and elder brother's wife). Junior members obey and respect their elders. Conflicts may, however, crop up on property matters. Inheritance is as per the rule of male-equigeniture and the eldest son succeeds the father. The status of women is usually low; some earn by working as midwives. They perform all household jobs, fetch water, participate in religious and other social ceremonies, but have little role in the mechanism of social control. Recently, women have formed a Mahila Mandal and assemble to discuss certain social and economic problems faced by their families. They regulate family expenditure, but may not take the final decision in important family matters.

The life-cycle rituals are observed as per the Hindu and Sikh tenets as the case may be. Post-delivery pollution and restrictions are maintained for forty days after which the woman is regarded pure and can cook. Purification comes with a bath and a sip of cow's urine and water of the Ganga. Sweets are distributed on the birth of a male child. Naming and cereal-taking ceremonies are avoided. *Mundan* is performed for the male child before the boy attains five years of age. Hair is shaved by the barber who may also be invited to the feast and the clan or family deity is propitiated. A feast may be given to the children of the *mohalla*. Thread-wearing or *janeu* ceremony is observed only at the time of marriage. Pre-marriage rituals such as *sagai, tika* and *thaka* (betrothal) are arranged when sweets, a token sum of money, clothes and ornaments are exchanged and given to the boy and the girl. *Haldi* (turmeric) and *mehandi* rituals are the preparatory rituals. The bride and groom circumambulate the sacred fire and take an oath for ideal happy living. The parents of the bride perform *kanyadan* and host a dinner to the groom's party. At his place, the *jathere* (a place in the courtyard to commemorate the ancestors) is propitiated, and some people take rounds of the branch of the berry shrub. The wedding ends with music and dance followed by a feast. Marriage is consummated on the next day.

The dead are cremated and the ashes are immersed in the Ganges. Usually the death rites are observed at the cremation ground. The pollution period lasts for thirteen days and *uthala* is observed on the tenth day. The *acharaj* performs a *havan* and seeks offerings. *Rassam pagri* (putting the turban on the son's head after the death of the father) is also performed on this day.

The Bharbhunjas are landless and depend on their traditional occupation of parching grain, maize, etc. They have also taken up various occupations as hawkers, grocers, fruit sellers, etc. Some are *dhaba walas* and cook meals whereas some are *kabaris* (collectors and sellers of rags or waste materials). In general, they remain petty shopkeepers and businessmen. Some of their women also are midwives. The linkages with the market are direct and daily. The dealings are on cash. Children assist their parents in their occupation.

The community has its own community council, called Kashyap Rajput Sabha, which is headed by a President elected by voice vote for an indefinite period or while he enjoys the confidence of the people. It holds its meetings on weekends or on days when the market is closed, and deals with certain social issues pertaining to marriage and other socio-economic problems of the locality or community. General welfare and developmental activities are under the purview of the Notified Area Committee. The community council cannot impose fines but those who deviate from social norms are penalised through social boycott.

A section of the Bharbhunja follow the Radhaswami socio-religious movement. They propitiate gods and goddesses of the Hindu pantheon. Besides, they propitiate family, clan, village or local deities. The *jathere* is propitiated on any ceremonial occasion. Guru is propitiated as a local village or town deity. The Bharbhunjas also propitiate various local/regional deities. Mansa Devi and Chandi Devi are regional goddesses, whose shrines are located on the outskirts of the city. The sacred specialists are from other communities. Magic men or spiritual specialists are also consulted whenever necessary. The major festivals of socio-religious and socio-economic importance are Dussehra, Diwali, Lohri, Baisakhi, Rakhi and Guruparabs.

Exchange of food occurs with all communities. Putative kinship-based friendship exists with other communities. Tap water is often shared with the next-door neighbour. The Bharbhunjas also share crematoria and religious shrines. They have developed modern inter-community linkages through small-scale business and shopkeeping. Political leadership is limited to the village or *mohalla* level.

Developmental programmes have had some impact in certain areas. The Bharbhunja have access to education up to secondary school for both sexes. But, in view of the prevailing unemployment problem they usually do not prefer higher or college education and hence engage their children in their own traditional work. In the sphere of health and medicare, modern treatment is usually taken but traditional methods are also followed wherever available and found effective. Attitudes towards family planning are favourable due to economic compulsions. Modern methods of sterilization are often employed and usually women get sterilized. Coal, fire-wood, kerosene oil, sawdust are the sources of fuel and some also have LPG. Provisions are available under IRDP programmes.

A.R. Sankhyan

# BHATIA

The Bhatias are originally from the countryside around Delhi. More recently they have migrated from Bhatner and Rajputana desert and claim to be of Yadubansi race, one branch of which became rulers of Jaisalmer, while the other took to commercial pursuits. The name would seem to show that they were Batis (Bhatti in the Punjab). The Bhatia or Bhatti, as they were called in olden days, claim with some probability to be of Rajput origin (Ibbetson, 1916). The Bhatias constitute a major group, termed a caste, which bears the ethnic rather than the occupational name. They have spread into the Punjab along the lower valleys of the Indus and the Sutlej. Sometimes, Bhatias are described as belonging to a 'widely spread and enterprising mercantile community'. They are often supposed to be Khatri, are very strict Hindus, far more so than the other trading classes of western Punjab. The Bhatias, like other Kshatriya groups of Punjab, are divided into seven *gotras* namely Prasana, Sanras, Bhardwaj, Sudhar Vans, Madhobadha, Devdas and Rashivans.

Unlike the *gotras* of other Hindu communities of the north these *gotras* serve no purpose other than for matrimony. The Bhatias are further sub-divided into sections called *nukhs* or *nookhs* which approximate to clans. These *nookhs* or clans have been formed on patronymic descent from an ancestor of fame or after the name of a particular village. Crooks (1896) classifies these 84 *nookhs* under the seven *gotras,* which would suggest common descent and close relationship. At present, there are a number of clan names among the Bhatias of Chandigarh which are either deviations of original clans or are new clans formed as a result of the need for contracting marriages. The community has been identified at the national level. Ethnographic and historical accounts of the community exist.

Punjabi is spoken within the family and kin group. The female dress is a typical Punjabi dress, i.e. *salwar, kameez* and *dupatta.* The male dress consists of *kurta, pyjama,* trousers, shirt and sometimes a *pagri* is seen on the head of old men. The *dhoti* is also worn by some old people.

The Bhatias of north India are characetrized by a high incidence of genes O (.603) and B (.229) at the ABO locus and genes M (.728) and S (.605) at the MNSs locus. The incidence or Rh -ve factor is low (.055). The results of Rh genotyping show a preponderance of chromosome R1 (CDe) (0.674). The recessive haplotype are (cde) is found to occur in low frequency (0.207). Other haplotyes ($R_0$, R', R", etc.) are present in much lower frequencies. Data is also available on some enzyme systems of serum proteins. The results show a high incidence of genes $p^b$ (0.566) and $p^a$ (0.431) at the AP (Acid phosphates) locus. The genes $Est_1$ (.796) and A $K_1$ (0.883) preponderate at the Esterase - D & AK (Adenylate Kinese) loci. At the $PGM_1$ locus the gene $PGM_1$ (.663) occurs twice as frequently as the gene $PGM_2$ (.337). The abnormal Haemoglobin is encountered with a fequency of .336. Analysis of Haptoglobin $G_m$ variants show high incidence of genes $H_p{}^2$ (.834) $G_m$-1-2 (.670) and at the respective loci.

Bhatias are traditionally vegetarian, but lately some of them have started eating non-vegetarian food as well. They refrain from eating garlic, onion and few other items of vegetable origin on account of their *tamasi* taste. Their staple food comprises mainly cereals like wheat, rice, *jowar, bajra,* maize and pulses of all kinds. Mustard oil, vegetable oil and *desi ghee* are mainly used as cooking medium. Non-alcoholic drinks like tea are consumed by both men and women. Some menfolk do take alcoholic drinks. They take seasonal fruits like banana, orange, grape, apple, etc. The consumption of fruits as a part of daily diet is on the increase.

The Bhatias are mainly Hindus while some follow Sikhism. Some of them switched over to the fold of Arya Samaj in the eighteenth century. They are mainly Vaishnavite, belonging to Vallabhacharya's sect, and visit holy places like Dwarka, Mathura, Gokul, etc.

The chief occupation of Bhatias is trading, shop-keeping and money-lending. The Bhatias were and still are inherently adventurous and enterprising people. There is no sphere of commerce or industry which they have not successfully tackled. They are in the forefront in textiles, cotton, iron and steel, mining, shipping and many other vital undertakings. The Bhatias unlike other Hindu communities, undertook sea voyages overseas and inland trade with immunity. As a class, they are vigorous and thrifty.

In the case of boys, marriage takes place around 26-30 years of age and in the case of girls the age at marriage is 22 to 25 years. Child marriage is on the decline now. Marriage is by negotiation and by mutual consent. Monogamy is the norm though a second wife is permitted in case of infidelity on the part of first wife. Levirate and sororate marriages are exceptional. Marriage among the Bhatias takes place according to Hindu rites and is associated with many customs and ceremonies. Betrothal or *mangni* is the first ceremony connected with marriage. Marriage rituals are performed at the bride's residence. The feast is given by the bride's parents on the wedding day.

The Punjabi Bhatias are divided into two subgroups, Bari and Bunjhar. Old men believe that their daughters should be given to western Bhatias as they are of superior status and wives are taken from the eastern Bhatias, considered inferior. In Chandigarh, the Bhatias are endogamous. Symbols of marriage strictly observed are vermilion, bangle, *bindi,* etc. Dowry in cash and kind exists. There are specific rules and regulations for divorce, which is permissible only on judicial approval. There may be various reasons for divorce; these are chronic sickness, maladjustment, etc. Divorce compensation is decided in court. Either party can seek a divorce. Both husband and wife have equal rights. Widower remarriage is permissible.

Rules of residence are patrilocal. Both nuclear and extended families exist. There is avoidance between daughter-in-law and father-in-law. Joking relationship is seen between sister-in-law and brother-in-law, grandparents and grandchildren. Property may be the major point of conflict among the relatives. Property is inherited through male equigeniture. Succession is by the eldest son. There is a rise in the formation of nuclear families and decline in the extended family system. Women have a role in economic activity, social functions, rituals, religious spheres, but rarely in political spheres. Women claim to have equal status and take part in important decisions relating to family matters. Besides attending to household chores, some of them also work in offices and contribute to family income; they also control expenditure.

The birth of a male child is heralded with great joy accompanied by many religious ceremonies depending upon the social and economic status of the parents. Naming ceremonies are held for the newborn of both sexes when the maternal uncle of the child presents gifts to its parents. The ceremony of first feeding is performed and is known as *annaprashan*. The *purohit* chants Vedic hymns, *dan-punya* is performed and the child is given *kheer*. When the boy attains an age of three, five, seven or nine years, his *mundan* is performed. Generally, the ceremony is performed in the temple. The Pandits find the auspicious moments for *kaan vedh* (piercing of ear) after consulting the *jantri* (almanac) and child's *kundli* (horoscope). During these ceremonies the ladies sing *mangal* (auspicious) songs.

Among the Bhatias, the dead body is draped in a white sheet and taken to the burning *ghat*. The pyre is lit by the son of the deceased. The mourners accompanying the dead body take a purificatory dip in the river before returning to their respective houses. The bones and ashes are collected on the next day. On the third day *teeja* is performed. The immersion of bones and ashes takes place between the third and the thirteenth day after death. On the thirteenth day obsequies are performed. A Brahman priest presides over the ceremony. Every year the *shradh* is performed and a number of Brahman are served pukka food.

To keep alive the social interactions and in order to maintain cohesion among *biradari* members a mechanism of gift exchange called *vartan bhaji* is mintained. Literally, *vartan bhaji* means exchange of sweets, fruits, food, money, etc. It also encompasses brotherly treatment including invitations extended on all ceremonial occasions.

Bhatias traditionally exchange water and food with 'high' caste communities, but not with Chuhras and Chamar. However the rules of commensality are breaking down. They share roads and places of worship with members of all communities. Attitude towards family planning and saving is favourable.

V. Bhalla
Achla Sood

# BHATRA

The Bhatras are mainly confined to the town of Manimajra, with only a few members living in the city of Chandigarh. They are also distributed in a few neighbouring states like the Punjab, Himachal Pradesh, Haryana, Uttar Pradesh and Delhi. The community perceives its identification at the national level.

In the *Mahabharat* and *Singhasan Batisi* it is claimed that one Madho Nai, a Brahman saint, who was well-versed in singing poetry, fell in love with, and married, a dancing girl named Kam Kundala. From these two persons descended the Madhwa, commonly known as Bhatra. Maharaja Ranjit Singh, while exempting this group from *tirni*-taxation, has referred to them as Madhwas, descendants of Madho, as can be proved by an original *parwana* dated 7 Assuj, Sambat 1866, to his governors, which is still in the possession of one Prithi Dass, Bhatra of Dhariwal. The term Bhatra is derived from the Sanskrit word *bhat*, and has been applied to the community, because Madho was himself fond of quoting poetry.

Madho claims to have lived in Ceylon (present day Sri Lanka). During the reign of Babar, Guru Nank visited Ceylon, where he became acquainted with Changa, an influential Madho or Bhatra, who became his disciple. Large numbers of Bhatras were converted to Sikhism, and when Guru Nanak returned to India they accompanied him. A Sikh temple, known as Dera Baba, was built in Ceylon in memory of Guru Nanak and the place where this temple is erected is the original home of Bhatras (Stewart, 1985: 315-16).

Rose (1919) has described the Bhatras as pedlars like the Maniars and Banjaras. According to him they first settled on the banks of Ganga in Bijnor district of United Province, where they worked as pedlars of cheap ornaments for women, and of Vedic medicines. They migrated to Sialkot and Hoshiarpur, and then settled in all towns and places of pilgrimage in India. They worked as magicians and astrologers. They often indulged in swindling. (Rose, 1919: 93-4). However, no crimes against property were reported against them, though they misappropriated the money collected for charities. These subscriptions were collected in the guise of *sanyasi, udasi fakir*, Bairagi Sikh or Brahman. Even now they remember their past activities, but the practices have completely been abandoned.

The community migrated to its present place from Patiala, where it had migrated earlier from Sialkot after the partition. The community remembers both these migrations. They speak Punjabi within the family and Hindi with others.

The people are accustomed to Punjabi food habits, on the whole non-vegetarian. Men drink liquor, purchased from the market, but abstain from smoking. There is a moderate intake of vegetables, pulses and fruits. However, the consumption has increased during the last few years. Pulses used include gram, *tur, urad, moong*, peas, *masur, moth*, etc. *Vanaspati, ghee*, mustard, sunflower and groundnut oil are most commonly used as cooking medium. Both wheat and rice are taken, but consumption of rice is very little; they prefer wheat to rice.

The community has many *gotras*. According to Stewart (1985) Bhotiwal, Lande, Digwa, Gamee, Kag, Lohi, Bhotti, Gojra, Bathaur, Kasba, Rod, Bhain and Lar were the 13 *gotras*, out of a total 22. These days the community records *gotras* like Takad, Galaya, Roe, Chandanpal, Sawali, Jagpal, Jogi, and Rathod. They believed that Galaya and Jogi *gotras* were same. All *gotras* are considered equal. The community is divided into Sikhs and Hindus. Hindu Bhatras continue the profession of astrologers and palmists. The Sikh Bhatras are mostly small shopkeepers in Manimajra. All Sikh Bhatras practise their trade in Manimajra, whereas Hindu Bhatras are working in Chandigarh city. These social divisions and differentiations help to regulate marriage alliances and indicate social status. The self-perception of the community is moderate. They consider themselves superior to many communities but inferior to Kshatriyas. However, other communities consider them of low status.

The Bhatras are endogamous at the community level, and exogamous at village and *gotra* level. Only *gotras* of father and mother are excluded. Marriages take place between Hindu and Sikh Bhatras as well. Marriages are performed at adult age. These are settled by negotiations, either directly or through *bicholas* (mediators); the consent of girls and boys is usually not asked for. Marriage symbols include vermilion, bangles, finger and ear-rings. Sikh Bhatra women do not use the *bindi* or *mangalsutra* as marriage symbols. Dowry is given in kind. Rules of residence are patrilocal. Divorce is permissible for various reasons but divorce cases are rare. Remarriage of widows is permissible with the consent of the parents in-law. Cases of *karewa* (marriage of widow with younger brother-in-law) are known. Remarriage of divorced women is also permissible. Rules of marriage have become liberal, and age at marriage has gone up.

The community lives in nuclear as well as extended families. There is avoidance relationship between *sas* (mother-in-law) and *jawai*, and *saura* and *nuhn* (daughter-in-law). However, *pardah* or *ghund* has declined. Joking relationships exist between *sali* and *jeeja,* and *bhabi* and *dewar.* Disputes arise due to property matters and challenge to the authority of elders. Inheritance is by the rule of equigeniture and succession is through the eldest son. The formation of nuclear families is on the increase. Women perform only household jobs and have low status as compared to men. However, they have decision-making powers and control family expenditure. They have a role in the ritual-religious sphere and in social control. Pollution is observed for thirteen days in the family. The new-born is baptised to Sikhism on the fifth day by the ceremony of *amrit chakhana.* The naming ceremony takes place as per the norms prescribed in Sikh religion which is termed as *vak lena.* The priest takes a *vak* from *Shri Guru Granth Sahib* and suggests the name. Among the Hindu Bhatras, it is done by the priest. *Mundan* takes place only among the Hindu Bhatras. Marriage rituals take place at the bride's residence. Marriage takes places as per *anand karj* or prescribed Sanatan Dharam rites are followed. The dead are cremated and bones are disposed of in water. The ceremonies of *satwan, daswan, satarwan* are performed after death. Pollution is observed until these ceremonies are over. Rituals have become more expensive these days.

The community was earlier engaged in astrology, palmistry and begging. During British rule, Bhatra was considered a criminal tribe (Gayer, 1985). But today, only a few members continue the profession of astrology and palmistry. The Bhatras of Manimajra have small businesses of ready-made garments, and bangle-selling. Due to a low level of education none of them is engaged in any white-collar job. As traders, they have a daily contact on cash basis with a fully regulated market. Children do petty jobs in shops. The community has a Singh Sabha Bhat Biradari Manimajra, which is affiliated to a regional body with head office at Ludhiana. It collects subscriptions from members and manages local *gurdwaras* of the Bhatra. Elections take place by voice vote. The sacred specialists, who are from other communities, perform worship, impart religious knowledge and preside over birth, death and marriage rites. Sikh Bhatras celebrate all Guruparabs. The Bhatras of both the communities celebrate Lohri, Baisakhi, Diwali, Dussehra, etc. Hindu Bhatras also celebrate Shivratri, Ramnaumi and other festivals.

The Bhatras have relations with other communities and exchange all types of food with them. They share water sources, crematoria, religious shrines and festivals with other communities. The community has a *gurdwara* of its own in Manimajra, accessible to all communities. People remember Makhan Singh Mirgind, a member of the community, who participated in *Jaito Morcha* during British rule.

The community has drawn selective benefits from the development programmes. Boys and girls generally go to school but only in a few cases up to a higher level. The boys drop out as they have to support families, but girls drop out because of social reasons, and also because they find it inconvenient to attend schools and colleges at distant places. Attitudes to modern medicare are positive. Some families have resorted to family planning after two or three children. Kerosene, coal and gas are used as fuel.

Virinder Singh
K.C. Kayastha

# BRAHMAN

The Brahman, according to Ibbetson (1916: 215), 'concerns himself but little with the spiritual guidance of the people but he is consulted as to omens and auspicious names, dates, and events, and he officiates at all ceremonial functions ... the Brahmans are ready to be fed or receive offerings in the name of God, but their sacerdotal functions [are] purely passive. ... In social position, the Brahman is of course pre-eminently first in the Hindu portion of the Punjab.'

Brahmans of Chandigarh speak Punjabi and Hindi and use Devanagari script. The males wear shirt, trousers, *pyjama* and the females wear *salwar, kameez, dupatta,* or *sari*. Traditionally, they are strict vegetarians. During marriage or any other ceremony they always offer vegetarian food to their relatives and guests. Staple food is *dal* and *roti*; *rajma, moong* and *urad* are some of their favourite pulses. Seasonal vegetables and fruits are eaten regularly. Roots and tubers are a common part of their diet. Their cooking medium is *ghee* and mustard oil. *Lassi* (butter-milk) and tea are the regular non-alcoholic drinks. Consumption of *desi ghee* is moderate due to its prohibitive cost. The males smoke *bidis* and cigarettes.

They recognize the *varna* system and place themselves foremost in the social hierarchy. There are seven *gotras*, Galib, Gaur, Saraswat, Prasar, Bhardwaj, Attari and Vasisht amongst the Brahmans. The two subgroups are Gaur and Saraswat. Regarding the origin of the *gotras* of the Brahmans, Ibbetson (1916) states that 'the word *gotra* means a family or lineage, the descendants from a common fold'. The Brahman say that their *gotras* are named after the great Hindu *rishis*, though it does not clearly appear whether the members of each *gotra* claim descent from the *rishi* whose name it bears, as from a carnal or as from a spiritual father. At any rate, whatever their origin, the Brahminical *gotras* have become absolutely hereditary and every Brahman, whether Gaur, Saraswat or otherwise, belongs to one or other *gotra*. But the Brahminical *gotra* extends far beyond the body of Brahmans.

'The *gotra* thus defined is used only at marriage, on the occasion of Sankalpa and in similar formal ceremonies.' In hierarchy and stratification, the Gaur occupy a higher social status than the Saraswat.

Brahmans arrange their marriages within their own community, but not between the same *gotra*. Earlier, child marriage was quite common, but at present the age at which a boy is eligible for marriage is twenty-one years, whereas the marriage age for girls is eighteen to twenty years. Generally, marriage is arranged by parents or by close relatives. Married girls use *sindur*, *bindi*, ear-rings, finger-rings, toe-rings and nose-rings which, along with glass or gold bangles, are regarded as symbols of marriage. However, the parents give clothes, utensils, etc., as gifts to ther daughters at the time of their marriage. The bride stays with her in-laws after marriage. In extreme cases of maladjustment, they go to court for seeking divorce. In Chandigarh levirate (junior) and sororate (junior) re-marriage is allowed. Brahmans used to maintain joint families but today nuclear families are coming up fast.

Traditional interpersonal relationships are strictly maintained amongst the Brahmans. Avoidance relationships exist between a mother-in-law and son-in-law, father-in-law and daughter-in-law. Joking relationship between *bhabi* and *dewar* is common. All sons inherit the property of their father equally. If there are no sons, daughters get equal shares in property. Succession is through the eldest son. Their primary duty still to attend to routine household chores, women have a low status.

Life-cycle rituals are observed in the family at the time of birth, thread wearing, marriage and death. After the birth of a child, the post-delivery pollution period ends on the eleventh day when the mother and the baby take a bath which is followed with offer of sweets to the neighbours. Usually, they use water of the Ganges for their purification. In the case of birth of a male child, most Brahmans give feasts to their neighbours. *Mundan* ceremony, in the case of a male child is observed in a temple with puja and *havan*. The sacred thread wearing ceremony is performed for boys at the age of five years or later. It is generally performed in the odd number of the years. In this ceremony, elderly members of the family invite their relatives and neighbours and serve a meal. A Brahman performs all the rituals and arranges *havan*. The new-born is confined to a dark room for three days; he should not see the sunlight nor the face of a non-Brahman. On the fourth day, he is given a bath and it is on this day he becomes a Brahman.

The marriage ceremony is held at the residence of the bride and marriage rituals are performed by the Brahman priests, partly at the bride's residence and partly at the bridegroom's. *Havan* is also arranged by a priest at the residence of the bride. A feast is given by the bride's parents as part of the marriage rituals according to Hindu tradition.

The Brahmans cremate their dead. Pollution lingers up to ten days. During the pollution period a male member (son) worships his ancestors. Only tea, water, and fruits are consumed by the sons of the deceased during the pollution period. On the eleventh day, they arrange *shradh* ceremony. They invite a Brahman to chant *mantras*, and to perform death rites. Many of them offer bedding and utensils along with some money to the Brahman at this occasion. Members of the community are invited and feasted. Death rituals are becoming less elaborate in the wake of modernization and due to rising prices.

The traditional occupation of the Brahman is to engage himself in priestly activities and to perform birth, marriage and death rites. However, many are now educated and occupy high positions in government service and various other professions like law, teaching, business, banking, or the defence services. They worship Hindu gods and goddesses such as Durga, Shiva, Krishna. Usually, women go to local temples to offer puja. Widows observe fast on *ekadashi* (eleventh lunar day), *sankranti,* the first day of the months of the local calendar. They celebrate festivals like Raksha Bandhan, Diwali, Dussehra, Holi and Lohri. Married women also observe fast on Karwa-chauth.

The Brahmans share sources of water, roads, schools, religious places with the members of other communities with whom they take part in traditional festivals. Earlier they used to accept water, kachcha and pukka food from the 'high' castes such as the Kshatriya and Vaishya. But today, they accept water, kachcha and pukka food from some other castes also.

Education is favoured for boys as well as girls. They get modern medical facilities. At present, there is marked awareness of various family planning methods and couples prefer two or three children. Fue-wood, cow-dung cakes, coal and kerosene oil are used for cooking purposes. Most Brahmans have liquid petroleum gas as an alternative source of fuel. They have easy access to medicare facilities like immunization for children and mothers. They mostly have saving accounts in banks. Most of them buy essential household commodities from shopkeepers on credit and maintain the system of monthly payment of cash.

V. Bhalla
Nupur Pathak

# CHAMAR

The term *chamar* comes from *charamkar*, i.e. worker and trader in leather products. Chamars are known today as Mochi or Muchi and have various names such as Ramdasia, Satnami, Raidas, Rohit, Rovidas, Ravidas, Ramnami and Rishi.

The Ramdasia are Sikh Chamars. The name Ramdasia was taken from Guru Ramdas, the fourth Sikh Guru who is said to be the first to receive the Chamars into the fold of Sikhism.

The community can be grouped into two major sub-castes, the Mochi and Muchi. This division depends on the nature of work. The Mochis make and repair shoes and *chappals* of leather. The Muchis are makers of the *mandar*, a kind of musical instrument. The Mochis do not make these and are generally superior to Muchis. Again the Mochis are divided into several exogamous clans such as Lakra and Dhusia.

Chamars are found in Punjab, Haryana and Uttar Pradesh. In Punjab, Sikh Chamars or Ramdasias have a history of about 500 years. They are to be found in northern, central, and eastern parts of Punjab. According to the Census of India, 1981, the total population of Chamars in Chandigarh is 20,128 which included 11,796 males and 8,332 females.

Chamars speak both Hindi and Punjabi. The Hindu Chamars speak Hindi with members of their own community and both Hindi and Punjabi with members of other communities. The Ramdasias converse in Punjabi with members of their own community.

Males generally wear loin cloth *(dhoti)*, and *kurta* whereas young men now wear trousers. The Ramdasia males wear turbans as well. Females wear *sari, salwar, kameez* and *dupatta*. Women adorn themselves with ornaments such as bangle, necklace, ear-ring, finger-ring, toe-ring, etc. The ornaments are made of gold or silver depending upon the economic condition of the family. The Chamars have been recognized as a Scheduled Caste community.

*Dal* and *roti* are the staple food of the Chamars. Pulses of all kinds, such as *urad, moong, kulthi*, peas, beans, *masur*, and *moth* are consumed. People are both vegetarian and non-vegetarian. Besides vegetables, they take egg, fish, meat, pork, etc. Onion and garlic are also used. *Sarson ka saag* and *makai ki roti* are favourite items. The food is generally cooked in mustard or groundnut oil. Roots and tubers are also consumed. Fruits such as mango, guava, orange, banana are eaten seasonally. Men consume alcoholic drinks very frequently. These are purchased from local market. Some men also take tobacco but the Sikhs do not touch it in any form.

Some of the common surnames are Karenwal, Nagwal, Chuhan, Simar, Rali, Bangar, Sidhu, Simri, Bahamaniya, Veerwar, Janagal, etc.

The Chamars marry within their own community. They also observe village exogamy. Monogamy is the general rule. Marriage involves three main ceremonies, the betrothal known as *mangani*, the wedding and the consummation of marriage or *gauna*. Child marriage is quite common. According to their belief, when a girl attains puberty she becomes polluted. So the girl should be married before puberty when she is unpolluted. Today however girls are married after fourteen or fifteen years of age. The usual age of boys at marriage varies from eighteen to twenty-four. Furniture, jewellery, clothes and other household material are given as dowry depending upon the financial condition of the girl's parents. *Kanyadan* is performed during marriage. After marriage, the girl stays at the residence of her husband. Divorce is also permitted with judicial approval. Remarriage of widows is also permitted, usually with the husband's younger brother. However, a widow can also marry outside her deceased husband's family. In such cases, the new husband has to pay some compensation to the late husband's family. The practice of child marriage is becoming less common day by day.

The Chamars have both joint and nuclear families. However, there is a rise in the number of nuclear families due to social and economic constraints. All sons inherit the property of their father equally. If there is no son, the daughters get equal shares of the property of their father. The eldest son gets the succession after his father. The status of women is generally low. The primary duty of women is to attend to various household activities, and help in looking after domestic animals such as cows, buffaloes, goats, etc. With the reservation policies of the government, expanding educational facilities and growing awareness, the number of boys and girls going for higher education is on the increase. Some women work in offices and hold good jobs, thereby adding to their status as well as to the income of their family.

When a child is born, the sixth day after the birth is celebrated as *chhatti*. The *mundan* ceremony is observed by Hindu Chamars. Ramdasias perform the *namkaran* ceremony also.

Marriage rituals are performed at the bride's residence. A feast is given by bride's parents to the bridegroom's family and friends. They perform marriage rituals according to the tradition of *phere*. These are held at the bride's residence.

The community cremates the dead and the bones are disposed of at Hardwar or some other sacred place such as Patalpuri. For the peace of the soul, *havan* or *akhand path* is performed. When an elderly person dies, a feast is offered to the members of the community. They also perform *shradh* ceremony.

The Chamars earn mainly from the sale of leather goods. Leather work is their traditional occupation. Previously they used to remove the skins from carcasses and after tanning they used to make shoes and *chappals*. But today, as chemically tanned skin has a great demand in the market, many of them are learning this particular process. Besides this, they also work as agricultural labourers in fields during the times of transplanting, reaping and threshing. They rear cattle as a subsidiary occupation. Members staying in towns and cities also work in industries and many of them are in government service. They have direct links with the market. Essential commodities are purchased either weekly or monthly, for cash.

The village Panchayat looks after the welfare of the people and implements schemes. But for the settlement of disputes, Chamars usually go to the police station or the court of law.

Chamars are Hindu or Sikh. They worship Guru Ravidas. All rituals related to birth, childhood, marriage and death are performed by sacred specialists from within the community. Chamars celebrate all festivals along with neighbouring communities.

They have oral traditions. Women sing and dance on important occasions. The Ramdasia women perform *giddha* and men perform *bhangra*. Folk tales also exist.

In recent times, they have found access to religious places and common water sources. The community has businessmen and teachers and some men work in the defence services. They also hold jobs as clerks and administrators in government offices. Political leadership has emerged at various levels.

Both boys and girls attend school. Boys study up to college level and some continue further. Girls usually study up to the secondary level and then help their mothers in household activities. The attitude towards modern medicare is positive. They get medical facilities from the local civil or government hospitals, including facilities of immunization. Most parents have more than three children. Drinking water is available within the locality. Taps, hand-pumps and wells are sources of drinking water. Wood, cow-dung, kerosene oil and gobar-gas are used for cooking purposes. Mid-day meals are served to children in *anganwadis* and primary schools. Many of them have savings accounts in banks.

V. Bhalla
Sushil Kumari

# CHHIMBA

The Chhimbas are stampers or dyers of cloth by occupation, but they are now turning to tailoring because dyeing and stamping has become unremunerative. Rose (1919: 166) gives Chhipi and Chhimpi as synonyms. In Chandigarh, they are also known as Darzi and Tank Kshatri. Ibbetson (1916: 321) has described them as calico-printers who can hardly be distinguished from Dhobis. He further adds that the Chhimbas often combine washing with dyeing and stamping, and they commonly work as *darzi* or tailors. Our study confirms their origin from Baba Namdev. There are two subgroups of Chhimbas based on the names of Namdev's sons, Tank and Rhilla, who were taught the art of dyeing, printing and washing clothes (Rose 1919: 166-68).

The community migrated to its present habitat from various parts of Pakistan, Burma, Punjab and Bombay and perceives its distribution at an international level. Chhimbas speak Punjabi and Hindustani and Gurmukhi and Devanagari are the scripts in use. They are occasional non-vegetarian and though women cook non-vegetarian food, generally they themselves do not eat. The staple cereals are wheat and rice, and pulses in common use are gram, *urad*, *moong*, peas, beans, *masur*, etc. *Vanaspati* and mustard oil are used for cooking. The menfolk consume both country and Indian-made foreign liquors on special occasions. These drinks are purchased from market. Fruit and milk consumption is moderate. Betel chewing is common and snuff is used. A change from vegetarian to non-vegetarian, decrease in the use of pulses and fruits, increased intake of vegetables are the few major changes found in food habits.

The Chhimbas in Chandigarh have the following prominent *gotras*: Jassal, Purba, Kainth, Pandeer, Raikh-Rai, Raikh-Rishi, Bedi, Bhatt, Bagri, Punjare, Vareh, Majedo, Toki, Mohel, etc. The function of these is to regulate marriage alliances. The community's self perception and others' perception about them, places them at the medium level. They recognize the *varna* system and identify themselves as Kshatriyas. The marriages are exogamous at *gotra*, village and surname level, and marriage partners of the mother's and father's *gotras* are avoided. Junior sororate and junior levirate are permissible. Marriage alliances are settled through negotiations between parents of the boy and the girl. Monogamy is the rule. Vermilion, *bindi*, nose pin or stud are symbols of married women.

*Kanyadan* is an important ritual during marriage ceremonies. Dowry is given by the bride's parents, both in cash and kind, to help establish an independent household, especially when the boy is in service or away from his parents and has to set up a nuclear family. The Chhimbas follow patrilocal residence. In some cases of maladjustment, they go for judicial dissolution of marriage. Widow and widower marriage is permissible. In the case of remarriage of a widow, ceremonies are minimum. Marriages are solemnized only after the boy and girl attain adulthood. Boys marry at about twenty-three and girls around twenty. Nuclear and vertically extended families are common.

There are conflicts and confrontations between the younger members and the elders of a family concerning property, the freedom of youngsters and elders' authority. Male equigeniture is the rule, but equal shares go to the mother and unmarried sisters also. Succession goes to the eldest son. Changes in the institution of the family include the rise of nuclear families at the cost of the extended family. Women have equal status. They contribute to family income by way of assisting in tailoring work and also manage family expenditure. They have their role in economic activity and in religious matters. Political activity and participation in the mechanism of social control is almost non-existent.

Post-delivery pollution and restrictions are observed. Mother and child are given a bath on *chhatti* for purification and again after *sava maheena* (forty days). The latter signals the culmination of all pollution and restrictions. Naming ceremony is observed. Marriage is solemnized at the bride's residence, where a feast is arranged by her parents for the *barat* (members of groom's party). Marriages are performed as per Vedic rites, or *anand karaj*. After marriage, the groom, or his parents, arrange a feast (reception) for their friends and relatives. The nuptial ceremony is performed at the groom's residence.

The dead are cremated; the dead body is kept on the pyre in the north-south direction; bones are disposed of at Haridwar in the Ganges or at Kiratpur Sahib. Death pollution is observed and all the rituals are completed on *kirya* or *tehravin* (the thirteenth day). *Shradh* (ancestor worship) is also observed. Life-cycle rituals are becoming more elaborate and more expensive over the years. The quantum of dowry and cash transactions as *shagun,* or in other ceremonies and rituals, are increasing.

Calico-printing and tailoring was the traditional occupation, but now tailoring is the primary occupation. All transactions are in cash. The traditional caste Panchayat of the Chhimbas is called Namdev Sabha which is located at Namdev Bhawan in Chandigarh. The Sabha's sole function is to look after welfare, especially that of the widows, orphans and the poor. The elders of this Panchayat are elected through voice vote and are seven in number. Funds are raised through donations.

The Chhimbas believe in the tenets of the Hinduism as well as Sikhism. They worship Jwalaji, Shivaji and *Guru Granth Sahib.* Sacred specialists are from other communities. Pandits in case of Hindus, and *granthis* in the case of Sikhs perform the life-cycle rituals, religious teachings and worship. Oral tradition exists in the form of folktales and folksongs. *Dhols* are the only musical instrument in use for celebrations. Light Hindi music is generally liked by members of this community.

The Chhimbas traditionally accept and exchange food and water from all communities, Bania, Rajput and Khatri, but not from Balmiki, Chamar, Bangale, Dhea and Muslim, but these rules are no longer observed. They share a crematorium with other communities and visit the same shrines. They participate in all religious festivals. Modern inter-community linkages can be seen in the form of entrepreneurship, and business. Political leadership has emerged at local, regional and national levels.

Boys' education is favoured but they drop out at secondary or college level due to lack of interest in studies. For girls, the attitude is partially favourable and they go up to secondary level. They drop out due to social reasons or poor academic performance and then help in augmenting family income by sewing. They make full use of modern medicare and have adopted family planning in a big way and couples prefer one or two children.

Drinking water is available in their locality through pipes laid by the Public Health Department and many households have hand-pumps besides pipes. Electricity is available in every house. Cow-dung cakes, coal, kerosene oil and LPG are the main fuel sources. Mid-day meals, ICDS and public distribution facilities are well utilized.

R. Malhotra

# CHRISTIANS

The Chrisitians of Chandigarh, also known as Isai, have a number of sects. The main sects profess their adherence to the Church of North India, Catholic Church, Baptist Church, Anglican Church, Church of God, St. Mary's Orthodox Syrian Church, Holy Trinity, Anglican Church, and Mathnoite, Syrian Jacobite and Salvation Army. There are no accepted titles used by the community, but many Christian migrants from Punjab use Massey with their names. The community is identifiable at regional, inter-regional, national and international levels. Both ethnographic and historic accounts of Christians exist. The Union Territory of Chandigarh was once part of Ambala district of unified Punjab before 1947 and also before 1966 (the bifurcation of Punjab). There are two views about the arrival of Christianity in north India. According to one view, Christianity came to these areas in the first century AD (McMillan 1982: 5). According to the second view Christianity was established in this area with the consolidation of the British rule (McMillan 1982: 140).

In 1971, there were 2,504 Christians in the Union Territory, with 1,280 male and 1,224 female in this population. Only 100 lived in rural areas. In Manimajra town the population was 37, and 2,367 Christians were in the city of Chandigarh (Census of India, 1971). In 1981, the Christian population of Chandigarh was 4,470 and there were 1,192 Christian households. Out of this total of 1,173 households, with population of 4,404, were in rural areas. There were 2,350 male to 2,054 female (Census of India, 1981). There is a clear pattern in the Christian settlement of Chandigarh. Protestant migrants from Punjab came mostly from Gurdaspur and Amritsar districts. However the migrants from south India are the Catholics. Only 150 Catholics are living in the villages of Chandigarh. Out of the total settled Catholic population of about 1,000, only 500 are from Punjab. Others have their origin in southern states such as Kerala and Goa. In the opinion of a priest of the CNI, there are 1,500 followers of this Church at the moment. Other churches have only a marginal following. A few of them, e.g. the Seventh Day Adventists, have a following mainly among the students from Nigeria. All of them remember the date when they migrated to this place.

In Chandigarh, Christians speak their own respective language, i.e. Punjabi, Hindi, Tamil, Malayalam or English. The script used is also according to the language spoken. In their dealings with other communities, English and Hindi are used. Church service is performed in Hindi in CNI and Catholic Church. Others perform services in English only. The Christain symbol of the cross is displayed prominently at Churches. The members of the community make a symbolic cross, to express sorrow and while remembering Christ. The use of European names like Emannuel, John, George, etc., by the community is another distinguishing feature. Under the Constitution, Christians are a religious minority.

Both women and men are non-vegetarian. Intake of vegetables and fruits is moderate. The use of alcoholic drinks is observed both in men and women. They smoke cigarettes and *bidis*. Milk forms part of their diet. There is distinction in food habits of Christians from south and north. Those from south continue their southern food habits. They eat rice, *dosa, vada, sambar, rasam* and various other south Indian food items. But those having origin in north India, eat *roti* made from wheat flour with pulses such as gram, *urad, moong*, peas, *masur, moth*, etc. While north Indian Christian use groundnut, mustard, sunflower and *vanaspati* as cooking medium, those from south India use coconut oil as essential cooking medium. Consumption of fruit and vegetables has increased. Southern Christians now consume *roti* as well.

Social divisions exist in the community at the level of various sects. According to some, the Catholic Church as an institution, is the oldest in the place. In March 1960, a place for a separate cemetery for Christians in Sector-25, was set up. Caste is prevalent to some extent among Christians from south India. Even Christians from the north are aware of their low caste origins. There is differentiation with hierarchy among the sects. The community is differentiated at occupational and economic levels. It holds positions in white-collar jobs. Although the educational background of Christians as a whole is good, not all are well educated. At social levels the Christians from the south can be distinguished by their dress and food habits.

These differentiations regulate marriages and are an indication of social status. The self-perception of the community is high; but others accord medium status to Christians because of their low social origins before conversion. The Christians of Chandigarh are generally endogamous at community and sect levels. However, there have been cases of inter-sect and inter-community marriages. Marriages between Protestants and Catholics are more common among Christians with origins in the north, than of those with origin in the south. Marriages can be endogamous at the locality level and are performed in the city itself. These marriages aim at 'social contracts and social relationships'. Personal attributes play an important role in mate's selection (Jatinder Kaur, 1977). More Protestants prefer inter-sect marriages than do Catholics. Even Protestant women are more economically independent and have higher status than Catholic women.

This study has also pointed out that among Catholics of the south, marriage is considered a sacrament and a contract. All Hindu customs of *arti*, distribution of *prasad*, wearing of *mangalsutra* are observed. While all Catholics prefer religious marriage, only a small percentage of Protestans prefer court marriage. The proposal mostly comes from boy's side. Engagement is performed by an exchange of rings. The presence of a priest at the engagement ceremony is compulsory. Date of marriage is fixed in consultation with the Parish priest. A proforma has to be filled by the groom and the priest checks the age at the time of marriage and verifies all facts against bigamy. Baptism is a must for the partners. The Parish priest announces the proposed union for consecutive Sundays. In case of no objection, a certificate is sent to the bride's church.

At the time of marriage the bride wears white, the sign of virginity. (These days red is also worn). The bride is accompanied by a bridesmaid. The bride stands to the left of the altar and groom's place is on the right. He is accompanied by the 'best man' and arrives before the bride. The bride's father or guardian gives her away and the bride and the bridegroom pledge themselves to each other. Both kneel and the priest blesses them. The priest takes the wedding ring from the best man, and sprinkles it with holy water, in front of Cross and gives it to the groom, who puts it on the third finger of the bride.

Mass is held after the wedding but it is not obligatory. Psalms are sung and prayer is said. Both sign the register in the presence of the witnesses. Dinner, or lunch, is served now (Jatinder Kaur, 1977: 43-53). Some social practices like dowry and *barat* have entered Christian marriages without religious sanction. After marriage newly weds live separately from parents. Divorce is permissible with judicial means, for various reasons. Compensation for divorce is given to the aggrieved party and children can be the responsibility of either parent. Remarriage of a widow, widower or divorcee is permitted. There has been liberalization of rules and symbols of marriage.

Christians prefer nuclear families. Joking and avoidance relationships among Christians of the north show the influence of local culture. Disputes arise due to property matters and checks on the authority of youngsters. These are mainly concerned with inheritance. All women have the right to inheritance but in practice male equigeniture is followed as a norm. Succession rules favour the eldest son. Women participate in economic activities and contribute to family income, generally. They have a say in control of family income, and have decision-making powers. In the formal sense they are equal to men as they participate in social functions, and also have a role in social control.

Christian children have to be baptised for entry into Christianity. The ceremony differs in different sects. The Church of North India performs the ceremony in the Church itself. Catholics do it in a lake, and all other sects follow this practice whereas the Salvation Army does it under its own flag. Marriage is solemnised in the church and the nuptial ceremony takes place at the groom's place or at any other place arranged for the purpose.

The dead are buried in a cemetery. The parish priest is present at the time of burial. There is no formal observation of pollution. It is desirable to wear black clothes at the time of burial. No ancestor worship has been reported. Rituals have not changed, but have become more expensive.

The Christians are a landless community with no traditional occupation, but are well represented in various white-collar jobs, defence service, nursing, etc. A large humber of its members are also engaged in unskilled labour. Christians from the south have comparatively better jobs and are mostly in government service. Christian migrants from Punjab are not as well placed as their counterparts from south India. However they have better living conditions than their kin in their natal villages. Some bodies, like the Common Cemetery Committee for all churches exist in the city. The Catholic Church has a Vincent Paul Society to help the poor. It also has a typing institute. Villages have Panchayats; these are heterogenous in nature and perform the usual statutory functions, and have statutory powers.

The Holy Bible is central to Christian teaching. Sacred specialists of the community are from the same community. They must also belong to the same sect. The priests perform functions of worship and ritual religious teachings. They perform ceremonies at the time of birth, death, marriage and baptism. The festivals of the community are of social and religious significance, Christmas and Easter being the most celebrated. All Christians are either converts or descendants of converts. Pre-conversion practices survive among Catholics from the south in the form of customs and caste system. Some of the Christians from the north, who were converted from lower castes, have changed back to pre-change practices to avail of the benefits of employment as Scheduled Castes, though the number of such cases is very small. The community is engaged in proselytising activities, but today insists upon a legal affidavit before the ceremony of baptism is performed.

The inter-community relations of the community are very good. It exchanges all types of food with other communities. However, the Catholics from the south observe the caste system in this regard. A few inter-community marriages have also taken place. Christians share water sources with other communities, but have a separate cemetery and separate religious places from other communities. Even different sects have different places for worship. Political leadership has not strongly emerged.

The developmental process has benefited the community. Education has been favoured for both boys and girls. Both try to get education up to post-graduation level. Though girls have special aptitude for nursing, a few have also got professional education in medicine and law. Some have doctoral degrees. Local Churches are also running many educational institutions in the city. The Church of North India has a nursery school, which was started in 1988.

The community makes full use of modern medicare. Both males and females have accepted the modern techniques of family welfare. Sometimes the Protestants resort to abortion.

Virinder Singh

# DHANAK

According to Rose (1919: 235), the name Dhanak derives from Sanskrit *dhanashka*, bowman. Dhanaks however are no longer hunters. They work at scavenging and do a great deal of weaving also. The Dhanaks also return themselves as Lal Guru, another name for Lal Beg, the sweeper Guru. But they were said to burn their dead and marry by *phera* and appeared to be closely allied to the Pasis. Crooke (1896) has also expressed similar ideas about the Dhanaks.

Dhanaks belong to Kallupanth as they are the offspring of Kallu Ram. Kallu Ram had one son Ekloa. Asthbakar was the son of Ekloa. Asthbakar had three sons, namely Dhanakmuni, Jharkanda and Markanda. Dhanakmuni is worshipped in Amritsar. The Dhanak also had Dhanakmuni's temple at Ratlam and Chakmanglur. Dhanakmuni spread the art of archery. Some of the Dhanak were commanders in the forces of Maharana Pratap. Aurangzeb converted them to Islam. The Dhanak were expert in archery like the Bhil. They went into the jungles in order to save their lives. Later on they adopted the occupation of weaving and became followers of Kabir. The Dhanaks are also known as Kandera in Rajasthan and Delhi, Sayeus in Uttar Pradesh, Neharya in Mathura, Bagri in Rajasthan, Thakur near Rajasthan, Koli in Uttar Pradesh and Julaha in Punjab. They have different names but the same origin.

The Dhanaks are concentrated in villages and also live in Chandigarh, having mostly migrated from Lahore to Sonepat in Haryana and from Haryana to Chandigarh. Some of the families have also migrated from Punjab. As they engage in weaving, they are also termed followers of Bhagat Kabir or Kabirpanthis. According to the Census of India, 1981, the total population of Dhanaks in the Union Territory is 609, which includes 336 males and 273 females.

They speak Punjabi and also Punjabi mixed with Hindi, within the family and with members of other communities. Those who are literate use the Devanagari script. The males wear *kurta*, *dhoti*, *saffa*, *juti*, whereas their females wear *salwar*, *kameez* and *chunni*. The females used to wear *ghagri* in the past. Some of the males also wear *pyjama* or pants. They have been recognized as a Scheduled Caste. *Dal-roti* forms their staple food. They take both non-vegetarian and vegetarian food. Their non-vegetarian food includes mutton, pork, and fish. They use alcoholic drinks specially on the birth of male child or a wedding. Wheat, rice, *bajra*, and maize are eaten as cereals. They also eat pulses which include *masur*, *moong*, *moth* and gram. Mustard oil or vegetable *ghee* is used as cooking medium. They take milk and milk products and smoke *bidis* or cigarettes; elderly persons smoke hookah. Some female also smoke *bidi*. Alcoholic drinks were not allowed earlier, but now intake of alcoholic drinks among the young has increased. Consumption of rice and fruits is only occasional and rare.

The Dhanaks have exogamous *gotras*, such as Bawania, Kat, Kanagwal, Saroha, Khichik, Khacherwal, Ladwal, Bansal, Solanki, Duggal, Mahar, Mahor, Bagri, Pharand, Dawla, Ninanya, Khahera, Athkan, Mundriya, Dilor, Indara, Kirar and Khundya.

Some other *gotras* of the Dhanak are Laungbarsa, Lakriha, Bhuseli, Garuharya, Garpelha, Alareha, Kacchwalia, Jugeli, Rureha, Tahdi, Ohakra, Dusadh, Kaithiya, Kalhareya, Kori and Rawat. Boys and girls are married at twenty or twenty-five. Age at marriage is increasing. Marriage is arranged with the help of the *vichola* by negotiations. Marriage is monogamous and residence patrilocal. Vermilion in the parting of head hair, bangles, *bindi*, ear and nose rings are marriage symbols. Dowry is allowed both in cash and kind. Dhanaks perform *kanyadan* of their daughters in marriage. Divorce is rare, but allowed due to adultery and maladjustment. Widows, widowers, and divorcees are permitted to marry again. The family type is mixed extended or nuclear. Levirate and sororate are also permitted. Joking and avoidance relationships are observed in the family. The *dewar* amd *bhabi*, *jeeja* and *sali* maintain joking relationship. Newly married girls maintain avoidance relationship with their father-in-law and husband's elder brother. Property and checks on the freedom of youngsters cause conflicts in the family. Sons inherit property equally; the eldest son gets succession.

The status of women is low. Women are consulted, while making decisions about marriage and household expenditure. They contribute to family income by working as scavengers. They have a role in the religious sphere, social functions, rituals, collection of fuel, and fetching water. Purificatory ceremony is held on the sixth day after delivery and post-natal restrictions are observed for forty days. They also have *mundan* ceremony for the male child, usually on the first birthday. They go to the *Mata* (goddess) for this. Marriage is performed according to the Hindu tradition of seven *phere* and the *mahurat* for *pheras* is fixed by a Brahman. *Pheras* are performed at the residence of the bride. Her parents host a feast to the members of the *barat* and close relatives. The nuptial ceremony is performed at the groom's residence.

Dhanaks cremate their dead and bury their dead children. The ashes of the dead are immersed in the Ganges at Hardwar. They perform the *shradh* ceremony.

They are employed as daily labourers, masons, weavers, scavengers and also play music at weddings. They have their own traditional Panchayat called the Dhanak Bradari Panchayat, which is registered. The *Pradhan* is elected by voice vote and his election is for his lifetime. The Panchayats also have a Vice-President, a Secretary and other members. They used to impose fines in the past, but these days they settle matters by mutual discussions and agreement. If both the parties do not agree to the decision of the Panchayat, they approach the court of law.

Dhanaks are Hindu by religion and worship Hindu gods and goddesses. The priest is from other communities. They celebrate various festivals such as Lohri, Diwali, Dussehra and Holi. They traditionally accept both kuchcha and pukka food and water from other communities except Balmiki, Chamar, Sansi and Sikligar. They share schools, roads, places of worship, and crematoria. They lack modern inter-community linkages. A few are in petty business, administration and in the defence services or work as office assistants, teachers and doctors.

Children of this community go to school. Some of them have studied up to the secondary level whereas a few are post-graduates. They take advantage of health and modern medical care, media and telecommunication facilities. Some of their houses have electricity. Hand-pumps are used for getting drinking water. Wood and kerosene oil are used as fuel.

V. Bhalla
Achla Sood

# DHEA

The name Dhea is variously pronounced as *dahiya, dahe* or *dhe*, meaning to surrender. The local people consider them similar to the Bangale. They trace their origin from the Chuhra or Balmiki. They tell a popular legend of two Chuhra brothers named Chhajju and Bhaggu. The Chhajju refused to continue the occupation of scavenging and learnt the art of making the *chhaj* (winnowing fan) of reed grass. Eventually, these winnowing fan-makers became a different community and being outcastes and in minority were named by the dominant group (the Chuhra) as Dahe. The people perceive their distribution at a regional level in the neighbouring areas of the Punjab and Haryana. They are immigrants to Chandigarh from the adjacent places of Punjab after partition. They have established temporary colonies at the suburbs of the city. They live in semi-circular small huts made of reeds and bamboo and covered by polythene sheets.

Dheas speak Punjabi but there are only a few who can write in Gurmukhi and Devanagari scripts. Men wear *kurta, pyjama* or trousers or *tamba* (waist cloth) and turban. Women wear *kurti, salwar* and shawl.

They are occasional non-vegetarians and consume fish, egg and mutton of sheep and goat. The common staple is wheat supplemented by rice and occasionally maize. All types of available pulses, *moong, urad, masur, kulth, arhar,* gram, peas and beans are eaten by cooking in vegetable *ghee* or mustard oil. Vegetables are purchased from the market and various roots and tubers are also eaten. Fruit intake is occasional. Mustard leaves are frequently taken as *sag* during winter season. Common festive preparations are *puri* and *kachauri* of wheat, *bhalle* of pulses and *halwa* (pudding). Non-vegetarian food is avoided during death pollution. Milk intake is poor and only available to small children. Elders drink tea as a common drink. Country liquor, purchased from the market, is occasionally drunk, especially on festive and marriage occasions.

The Dheas recognize *gotras* such as Ladhar, Bahmbi, Marar, Kandara, Sahote, and so on, and these function as exogamous units to regulate marriages and also denote ancestry. The community accepts its low social position among the unclean Shudra in the Hindu *varna*. But they still regard themselves as superior to the scavenging Chuhra, Bhangi and Balmiki. Yet the Chuhra treat the Dhea inferior to themselves, probably in view of their poor socio-economic condition.

The community is endogamous and adheres to *gotra* exogamy; but village endogamy is allowed. They practise consanguinity at cross-cousin level (FSD and MBD). Adult marriages are common though earlier, child marriage was also in vogue. Negotiation is the usual mode of acquiring mates and monogamy is practised. Men may go for second wife if the first is unable to produce any child. They follow *kanyadan* practice and also give some petty household articles, if possible. Marriage symbols are *sindur*, glass bangles and a nose ornament. The bride lives patrilocally. Widow remarriage as junior levirate is socially approved, but no ritual is performed. Only a small feast is hosted by the new husband. A widower may marry a woman other than his deceased wife's sister. The community allows divorce in case of maladjustment, cruelty and adultery and compensation is paid to the aggrieved party. The children remain their father's responsibility. Either of the divorcees is free to re-marry. The community Panchayat gives three chances for reconciliation for a couple seeking divorce.

The family pattern is mainly nuclear as Dheas have small huts only sufficient for small family. The married sons get separated. *Nuh* (son's wife) avoids her *saurah* (husband's father) and *jeth*. Joking relation generally occurs between *dewar* and *bhabi*. The inheritance of paternal property is as per the rule of male-ultimo geniture, i.e. the youngest son inherits, but the eldest son succeeds father at his death. Points of conflict are generally on domestic matters, division of work and on property. The inter-family bonds are strong. Though placed in low social position, women have considerable freedom on the domestic front. They collect fuel and water and also help men at work. They participate in social and religious ceremonies, regulate family expenditure, but don't have social control in their hands.

Post-delivery restrictions are imposed on women. The *sutak* (birth pollution) is maintained for ten days but the first purification ceremony called *gunti* (taking of cow's urine), may be observed on the third day. The *dai* (midwife) suggests a name for the child. The cereal taking ceremony is observed, in which parents propitiate their clan or community deity, Rishi Balmiki, whose *marhi* (place of worship) is located in the locality. *Mundan* is done at the end of *sutak* and the *mama* (mother's brother) or the *nai* just touches the razor on the head of the infant and seeks five rupees as honorarium. A feast may be given to the young children.

The pre-marriage rituals are called *sagai, mangni and karmai*. The girl's father offers a finger-ring and a nose pin or ring to the girl along with cash and sugar. A priest is consulted for adjudicating the planetory position of the boy and the girl as per their horoscopes and the marriage day is fixed. The marriage occurs through *agni-phera* in which the bride and groom circumambulate the sacred fire, where four twigs of *chandan* (sandal wood) are erected. The bride's parents give a feast to the groom's party. The consummation of marriage occurs on the third day. The bridegroom comes to his parents-in-law, stays for a day and takes the bride with him. The first delivery should occur at the husband's place.

Earlier, the Dhea used to bury their dead. But now they have a common cremation ground. The ashes are collected on the third day and immersed in the local river Ghaggar and on the same day. Ancestor worship is performed by their community priest, who is offered some cash.

The community traditionally survives on reed work and basketry by making *chaaj*, mat and *moorha* (sitting cushion). Of late, they also have started collecting waste material—paper, rags, metal and plastic pieces and selling these to wholesale dealers. A few may also keep a snake for exhibition to seek alms. Some are engaged as casual daily wage labour on roads, quarries, factories, etc. Child labour exists.

Dheas are generally governed by the dictates of their conmmunity Panchayat which is headed by a *Pradhan* elected by voice vote. Each family contributes rupees five per month to maintain the Panchayat which solves their socio-economic problems. The Panchayat's decision is final and has to be obeyed; otherwise a person may be fined in cash or may be ex-communicated (*hukka pani band karna*). The Panchayat also solves marriage and divorce related problems. The town area committee also exercises some control over the community and performs social welfare and developmental activities.

Dheas propitiate Rishi Balmiki (popularly called Baba) as well as the village deity, on child birth and marriage and other festive occasions. Guga is also worshipped as a local deity. Regional deities of special reverence are Mansa Devi, Chandi Devi and Kali (the forms of goddess Durga/Shakti), whose shrines are located at a short distance and are visited from time to time and during the fairs for blessings and for ensuring happiness in the family. Major festivals celebrated by the Dhea are Lohri, Holi, Baisakhi, Diwali and Baba Balmiki birthday. The main fairs are Dussehra fair and Mansa Devi fair. Folk tales and dances like *Bhangra* and *Giddha* are commonly practised. Percussion music by drum is the common musical apparatus. They know basketry.

They accept kachcha and pukka food from other communities. Water, available through taps may be shared with other neighbouring people. The crematorium is common; so are the various religious shrines. But the Dheas also have their own *marhi* in their settlement colony. They have occupational linkages with other agricultural communities to whom they supply winnowing fans.

The developmental programmes have made very little impact on the community. Their children do not attend school because of their poor social and economic conditions. They sometimes avail themselves of the modern medicare facilities, available in the town. Recently some persons have adopted sterilization for checking family size. They use kerosene oil for lighting and burn fuel-wood, cow-dung cakes, saw-dust, coal, etc. as energy sources. Potable tap water is available in the neighbourhood.

A.R. Sankhyan

# DHOBI (MUSLIM)

Dhobi and Chhimba are sometimes considered synonyms, but traditionally a Dhobi is a washerman as the name is derived from *dhona,* to wash, whereas the Chhimbas are calico-printers. The Chhimba or Dhobi are Hindu with Tank and Rhilla as two groups (Rose, 1919), but in Chandigarh a Dhobi is commonly a Musalman. Rose (1919: 239) mentioned Barita or Khalifa as titles of the Dhobis. They were converted to Islam during the regime of emperor Aurangzeb. The community is mostly urbanised. They perceive their distribution at regional and inter-regional levels in Nahan (Himachal Pradesh), Dehradun and Saharanpur (Uttar Pradesh) and Patiala (Punjab).

Earlier, Dhobis used to keep donkeys. Today they wash and iron clothes at laundries and do drycleaning also. Men usually wear a *kurta,* or shirt and *lungi* or *tahmat*, or *pyjama* or trousers. Some also wear caps. Women's dress is *kurta* and *salwar* along with *dupatta* or *chunni.* They don't wear the *burqa* (veil). Ear, nose, neck and wrist ornaments of gold or silver are worn.

Dhobis share food habits of the region and are non-vegetarian, but eat only *halal* meat; fish and eggs are eaten occasionally, as also meat. During Id-ul-Zuha they feast on meat. Staple foods are wheat, rice and maize. All pulses, available in the market, like *moong, urad, masur, arhar,* gram, peas and beans are eaten along with roots and tubers and seasonal vegetables. The cooking medium is vanaspati *ghee* or mustard oil. Mango, banana, apple, peach, guava, *ber* and *jamun* are the fruits occasionally eaten. Milk consumption is occasional for adults, but regular for children. Tea and *sharbat* (sweetened water) are the common drink. Some men occasionally take country liquor which is purchased from the local market. They also smoke hookah, *bidis* or cigarettes. Meat, pudding like *halwa* and *kheer, poori* or *bhatura* and *chhole* (gram preparation), *dahi* (curd) and *bhalle* (cakes of pulses), *savian* (vermicellis), are cooked on festive occasions.

The community recognizes *gotras* like Gaur, Kampoo, Kashoi, Sahote, etc. But the eleven Dhobi *gotras* mentioned by Rose (1919: 239), are not known to the community in the study area. These are suggestive of their descent from a particular ancestor and sometimes also regulate marriages. In the Muslim regional social hierarchy the Dhobi is in a low position.

The community is endogamous and practises clan exogamy and village or *mohalla* exogamy. Consanguinity is followed at cross cousin (FSD and MBD) levels. *Mehar* is promised in marriage contract for future payment. Traditionally the minimum amount of *mehar* was equivalent to thirty-two and a quarter silver rupees, but at present about a thousand rupees are promised as *mehar*. Dowry or *daj* in the form of household articles are given. Men can divorce and pay compensation; children stay with their father. A divorced woman can also remarry after completing the duration of *iddat* (three months and ten days). Widow remarriage is allowed only after four months from the death of the husband. Junior levirate and sororate are allowed, but junior sororate is not a common practice. There has been a rise in marriage age and in the amount of *mehar*.

The Dhobi family pattern is almost nuclear and the main reason for breaking of joint families is limitation of space in urbanized dwellings. In joint families, the *nuh* or *bahuti* avoids her *saurah* and *jeth*. Informal talk and joking may occur between *dewar* and *bhabi; jeeja* and *sali*. The inheritance is as per the rule of male equigeniture and rarely does a divorced and widowed daughter claim a part of her father's property. The eldest son becomes successor to his father.

Women are given low status though they do various types of jobs and contribute to family income. Besides household chores, they assist men in washing and ironing, stuffing and stitching quilts, pillows and mattresses. They also participate in social and religious ceremonies and regulate family expenditure and have a say in decision-making in the family.

Post-delivery restrictions and pollution are maintained for 40 days, after which the woman takes oblation. *Azan* is chanted in the ears of the new- born child. A *maulvi* (priest) may be fed on the fortieth day after birth and a name is given by him from the Quran. The *aqiqa* ceremony is observed on the fortieth day and after one year. The *maulvi* is fed along with the poor of the neighbourhood. *Sunnat* or *khatna* (circumcision) is a major childhood ritual which is performed before the age of ten years. It is performed by a *nai* or *abdal* but recently some educated persons prefer it to be performed by a medical man to avoid injury or infection. Friends and relatives are feasted on this occasion and the *maulvi* is offered some cash for his religious performance.

*Mangni* or *sagai* is the pre-marriage ritual in which sweets and some ceremonial cash is offered to the prospective spouses. *Nikah* is performed at the bride's residence. The *qazi*, along with two witnesses, takes the consent of the boy and the girl three times in audible voice for acceptance of marriage. A marriage *sharatnama* (contract) is signed after fixing the amount of *mehar*. The bride's parents give a feast to the groom's party. Marriage consummates on the day after marriage and the nuptial ceremony occurs at the bridegroom's place.

The dead are buried in the common burial ground. Death pollution is observed for 40 days. Rituals are held on the third, seventh, tenth, twentieth and the fortieth days. A *maulvi* offers prayers on the last day. The poor are given some cash and cloth. A ceremonial meal, normally non-vegetarian, with *halal* meat, is served to relatives and friends.

Dhobis depend traditionally on washing and ironing clothes. At present, they are dry cleaners and dyers. Many have taken up miscellaneous occupations as milkmen, masons, timber and wood-sellers, cotton scutchers, etc. A few are truck drivers. There are some who work as daily wage labourers.

All Muslim communities of the area also have control on the Dhobi in matters of disputes and social problems. This community is headed by the *imam* of the local mosque who generally encourages Muslim brotherhood and advises on social problems related to marriage and divorce. The head is elected by voice vote for the period that he enjoys the confidence of the people. The committee has little power to punish, but certain social restrictions in terms of ex-communication may be imposed on the person who does not obey decisions of the committee. The Town Area Committee does the general welfare and developmental activities for the wards.

Dhobis belong to the Sunni sect of Islam. Hindu Dhobis are also found in the area, but not in a sizeable number. Hindu Dhobis worship Hindu deities and follow Hindu ritual traditions and rites on birth, marriage and death. Sakhi Sarwar, locally called Lallaanwala Pir is their patron as well as the village or local deity who is also propitiated by other communities on fulfilment of a vow or desire. Some persons also have *silsila* affiliation to the deity. They also have faith in the regional deities Mansa Devi and Chandi Devi, whose shrines are located on the outskirts of Chandigarh. People have faith in medicine men usually the *imam* and *maulvi* also know the art of healing. Their main festivals are Id-ul-Fitr, Id-ul-Zuha, Shab-e-Barat and Barawafat. Muharram is a solemn mourning occasion. Local fairs, generally the annual Dussehra fair is common. Weekly wrestling matches are also held in the town. The common source of entertainment, however, is cinema. *Qawali* and various Panjabi folk songs and tales are shared by Dhobis.

The commensal relations in terms of exchange of food and water are confined to Muslim communities. Dhobis accept kuchcha and pukka food and water from all Hindus except the Chuhra, Chamar and the like. Putative kinship-based friendship exists. They share common water taps and burial places. They have access to the house but not the kitchen of a caste Hindu. They have linkages with all communities through their occupation.

Developmental programmes have made some impact on the Dhobis. They give school education to their boys and girls generally up to the middle and secondary levels. Only a few boys go for college education.

They use both traditional indigenous as well as modern medical and health care facilities. Some women have adopted sterilization as a family planning measure, after having three or more childeren. They would prefer at least one male child before using any birth control measure.

Drinking water is available through taps and their houses have electricity. *Pathis* (cow-dung cakes), firewood, charcoal and kerosene oil are the sources of energy. Children undergo immunization. They are dependent on the local shopkeeper and moneylender.

A.R. Sankhyan

# GADERIA

The Gaderia, Gadaria or Gaderie, are shepherds who subsist on rearing sheep and goats. The word *gaderia* is derived from Hindi word *gad,* meaning herd and denotes a shepherd, the one who keeps, or tends, the herd of sheep (goats included). There are sporadic ethnographic notes on the community in old ethnographic accounts (Rose 1919; Ibbetson 1916; Crooke 1896, etc.). In the Union Territory of Chandigarh, the community perceives its distribution in the villages of Burail, Ahlumajra, Faidan, etc., which have now been included in the urban conglomerate and have nearly lost the character of rural settlements. In addition, the community perceives its distribution in some adjoining districts of Punjab, viz., Patiala and Ropar.

Men dress in shirt and trousers or *pajamas*; women wear *kurta, salwar* and a *chunni* or *dupatta.* Common ornaments are nose pins or studs, ear-rings, neck-chains, wristlets and anklets made of gold or silver.

Their staple food is wheat supplemented by rice and sometimes by maize. Various types of pulses like *urad, moong, kulthi, arhar, masur,* beans or *rajma,* grams and peas are eaten moderately. Green vegetables, roots and tubers are consumed. Non-vegetarian food is taken occasionally whereas milk is used almost daily. Fruits available in the market are eaten less frequently. Some men consume liquor purchased from the local market. Men also smoke *bidi,* cigarette and loose tobacco through hookah.

They recognize clans, called *gotra,* such as Kauwa, Chandel, Pandwar, Hiranwal, Phulisange, etc. These clans are social units that regulate matrimony and are exogamous; they also denote descent from a particular ancestor. There is some sectarian differentiation as some persons follow the Radhaswami sect, but this does not discriminate while seeking marital alliance. The Gaderia are placed among the clean Shudra in the Hindu *varna* system at par with the Kumhar and the Lohar, and they also accept this social hierarchical position.

The community is mainly endogamous, but village or *mohalla* and clan or *gotra* exogamy is followed. Marriages occur through negotiation and after attaining adulthood. Gaderias perform *kanyadan* and also give a little *dahej* to their daughters in the form of household goods for setting up a new home. *Sindur,* glass bangles, nose and ear ornaments are the symbols of married status. They practise monogamy. Man may acquire a second wife in case the first is barren. Residence is patrilocal. Widow remarriage, junior levirate and junior sororate, are allowed but are rarely practised. Divorce is a rare event and may be permitted on grounds of maladjustment and cruelty and is effected either by social approval or through judicial verdict. Either spouse can seek divorce, but legally the man is bound to pay maintenance to the woman and also bears the liability of the children. Divorcees of either sex may remarry.

Gaderia families are nuclear at present, but earlier vertically extended families were common. The main reasons for the decline of joint families are limited economic resources and residential space. Avoidance relationships may be observed among the older women. The *bahu* covers her face from her *saurah* and *jeth*. Joking relationships between *dewar* and *bhabi*, *jeeja* and *sali* exist. The junior members are expected to respect their elders. Inheritance is in the male line, male-equigeniture is followed and succession goes to the eldest son.

Women's status is low as compared with that of men. They often work in the houses of rich persons of their *mohalla*. They do all types of household work like making *pathis* for fuel. They are also engaged in animal husbandry, but generally men attend to sheep and goat grazing in the pastures. Women take part in social and religious ceremonies, but have little say in the political sphere and in social matters. They do have influence in domestic and social matters for taking decisions and also regulate family expenditure.

Life-cycle rituals are performed by a Brahman priest as per the Hindu custom. The Radhaswami, however, observe brief rituals and arrange a *satsang* (religious gathering). Pre-delivery and post-delivery pollution called *sutak* is observed for forty days, after which the woman is purified by ritual oblation. *Mundan* of male children is performed by a *nai*, who is offered eleven rupees.

Horoscopes are consulted for choosing a spouse. *Mangni*, *sagai* or *thaka* (betrothal) are pre-marriage rituals when sweets with ceremonial cash and a few ornaments and cloths are exchanged by two parties. On the wedding day, various rituals are observed; *agni phere* is performed at the bride's place, when the bride and groom together circumambulate the sacred fire; the parents of the bride perform *sankalapa kanyadan*. They also serve food to the *baratis*. The bride departs on the next day. *Gauna* or *muklawa* of the girl takes place on the same, or the next day, when marriage is consummated.

The dead are cremated and the ashes, collected on the third day, are immersed in the Ganges at Hardwar. The Radhaswamis usually immerse ashes in the Beas in Amritsar district. Ancestor worship is performed on the tenth day, when the *acharaj* officiates and seeks offerings. The pollution period lasts seventeen days. On the last day *rasam pagri* (succession of the eldest son) occurs and Brahmans are fed. This is called *barha* and is performed on the father's death.

Today, only a few Gaderias have retained the traditional occupation, as pastures are rarely available. The pastures are obtained on yearly contract. They also breed cattle (cows and buffaloes) and sell their milk. Some are also engaged on daily wages as road labourers or as industrial workers. A few are in government service in lower posts. Children are also engaged in grazing sheep and goats.

The community has its own Gaderia Panchayat. A *pradhan* is elected by voice vote for an indefinite period or as long as he enjoys the confidence of the people. Problems of illiteracy and socio-economic development are resolved in the Panchayat. The Panchayat may impose ex-communication or a cash penalty. The Town Area Committee looks after only the general welfare and development of the area.

The Gaderias are Hindu and most of them follow Sanatana Dharam. During the post-independence period some have also become followers of the Radhaswami sect which has reduced the influence of Brahminical rituals. However, faith in family, village and regional deities is still strong. Talokpara, near Kala Amb in Haryana, is a clan deity propitiated on various festive occasions and life-cycle rituals. *Bar badere* (ancestors) and *sati* idols are propitiated for the well-being of the family. Lallanwala (Sakhi Sarwas) Peer, a village deity, and Guga *marhis* are propitiated. Mansa Devi, Chandi Mata and Naina Devi are the main regional deities. The main festivals celebrated are Diwali, Dussehra, Holi, Lohri and Baisakhi. On the Baisakhi Amavasya, Gaderias prepare *poori* and *kheer* (milk pudding) and on that day they do not sell milk. The sacred specialists are from other communities. They share various regional Punjabi oral traditions—folksongs, tales, music and dances.

The connubial norms of the community are confined to itself but putative kinship-based friendship occurs with other communities. The commensal norms in terms of exchange of kachcha and pukka food and water apply only to caste Hindus, and the clean castes. They traditionally do not accept or exchange kachcha food and water with the Banjara, Chuhra, Chamar, Dumna and Muslim but the barriers are gradually giving way. The caste Hindus (Brahman and Rajput) do not offer them their smoking pipe. The cremation ground is shared with other communities as are the various religious shrines and other public places. Traditional *jajmani* (patron-client) relationship exists only with Brahman priests. Symbiotic relationships and modern linkages have developed to some extent.

Modern developmental programmes have had their impact. The Gaderias now send their children to school up to the secondary level. Modern methods of medical care are used but the indigenous methods are still utilised. Houses have electricity and tap water is also available. They commonly use cow-dung cakes, fire-wood, coal, coal-dust balls, saw-dust and kerosene as fuel. ICDS immunization is availed. The benefits of the small family (generally three children) have recently been realised and sterilization is being adopted as a birth control measure.

A.R. Sankhyan

# GUJJAR

The Gujjars take their name from Sanskrit *gurjara*, the original name of Gujarat or else from *gaucharana*, meaning to graze cows. An equally imaginative origin is in the Hindi word *gajar* (carrot) from the belief that the Gujjar fed their cattle on carrots (Bingley 1904).

The Gujjars are said to have originally established themselves in Kabul, Kashmir and the northern Punjab, where their settlements may be traced to the names of places and districts such as Gujranwala and Gujrat. About the migration of Gujjars, Ibbetson (1916) says 'Before the end of the third century, a portion of the Gujjars had begun to move southwards down the Indus and were shortly afterwards separated from their northern brethren by Indo-Scythian wave from the North. In the middle of the fifth century, there was a Gujjar kingdom in the South-Western Rajputana, whence they were driven by the Balas into Gujrat of the Bombay Presidency; and about the end of ninth century, Ala Khana, the Gujjar king of Jammu, conceded the present Gujar-des, corresponding very nearly with the Gujrat district, to the King of Kashmir. The town of Gujrat is said to have been built or restored by Ali Khan Gujjar in the times of Akbar.'

In Chandigarh, the Gujjars are migrants from Jalkheri, which is near Delhi. Gujjars are settled in the villages of Kansal, Nada, Jyanthimajra and Burail.

The dress of the male Gujjars is *dhoti* and *kurta*, over which, in the cold weather, is worn a bright coloured waistcoat. On ceremonial occasions, such as a wedding, some Gujjars may wear a coat called an *angarkha* reaching the knees. The *chadar* or shawl is worn across the shoulders over the *angarkha*. The *pagri* or turban is invariably worn. The men have a custom of boring their upper front teeth and inserting some gold in the cavities. They also wear ear-rings and necklaces of gold and coral beads. Armlets are worn for protection against malevolent spirits. The Gujjar women wear *salwar* and *kameez* with an embroidered *dupatta*. Ornaments of all kinds such as ear-ring, nose-ring, necklaces, *payal*, bangles, finger-ring, etc., are worn.

*Dal* and *roti* are their staple food. Their favourite dish is *rabri*, i.e. gram or jowar fermented in buttermilk, and *khichri* made of *bajra* and *dal*. *Daliya* is prepared from wheat, *jowar* and *makkai*, the grain being bruised and then boiled in a couldron, with salt and *dal*. *Misi roti* is also relished which is prepared from *chana* mixed with wheat flour. Pulses such as gram, *urad*, *moong*, peas, beans, *masur*, *moth*, etc., are consumed. The cooking medium is mustard and groundnut oil. Roots and tubers are also eaten but fruits are taken only occasionally. The Gujjars take tobacco, which they chew as well as smoke.

The community has a number of clans. The principal clans are Barsoi, Dhanga, Chamayan, Chhokar, Khatana, Rawal, Khare, Seradra, Pilwara, Awana, Kumbar, Madi, Chechi, Koli, Chadri, Chanda, Mutan, Nikari, Rawat, Rajana, Budana. The clans regulate their marriage alliances.

They are endogamous, but maintain exogamy at village and clan level. Marriage is arranged by negotiation when boys and girls become adult. Monogamy is practised. Vermilion, *bindi*, nose and finger-rings are symbols of marriage. Dowry in kind, which includes household articles, is allowed. Residence is patrilocal. Divorce is very rare and re-marrriage is permissible.

The rite called *karao, karewa or nata,* practised by the Gujjar, is in essence, identical with the levirate system. On the death of a man, his younger brother has the first claim to the widow, then his elder brother and after them other relations in the same order. The *karewa* cannot be performed while the girl is minor or if she has not extended her consent. The main objective of *karewa* marriage is to transfer control of her deceased husband's land from the widow to his brother, or some other near relation. Where children are born to the deceased husband, *karewa* seldom takes place.

The status of women is low. They grind corn, cook food, spin, bring wood and fuel, draw water for their families. Pre-delivery restrictions and post-delivery pollution, *annaprasana* (first taking of cereals by child) and adolescence ceremonies are observed.

Marriage rituals are performed at the bride's residence. Her parents offer a feast to the marriage party. The actual marriage ceremony takes place at the bride's residence.

The Gujjars cremate their dead and the bones are disposed of in the Ganges at Hardwar. They also worship their ancestors. Tiny shrines, dedicated to the memory of ancestors, are commonly found in their agricultural fields.

The primary occupation of Gujjars is to keep flocks of sheep and herds of cattle apart from being good cultivators. Some are now employed in private or government service, whereas others work as labourers on daily wages. As their land has been acquired by the government, they have become a landless community. The community Panchayat now plays a less important role in social control of the people. The village Panchayat is elected by secret ballot and attends to various problems.

The Gujjars in Chandigarh are mostly Hindu and their birth, marriage and death rites are performed according to Hindu traditions. They are usually Saivas or Saktas and also worship Sitala Bhawani, the small-pox goddess. They also worship gods like Pyareji and Baba Sabha Ram. The temple of Pyareji is at Randewa in Saharanpur district.

The Gujjars celebrate Holi, Diwali, Dussehra and Lohri which are of

Mansa Devi

Mansa Devi temple

Chandi Mandir and its *pujari* (priest)

The Rock Garden

A Gaderia grazing sheep

A Sunar in his jewellery shop

A Chhimba (tailor) in his workshop

A Barhai in his workshop

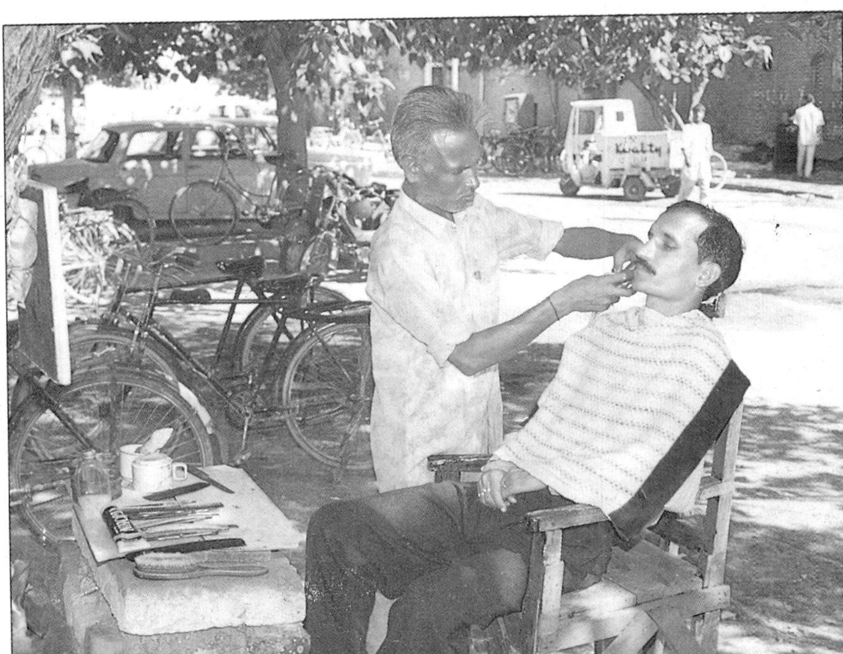

A road-side Nai

A Julaha female with a spinning wheel

The Bhari women

A Dhea male

The Bharai male and female and their drum

A Mochi doing shoe shining

A Kumhar making earthen vessels

religious significance. The shrines constructed in memory of their ancestors are commonly worshipped. Among Gujjars, the river Jamuna, always called Jamunaji, is highly revered.

Gujjars traditionally accept from and exchange food and water with the Brahman, Jat, Bania but not with Balmikis, Chamars, Pinjas and Musalmans. Boys study up to college, while girls study up to primary level only, either due to poor economic conditions or social reasons. They have been benefited by health and medical care, family welfare and drinking water facilities. They have taps, and wells for supply of water. Their houses are provided with electricity. They use cow-dung, fire-wood, kerosene oil, and gobar-gas as fuel. The mid-day meal scheme and ICDS are available. Although the attitude towards saving is favourable, they depend on the moneylenders or banks for loans to purchase livestock.

V. Bhalla
Sushil Kumari

# JAIN

'Jain' is a generic term used for those who follow the religion of that name. (The word *jina* is derived from the Sanskrit root *ji*—to conquer.) A *Jina* literally means one who has conquered the inner passions of desire and hatred. Formerly, the religion was known as *nirgrantha* religion—a religion of one who has got rid of all knots. A *Jina* is variously mentioned by the Jainas as *arhat, arhant, arihant, tirthankara,* etc. Of these, the word *tirthankara* has a special significance. It implies one who is the founder of four-fold order of monks and nuns and of lay-followers, male as well as female. A *tirthankara* is also its supreme law-giver. The twenty-four *tirthankaras* are also called *Saraogis*, a corrupt form of *Sharawaka* disciple (*sewak*). Jains are recruited from various groups of the Bania, such as Aggarwals, Oswals, Shrimals and Khandelwals, the last three of whom are also called Bhabra—a corrupt form of *bhaobhala* (from *bhao*, motive and *bhala*, good, i.e. those of good intent).

Of the twenty-four *tirthankaras* who were born in India, Risabha was the first. He was not only the first *tirthankara* who preached religion, he was also the first sovereign monarch to rule and teach people their household duties. He taught the art of cultivation, of cooking and of making earthen pots. Risabha, after many years renounced the world and took to penance and preaching. As he was the first among the *tirthankaras*, he is also known as Adinatha or Adideva. Mahavira, the elder contemporary of Buddha, was the last *tirthankara*. The chief tenet of Jainism is not to injure any living creature and to attain *nirvana* or salvation. Among Jains, it is a strict rule that flesh or intoxicants should not be touched. The monks of this community are held in the highest respect. They live a hard and austere life. They also observe five great vows or *maha vratas*. These are *ahimsa* (not to kill), *satya* (not to lie) *acaurya* (not to steal), *brahmacharya* (to abstain from sexual relation) and *aparigraha* (non-attachment to worldly things). *Ahimsa* implies not only abstaining from killing, but also from torturing or forcing a living creature to act against his will. This is the first great vow and is known as *ahimsa* or *pranatipata vira mana*.

Not to lie is the second great vow. This is known as *satya marsavada virmana*. In case a truth uttered causes pain or death of a living being, one should remain silent, not utter what is not true.

The third great vow is *acaurya* or abstention from theft. To take more than one's requirement is also theft.

The fourth great vow is *brahmacharya* or *maithuna virmana*—abstention from sexual relation.

The fifth great vow is *aparigraha* or *parigraha virmana*—renunciation of all interests in mundane things.

Along with these five great vows, monks strive after the ten-fold virtues of a *yati,* or a self-controlled ascetic. They do not take food at night, and live on alms without using any kind of conveyance in their movements from one place to another. They neither keep money nor accept it. They have no property and no personal belongings.

As a religious community, the Jains are divided into two great sects, viz., Swetambara and Digambara. The Swetambara worship idols, which are often adorned with gold and silver ornaments set with jewels, such as *mukta, angia,* etc. They have eight sacred days, viz., the *pajusanas* beginning on the twelfth Badi to the fourth Sudi (both days inclusive) in Bhadon, the eighth day being called Chhamachhri, the holiest day of Jains. During these days the holy scriptures, Sutras, are either read or listened to and a fast is kept. Swetambaras believe that a woman can attain *nirvana* salvation, while the other Jains hold that she must first be born as a man.

The Swetambaras have ascetics who are initiated as follows. An aspirant must live for some time as ascetic and become fully acquainted with the austerities which he will have to undergo. On an auspicious day, the *Saraogi* of the neighbourhood are invited. The person is first rubbed with *batna* (mixture of barley, flour, oil and turmeric) and then bathed. He is dressed in handsome apparel and seated on an elephant and is carried in procession through the *bazars* to a Jain temple or such other place as may have been made beforehand for the purpose, or a place that resembles a Jain temple. There, his head is shaved, and his tutor or guru, after performing certain religious rites, gives him saffron clothes, the *ugha* or *rajoharna* (a kind of brushing stick), the *munch patti* (a piece of cloth which is placed over his lips before speaking or reading), *patras* (wooden utensils) and a stick. He accepts these things and takes vows ( *panch mahabratas*). Thus he becomes a monk and is often styled as a *sambegi sadhu.*

A *sadhu* has to walk bare-foot; he is not to use any conveyance while travelling; he is to take no food or drink after sunset; and abstain from touching a female. He is to refuse to accept uncooked vegetables, and only to eat certain of them if cooked, to use wooden utensils, never to prepare his own meals but always to beg and always drink boiled water and never to give an opinion on any worldly matter.

The Digambaras worship naked idols and their monks are also naked. They also keep fasts and have eight sacred days called *athai,* which occur every fourth month in Asharha, Kartika and Phalgun of each year. In addition, they have ten more sacred days, called *das lakshmi,* from Bhadon Sudi five to fourteen. Many of their tenets agree with those of Swetambaras. They are divided into two sects, Bispanthi and Terapanthi.

The Bispanthi revere the twenty-four *arhats*, the guru and the *shastras*, while the Terapanthi hold there is no guru, save the *shastras* themselves. They clothe their idols, worship seated, burn lamps before them, but present no flowers or fresh fruit to them, holding it to be a sin to destroy even vegetable life though they will eat vegetables if any one will give them readycut and prepared for cooking.

The birth of a man is considered very important in Jainism; the moment a male infant is born, a brass tray is beaten by the proud father or other relatives in order to announce the happy event, and also to get the infant used to noise and to ensure that he will never be frightened. The baby is then bathed in water and its mouth is washed with wool dipped in a mixture of sugar cane water and melted butter. If the baby is the first son in the household, the parents send presents of such things as sweets and fruits to their friends; but of course no such extravagance is indulged in if the neonate is a girl. A Jain believes that a boy's future is decided the night he is six days old, and on that night Mother Chatthi is worshipped. On the ninth day (or with some sects, the eleventh), after the child's birth the mother is bathed. After bathing, she stands so as to face the sun and shakes from her finger a drop of *kanku* (turmeric).

When the baby is twelve days old, it is named with ostentation. The child is dressed in a silk *sari* and given some grain, the leaf of a *pipal* tree, a copper coin and a betel nut, and then four boys (or, if the baby is a girl, four girls) are called. As the children rock the *sari* and sing, the aunt (father's sister) at the right moment declares the baby's name.

Fifteen days after the birth, the mother goes to the river to fill the water vessels. She takes with her seven kinds of grain and a coconut. As she arrives near the river, she lights a tiny *diva* (earthen lamp) containing *ghee*, splits open the coconut, and after arranging grain in seven rows, she puts it in her lap. As she walks home carrying the filled water vessels, she scatters the grain.

The cutting of the infant's hair is done either in the third, or the fifth, or the seventh or the ninth month. The barber is called for this, and after the hair-cutting, he is given a special present, and a lucky mark is made on child's forehead.

On some auspicious day during the early months, *abotava,* first feeding of cereals, takes place, at which the father's sister again presides, but this time she receives presents.

In another ceremony, *jotri jharanam,* which takes place when the child is three months old, all women of the household join in preparing specially dainty food for a feast, and then place some grain, betel nuts, small copper coins and one silver coin on a stool. The baby is then made to bow to this collection. The father presents a piece of silver to his sister and entertains all his friends.

Among the Jains a boy is usually betrothed at twenty or twenty-five and a girl slightly earlier. When a suitable match is found, the girl's father sends a coconut and a rupee-coin to the boy's father. Then a priest is called to put an auspicious mark on the forehead of the boy and his relatives with sandal. A lucky woman or virgin then takes the coconut and marks it with sandal and puts one rupee on it. Later boy's father invites all his friends to a feast, to which each of the guests brings a coconut. After two or three days a present consisting of one coconut and ten rupees, is sent back to the girl's house as a sign of goodwill.

First, the boy's father invites the prospective daughter-in-law and some other children to a feast and gives her three silk dresses. Afterwards, the girl's father invites the boy and some children to a feast in his house and offers him a gift.

At the time of *lagnapatra*, an astrologer is called who decides about the time when everything will be auspicious, and fixes the day. This date is written in old ink and carried by children from the bride's house to that of the boy's parents. About three days before the actual wedding ceremony a *mandap* is erected, where appropriate songs are sung, and dates and sugar are distributed amongst those who are present.

As the wedding day arrives, the family goddess is worshipped and fourteen girls are fed. The marriage ceremony takes place after sunset.

When a person is about to die, his relatives summon a monk or a nun to give sermon to the dying person. As an ascetic is not allowed to sit, he cannot continue for a very long time, so any devout man or woman can supplement his performances. As soon as the person dies, the body is removed from the bed and placed on the floor, which has been previously covered with a preparation of cow-dung. The corpse is so kept that the face of the dead is towards the north. An earthen lamp, filled with *ghee,* is lit by his side.

When a woman dies, she is dressed in her best, as far as possible, in a *sari* with golden border. Formerly, these things were burnt along with her, but these days they are removed before actual cremation. The corpse is swathed with green cloth from knee to waist underneath the silken garments. If the corpse is that of an ordinary widow, she is not dressed in silk, but in black.

If the woman is a *vesa* widow (i.e. one under thirty, whose husband has died whilst she was still a little child), her corpse is not dressed in black. When a man dies and leaves a widow, her ivory bangles are broken, except one of them which is tied to the bier and the rest are taken to the river by women. Even if the wife is a virgin, she must take off her jewels and wash off the red auspicious mark from her forehead. However, she is not always compelled to wear black dress, abstain from sweet-meats, or sleep on the floor, until she attains womanhood. The corpse, in case of a man, is dressed only in loin cloth.

The dead body is placed on the bier and carried by near relatives to the cremation ground, where a pyre has already been arranged. It is lit by the son of the dead man. The fire which lights the pyre is taken from the house, and special attention is paid by the relatives and friends to the manner in which fire is carried from the dead man's house to the cremation ground. After the body is cremated, most of the relatives go back home, but one of them goes to get a water pot, which is filled, by the next of kin, four times and poured over the ashes each time.

Strings and knots serve as a protection and have many magical powers. At the initiation of a boy, a Jain knots his scalp lock, puts the cord over his shoulder, and a string of the sacred *kusa* grass round his waist.

At present, Jains can be found to be engaged almost in every walk of life. They have been benefited by the developmental programmes on education, health, communication, media, public distribution and employment opportunities.

V. Bhalla
Achla Sood

# JAT

According to Ibbetson (1916) the Jats were of 'Indo-Scythian stock' and 'probably entered the Punjab from their home on the Oxus' and moved into the Indus valley about a century before Christ, as far down as Sindh, and spread into the Punjab proper, where they were firmly established in the beginning of the eleventh century just before Muslim invasion. According to Khushwant Singh (1977: 14-16) the Jats, who 'made northern plains of India their home were of Aryan stock, brought with them certain institutions, the most important being the Panchayat, an elected body of five elders, to which they pledged their allegiance. Every Jat village was a small republic made up of people of kindred blood, who were as conscious of absolute equality between themselves as they were of their superiority over men of other castes who earned their livelihood as weavers, potters, cobblers or scavengers. The Jat is a born worker and the warrior. He tilled his land with his sword girded round his waist. He fought more battles for the defence of his homestead than the Kshatriya, for unlike the martial Kshatriya, the Jat seldom fled from his village when the invaders came. And if the Jat was maltreated or if his women were molested by the conqueror on his way to Hindustan, he settled his score by looting the invaders' caravans on their return journey and freeing the women he was taking back. The Punjabi Jat developed an attitude of indifference to worldly possessions and an instinct for gambling with his life against odds. At the same time he became conscious of his role in the defence of Hindustan.' This statement also reflects current Jat perceptions of identity.

The Jats migrated recently from Punjab or Haryana; many are concentrated in large numbers in the neighbouring states of Punjab, Haryana, Himachal Pradesh and Uttar Pradesh. They speak Punjabi and Hindi and use Gurmukhi and Devanagari scripts. The men wear turban, shirt and *chadra* (*dhoti* ). Those who are educated wear trousers and shirt. The women dress is *salwar, kameez* and *dupatta. Dal* and *roti* is their staple food. *Moong, masur, moth, urad* and *rajma* are the pulses taken by them. They take alcoholic drinks on special occasions, such as the birth of the male child or a marriage in the family. Groundnut oil and *desi ghee* are used for cooking. Tea, *lassi,* curd and milk are consumed in large quantity.

Jats are endogamous and strictly observe village and *gotra* exogamy. They are divided into different *gotras* such as Dhillon, Virk, Sidhu, Bhular, Mann, Gill, Bal, Panu, Brar, Dhariwal, Mangat, Dhindsa, Grewal, Chahal, Mahal, Aulak, Her, Randhawa, Kang, Sohal, Bains, Sahi, Chimma, Bajwa, Punia, Ghaman, and according to Ibbetson (1916: 100), those who hold these clan names are *asl* or original Jats, because they claim no Rajput ancestry, but are supposed to be descended from the hair (*jat*) of the god Siva. These *got* divisions regulate marriage alliances. According to members of other communities, and in their own perception, Jats are of high status and they recognize their place in Kshatriya *varna* order.

Monogamy is the form of marriage. Boys and girls marry when they are around twenty to twenty-five years of age. Marriage is arranged by negotiation with the help of a *vichola*. Married women wear ear-rings and glass bangles. Depending upon the financial condition of the girl's parents, dowry in kind is allowed. Residence is patrilocal. Divorce with judicial approval is permitted in case of maladjustment. Remarriage is allowed. Among changes in the marriage rules, there is an increase in the marriageable age. There are also a few cases of inter-caste marriages in Chandigarh.

Joint families are common but nuclear families also exist. Joking relationship among the *dewar* and *bhabi, jeeja* and *sali*, grandparents and grandchildren are observed. Conflicts due to disputes related to property, check on freedom of youngsters and challenge to the authority of the elders, exist. All the sons inherit property of their father equally; the eldest son gets the succession. Among changes in family, it may be mentioned that there is increase in nuclear families and joint families are on the decrease. Women attend to various household jobs, apart from helping men in the agricultural fields and animal husbandry.

Post-delivery pollution is observed for six days and restrictions on the mother are observed for forty days. They observe naming ceremony and offer *roti* to the community. *Mundan* is done.

Marriage rituals are performed at the bride's residence, according to the Sikh tradition of *anand-karaj* in Sikh Jat and according to Hindu Vedic rites in Hindu Jat. *Roti* is given by the parents of the girl in marriage after the *phere.* Consummation of marriage takes place at the bridegroom's residence.

The Jats cremate their dead. *Phul* (charred bones of the dead) are collected on the third day and immersed at Kiratpur Sahib among Sikhs and at Hardwar among Hindus. They perform the *shradh* ceremony and also observe pollution period at the time of death. On the tenth day *dasai* is observed and after the twelfth day *rasam pagri* or *kriya* ceremony is arranged. Rituals have been curtailed as they have become more expensive.

Agriculture is the primary Jat occupation. As some of their agricultural land has been acquired by the Chandigarh Administration for the construction of houses, some Jats have shifted to dairy farming and poultry. They are also employed in civil, police and defence services. The formal village Panchayat, elected by secret ballot, also looks after their interests and attends to various disputes related to land, marriage, divorce, etc. In case the village Panchayat is unable to settle their disputes, members approach the court of law. Some profess Sikhsim while others follow tenets of Hindu religion and perform various rites associated with birth, marriage and death, accordingly. They celebrate Guruparab, Diwali, Lohri, Baisakhi and other local festivals. Some women weave *daris*. Ladies sing *ghorian* (folksongs) and *suhag geets* on the occasion of marriage. They have folklore, folk-tales and folk-dances which they share with neighbouring communities from Punjab and Haryana.

The Jats traditionally accept food from and exchange water and food with the Rajput, Saini and Bania but not with the Balmiki, Chamar, Sansi and Gaderia. However due to the impact of education and urbanization, such restrictions are not observed rigidly. Patron-client relationship with Chamar, Balmiki, Lohar, Tarkhan, Mirasi and Bharai, were prevalent in the past. But at present, in the villages, their services are rendered in lieu of cash. There are Jats in administration, other white-collar jobs and the professions. Political leadership has emerged at the village level.

Both boys and girls go in for formal education. They have benefited from various developmental schemes, and as a dynamic and progressive community they are doing very well.

Swaran Singh

# JHEEWAR

Regarding the origin of this community one account has it that Ak was a Chauhan Rajput of Garh Mukhiala (in the Salt Range), who died leaving a son of tender age named Dhingar. The people treated him as a servant and nicknamed him Jhiwar. Bhat, his son, who fed the people at each full moon with rice, had four sons, founded four *muhins,* each containing several *gotras*: *muhin* Lungo with four *gotras* Makhu, Store, Dhain, Dhengi; *muhin* Ghul had Gadri, Haremi, Waddan and Malle *gotras*; Dhengi *muhin* also had four *gotras,* i.e. Manni, Mande, Langtra, Bhal; and Tak *muhin* had Khone, Gadri, Dhogle as *gotras* (Rose 1919: 382-3).

The Jheewars are also called Dhenwar, Dhimar, Dhiwar, Jhinwar, Kahar, Kashyap Rajput, and Mallah. According to Ibbetson (1916: 306), they supplied all the baskets needed by cultivators and brought water to the men in the fields at harvest time, to the houses where the women were secluded, and at weddings and other similar occasions. According to Rose (1919: 381-2) the Jheewar is the carrier, water-man, fisherman and basket-maker of eastern Punjab, is concerned with water, in so much that the cultivation of waternuts and the netting of water fowl are for the most part in his hands, and he is the wellsinker of the province.

The Jheewars today live in the villages of Bhagwanpura (about 25 families), Maoli (50-60 families), Makhan Mazra (34 families), Hallo Mazra (20-5 families), Manimajra (15 families). They are also called Jheor and the other groups identified with them are Kashyap Rajput, Panch (in Jallandhar area), and Bharbhunja. The Jheewar of Chandigarh consider the Bharbhunjas lower in status and hence do not intermarry with them.

The Jheewars of Bhagwanpura are immigrants settled by the raja of Manimajra over a century ago. They speak Punjabi with members of their family but with outsiders they can also speak in Hindi. They use both Gurmukhi and Devanagari scripts.

Jheewars are also distributed in the neighbouring states and identify themselves at the regional level. Where the Dhimars have migrated they speak Hindi and use Devnagari script. Men wear *dhoti, kurta* and trousers, and women's attire includes coloured *ghagra* or printed cotton *sari* and blouse. Some of them also wear *salwar, kameez* and *dupatta.* Females have tattooing marks on their body. The ornaments used by them are *koka* (nose-stud), ear-rings, *hansli* (necklace), *churian* (bangles), *pazeb* (anklet) and *bichoo* (toe-ring).

*Dal-roti* is their staple food. They take wheat, rice and maize as cereals; gram, *urad*, *moong*, *masur* and *moth* as pulses and mustard oil as cooking medium. They eat fish, mutton and pork occasionally as they are changing from vegetarians to non-vegetarians. Vegetables are eaten in moderate quantity. Alcoholic drinks and fruits are taken occasionally. They consume milk and milk products. Some smoke *bidi* and hookah and chew *pan*.

The Jheewars are endogamous but observe exogamy at village and *gotra* levels. Some of their *gotras* are Bathina, Bot, Bhuriya, Gharak, Jaismar, Kaukon, Mahar, Khaviar, Mallah, Rawant, Peechan, Panan, Sansol, Pathyarae, Langsar and Turai.

Earlier in addition to the *gotras* of the mother and father they used to avoid the *gotras* of the *nani* (mother's mother) and *dadi* (father's mother). They are aware of the *varna* system and consider themselves Shudras. They marry their boys and girls either by negotiations or through mutual consent, when they are twenty or twenty-five. Monogamy is the form of marriage. Married girls use vermilion, bangles, *bindi*, toe, finger, ear-rings and nose-studs as symbols of marriage. Dowry in cash and kind is permitted. They are patrilocal. Divorce is allowed due to maladjustment. Widow, widower and divorcee remarriage is permitted. There is increase in the age at marriage, bride-price has been replaced by dowry rules of remarriage are now more liberal.

The Jheewar family is either nuclear or extended; avoidance and joking relationships exist. Conflicts in a family due to property or check on the freedom of youngsters are reported. Sons inherit property of their father equally. The eldest son gets succession. Nuclear families are on the increase and joint families are on decrease. Women have a role in agricultural operations, fetching water, and social religious spheres. They have low status.

A post-delivery pollution period is observed, and on the sixth day, *chhatti* is observed; post-natal restrictions continue for forty days, though in most cases the mother starts attending to household work as soon as she feels fit. The Jheewars observe *mundan* and naming ceremonies.

Marriage rituals are performed according to Vedic rites of seven *pheras* at the residence of the bride. A feast is given by the parents of the bride. Consummation of marriage takes place at the residence of the bridegroom.

Jheewars cremate the dead and the ashes of the dead are immersed in the Ganges at Hardwar. *Shradh* ceremony is also observed.

Rose (1919: 383) described the Jhinwar as a remarkably composite caste who comprised several groups whose names depended on their various occupations, and indeed probably varied with the occupation they pursued from time to time. Sikh Jheewars were employed as *jhatkais* (butchers), and in Sikh regiments they worked as *langris* (bakers). The Jheewars were the drawers of water and palanquin-bearers of Hindu communities, and Panihara and Kahar were synonyms of the caste, Sodia being restricted to the Sikh Jheewars.

Today they are landless and the forest is the main natural resource for livelihood. Settled cultivation was their traditional occupation and a few of them are still engaged in agriculture. They are employed in government and private offices. At present, many make *moorahs* (stool) and mats. Some of them also work as labourers. They have their caste Panchayat. The village Panchayat is also approached to settle disputes. The Jheewars are Hindus and worship all the Hindu gods and goddesses. Those who belong to Sikh religion, visit the Gurdwara. The *pujari* or *pandit* is not from their own community. They also approach the *siana* for exorcisms and healing. The *pandit* performs various rites associated with marriage, birth and death. They celebrate Holi, Baisakhi, Diwali, Dussehra and Lohri festivals along with the members of other communities. Women sing folksongs on the occasion of marriage and use *dholak* as the musical instrument. They worship Sanjhi on the eve of Dussehra.

Jheewars accept food from, and exchange food and water with, all except the Chamars, Chuhra and the Dhobi. Kanaujiya Brahman do not accept their food and water. They share roads, places of worship, sources of water and crematoria and participate in the traditional festivals and festivities along with the members of other communities.

Both boys and girls study up to secondary level only, because of poverty. They take advantage of health, medical care and family planning programmes. Hand-pumps are used to get drinking water. Though they utilise media and communication facilities, electricity is available only at some locations. Fire-wood, cow-dung cakes and *chitia* (dried cotton plants) are used as fuel. Kerosene is also sometimes used as fuel. School-going children in the nursery classes do not get mid-day meal scheme facilities at all places. They help each other at time of need instead of approaching moneylenders for loans.

V. Bhalla
Achla Sood

# JULAHA

The name 'Julaha' comes from the Persian *julah*, a ball of thread. They are an exceedingly numerous and important artisan class. The Julaha did not work in impure leather, he eats no carrion, he touched no carcasses and he was recognized by both Hindu and Musalman as a fellow-believer and admitted to religious equality. In a word, the Julaha was an artisan.

According to Rose (1919), the Kabirbansis lived in Ambala and Kangra. This word was 'derived from the great Bhagat Kabir of Banaras who was himself a Julaha and whose teaching most of the Hindu Julahas profess to follow'. The eastern Julahas were divided into two sections, Deswale or those of the country, and Tel, the latter descended from a Julaha who married a Teli woman, the latter considered inferior.

The Hindu Julahas of the Phulkian States were again divided into groups such as the Ramdasis and Kabirpanthis, the former being the followers of Ram Das, who was a *chela* of Lakhmir. 'Having abandoned his calling as a shoe-maker, he took up weaving and followed the teaching of Granth. The Ramdasis do not eat, smoke or inter-marry with the Chamars', Rose (1919).

The Julahas are identified and distributed at the regional level. They have been living at Maloaya village for the last 150 years. According to the Census of India, 1981, their total population in Chandigarh is 2,109 individuals, which includes 1,163 males and 946 females. They speak Punjabi and use Gurmukhi script with members of their own community and outsiders. Men wear turban, *kurta, pyjama*, or trousers and women, *salwar, kameez* and *dupatta.* They are classified as a Scheduled Caste. They are generally vegetarian and eat vegetables in moderate quantity. But some occasionally take non-vegetarian food which includes mutton, eggs and chicken. Staple food includes wheat, maize or rice as cereals, *urad, moong, masur* and *moth* as pulses. Groundnut and mustard oil are used as cooking medium. They take milk and milk products. Use of pulses has decreased while use of vegetables and fruits have increased.

The Julahas are now divided into different *gotras* such as Saroal, Bagri, Dabdya, Kalair, etc. They consider themselves of 'high' social standing, but the perception of other communities is that they are of low status. They are aware of the *varna* system and place themselves as Shudras. They are endogamous but observe exogamy at village and *gotra* levels. The age at marriage is about twenty-one for girls and twenty to twenty-five for boys. The parents arrange the marriage with the help of a *vichola* by negotiation. The marriages are monogamous. Dowry in kind, including utensils, bedding, ornaments, clothes, etc., is allowed. Julaha post-marital residence is patrilocal. Divorce due to adultery, barrenness, maladjustment, impotency or cruelty, is allowed with judicial approval. Remarriage is also permitted. There is increase in age at marriage and the divorce incidence is on decline. Nuclear and vertically extended family types are prevalent. Conflicts due to property, checks on the freedom of younger members and challenge to the authority of elders in a family are reported. All children equally inherit their father's property. The eldest son gets the succession. Changes in family include rise in the formation of nuclear families and decline of extended family system. Women have low status and attend to household jobs in addition to their duty of attending to the domestic animals and bringing potable water. They have role in social functions and rituals. They contribute to family income.

Post-delivery pollution restrictions are observed. The Julahas have the naming ceremony and *chhatti*. Marriage rituals are performed at bride's residence according to the tradition of *lavan-pheras* after which the *roti* or feast is offered to the marriage party and close relatives. Consummation of marriage is at the groom's residence, one day after the wedding. The Julahas cremate their dead. On the third day, the bones of the dead are collected; on the tenth day *dasai* is observed; and after twelve days, the *sadharan path* is performed followed by a feast to the members of the community. The bones of the dead are disposed of either at Hardwar or Kiratpur Sahib. They also observe *shradh* ceremony.

The Julahas are landless and weaving is their traditional occupation. They are also engaged in business, government or private service. They are teachers, doctors, engineers and are in defence services and also in white-collar jobs. They follow the Sikh religion. Sacred specialists, from other communities perform various rites associated with birth, marriage and death and imparts religious teachings. Weaving and embroidery on cloth are their craft. Men and women both sing folksongs on occasions like marriage and participate in *bhangra* and *giddha*.

They traditionally accept food from, and exchange it with, all communities except Chamars and Balmikis and share roads, places of worship, sources of water with neighbouring communities and participate in various local festivals. Political leadership has emerged at only the village level.

Julaha houses are provided with electricity and have piped water. Fire-wood, coal or kerosene oil are used as fuel. They have benefited from the mid-day meal scheme, ICDS and ration distribution system.

Swaran Singh

# KAMBOH

The Kamboh have been described as the finest cultivating caste by Ibbetson (1916: 201-2) and Rose (1919: 442-46). In the early ethnographic accounts, they are divided into two groups, Lammawalas who came up the river from Multan and Tappawala from Kapurthala. There was also a professional division between the Qalmi (men of the pen)—who are engaged in military, mercantile and white-collar jobs; and the Khaki who worked in agriculture. When the earlier ethnographic accounts were written, the Kambohs were concentrated in Sohana, Patiala and Nakodar. However, the accounts of various sections noted above are not admitted as true by the Kamboh of Chandigarh.

Historically, the community traced its descent from Raja Karan; and claimed that their ancestors had fled to Kashmir. They traced their origin to a trans-Indus country; and some claimed to be ancient inhabitants of Persia. However, Rose (1919 : 444) and Ibbetson (1916 : 201) had not accepted their extra-Indian origins, because at that time 40 per cent of them were Hindus and 23 per cent were Sikhs. The community in the past had also claimed the Surajbansi Rajput origin. According to this account they came from Kamrup in Brahmputra valley to Delhi during the reign of Humayun (1530-56). Then one ancestor, Bodh Rae, migrated to Lahore and another, Dalu Rae, to Jallandhar district. Another version, traces their origin to the Kshatriyas of Mathura. When Parsuram was slaughtering Kshatriyas, he found the ancestor of this community, Bhup Rai, heavily armed. The latter was about to be slain, when he denied his Kshatriya origin. But Parsuram replied that he was armed and a relation of the Kshatriyas—(*kam bu hai; yaane teri bu kshatriyanwali*). Bhup Rai said he was not *quambu* (of any fixed order), and so got off. He was known as *quambu*, which later on changed to Kamboh (Crooke 1896: Vol. III, 118-19).

Recent historical accounts of the community claim even earlier origins. According to Kamboj (1980: 1-10) the community is the twelfth in descent from Rishi Bhrigu. The community is true Aryan and is well versed in *sastra* (weapons) and *shastra* (holy books). So they are true Kshatriyas and true Brahmans. The rule of Kamboja prevailed until the first century BC. Then it changed to Kambu and later to Loh, which was lost to the Hindu kingdom of Afghanistan. The *Ramayana* refers to good quality horses of Kamboj rulers, who ruled hundreds of years before the *Ramayana* was written.

Another recent historical account of the community by Baijnath Puri traces its origin to Kamboj Rishi. According to some members of the community at Manimajra some Saman Shah Halwai from Sultanpur Lodhi (now in district Kapurthala) was blessed by Guru Nanak. The Halwai belonged to this community. From there the community adopted its traditional profession of Halwai. The oldest Halwai shops have been claimed to belong to this community. Of the gathering at Gurdwara Ber Sahib in Sultanpur Lodhi, 80 per cent are Kambohs. The community is conscious of its present distribution at national level.

The community speaks a Punjabi dialect within its kin group. Migrants from Haryana speak Haryanvi dialect. They use Gurmukhi and Devanagari scripts. In addition, some of them also speak Hindi and English in their communication with the members of other communities, and use Roman and Devanagari scripts.

The Kambohs eat vegetarian and non-vegetarian food. There is moderate consumption of vegetables and fruit, which has increased in the last few years. Consumption of pluses has also increased; main pulses used are gram, *urad, moong*, peas, *masur, moth,* etc. Cooking is done with *desi ghee, vanaspati,* groundnut, mustard and sunflower oil. Some male members occasionally take alcoholic drinks purchased from the local market. They are fast changing from vegetarianism to non-vegetarianism and prefer *roti* to rice, though consumption of rice has increased recently.

Within the community differentiation at social, economic, religious, occupational and educational levels has taken place. Its members are Sikhs, Hindus or Muslims. They have various occupational pursuits like trade, white-collar jobs; medicine, law and administration; they are also in defence services. The community, though on the whole well-educated, has variable standards of education ranging from illiteracy to the highest university education. Males have higher education than females; education is also differentiated at the social level. Ibbetson (1916: 202) noted nine largest *gotras,* Thind, Jausan, Jahra, Darut, Nahrok, Sande, Jammun, Jhande and Unmal. Names of a few sections of the community resemble those of Rajputs such as Chhatri, Raghubansi, Rajput and Surajbansi. Others were Chaurasi, Chaurasi Goli, Chaurasi Kanha; and Bawan, Bawan Goli, Bel, Bendpari, Chodsi, Dangan, Dewasi, Dhaman, Dhani, Dholdhar, Gadi, Ganaiti, Gatru, Hatthi, Kamoji, Kakli, Karai, Kara, Karni, Khattari, Luruaji, Makotri Mal, Muki, Murli, Rajwani, Sankla, Thapri, etc. (Crooke 1896: 121). According to some informants the community is divided into two sub-castes, one having eighty-four *gotras* and the other fifty-two. Earlier, no marriages were possible between the two sub-castes because the latter indulged in the practice of *wata* (exchange marriage).

However, due to change in these practices, there is growing interaction between the two. Muslim Kambohs had two groups, Bawan Gota (52 *gotras*) and Chaurasi Gota (84 *gotras*). These groups did not intermarry with Hindu

Kamboh. According to one version when Garh Gajni was destroyed a Chaurasi Kamboh took refuge with a bard named Kamagh. So, ancestors of Bawan Gote severed all connections with him. According to another version it were Bawan Gote of Lalachi in Patiala, who got converted to Islam but Chaurasi Gote remained Hindu (Rose 1919: 445).

A recent study claims that the community was divided into these two groups since the times of *Mahabharata.* These groups hated each other, and did not intermarry, but the situation has changed since the turn of this century. It further points out that names of *gotras* originated from names of places. Those who arrived from Basara in Egypt were called Basare, those arriving from Gandhara, were called Gandhare. The various *gotras* are: Ajapal, Abdal, (Abdal); Angiare, Amlawe, (Amlawe); Angotre (Angotre); Ambre, Gandhe, (Sandhe); Soeyah, Sawan, Same/Siame, (Same); Suner, Sarkude, Sone, Sulhare, Soki, Sanik, Sandhere, Suhage, Senapati, Sarang (Mamsarang), (Sarang); Hande (Hande); Harse (Harse); Rashyap (Kashyap); Karanpal, Kosale (Kosale); Kayar (Kayar); Kodhe (Kodhe); Kalare (Kalare); Kukad, Kukede, Kukadi, Kakad (Kukad); Kals (Kalsi); Khits, Khande, Khinde (Khinde); Khokhar, Gandi/Gande, (Gande); Gagade (Gagade), Gugan (Gogan); Gandhare, Gandhi, Gadhi (Gandhi); Goase, Gore (Rai Gore); Gilawe, Gadade, Gayale, Ghasete, (Ghasete); Chandane/Tandane, Chandi, Chaandi, Chunni (Chandi); Chaak (Chaak); Chatrath (Chachare); Chamade (Chimde); Chimne, Cheene, Chakhote (Chachote); Chanan, Josan ( Josan); Judge, ( Judge); Jammu ( Jammu); Jaode ( Jaode); Jai ( Jai); Jatmal, Jagpal, Jangle ( Jangle); Jamaan, Jham/Jhab, ( Jham); Jhand ( Jhand); Toorne (Toorne); Dhote/Dhate Doliyan (Doliyan); Dode Dange (Dange); Dahre/Dhare (Dahre); Dhot (Dhot); Dhil, Dhade/Thathe (Dhade); Dare, Tirakh, Toome, Tapadiah, Tamal, Topachi, Thind (Thand); Thogade, Dutane (Daotane); Dehal/Daharal (Dehal); Dehar (Dehar); Diode (Diode); Dhawade (Dhawade); Dhanjv/Dhijv (Dhanju); Dhinjal (Dhinjal); Nande/Lande (Nande); Nagare, Nagpal, Nandan, Naipaul, (Naipaul); Nuri, Ningbar, Nohariah/Nahare (Nahre); Nimbore (Nimbar); Pandhu, Pande, Pandhiae (Pandhe); Patanrai, Puraan, Fokani (Fukani); Barad (Barad); Bajane, Badgote (Badgote); Badban Bagban, Bagyan, Behhad (Bihad); Baihman, Bastod, Barham, Bassi, Banjhaal, Bangaare, Bangwaie (Bangwaie); Basara (Basara); Bhon/Ban (Bhon); Bhojrath, Bhatti/Batti (Bhatti); Bhunjaaj/Banjahal (Bhunjal), Bhunang (Bhujang); Makode/Makodi/Makad (Makad); Machaliae (Machale); Malhe/Mele (Malhe); Multani, Ratanpal (Ratanpal); Rudra/Rutri (Rudra); Ore (Lokee); Late, Latambe (Latambe); Lahang (Lahang); Langhade (Langhade); Lande (Lande); Yanayak/Athane (Pathane). (Names in brackets are the present names of the *gotras*). A few *gotras* like Thind are also found among Jats. Some of them have intermarried with Jats. Those who adopted the profession of Darzi, Nai, Tarkhan, Lohar, etc., started intermarriage with those castes as well (Kamboh: 1980: 365-6). The social divisions have been used to regulate marriage alliance.

Kamboh self-perception is very high; however, other communities consider them of medium status. In the *varna* hierarchy it considers its status equal to Kshatriyas. A few authors consider them equivalent to Brahmans (Kamboj 1980). Another study (Singh 1977: 70-1) points out that one of the reasons cited for not giving a higher rank to Kambohs was that now they were no longer priests, but engaged in trade. The same reason was given for putting Kambohs, who were agriculturists, lower in rank than Jats. Some Kambohs are running grocery shops, a thing that the Jat will never do. Kambohs claim higher status than Jats because the latter practise hypergamy.

The Kamboh is an endogamous community. Earlier endogamy was practised at the sub-caste level as well. The group of 84 *gotras* did not intermarry with the 52 *gotras*. The Khaki group did not marry with the Qalmi. These divisions do not exist anymore. There is exogamy at *gotra* level. Only two *gotras* are excluded, that is of the mother and of the father. The community is exogamous at village level as well. Most marriages are performed in the places of origin in Punjab and Haryana. These days, all marriages are adult marriages and are monogamous. These are arranged by negotiation. A system of *vichola* prevails in settlement of marriages. There is increasing tendency to find spouses through matrimonial columns of newspapers.

Usual symbols of marriage are vermilion, bangles, *bindi*, finger-ring, toe-ring, ear-ring, nose-ring, etc. Muslim Kamboh marry according to Islamic rites whereas Hindu marriages have a custom of *kanyadan* and dowry is given in kind. In the case of Muslims, *mehar* must be settled. The rule of residence is patrilocal. The community allows divorce by judicial methods. Both parties can seek divorce. Compensation and custody of children are settled through court. Remarriage of widows and divorced women is allowed by the community. However such cases are very few. Sororate or levirate is absent. There has been liberalisation in the rules of marriage. Age at marriage has also increased.

The families are mostly nuclear, However, a few families are also vertically extended. Avoidance relationships between father-in-law and daughter-in-law and mother-in-law and son-in-law exist. Joking relationship exists between *sali* and *jeeja*; and to a lesser degree between *bhabi* and *dewar*. Disputes in families arise due to property matters. Inheritance is by male equigeniture and succession rules favour the eldest son. Legally, a daughter has been allowed to share in parents' property. Status of women continues to be low. Women have roles in social functions, rituals, religious sphere and in social control. They are engaged in economic activity, contribute to family income and control family expenditure. They also take part in decision-making at the family level.

Pollution is observed for eleven days after the delivery of the child. (Earlier, it used to be up to forty days). The mother of a new-born baby is not allowed to work during this period. On the eleventh day, she resumes normal work and it is known as *chaunka chadana*. In Hindu families, *namkaran* takes place by *havan* ceremony performed by a *Pandit*. In Sikh families *namkaran* is done according to Sikh rites. Hindu families observe *mundan* ceremony at some shrines. These shrines are affiliated to *gotras*. The community belonging to Gugal *gotra* does it at the Mandir of Mata Kalka Devi near Ambala. A few perform *mundan* at temple of Mansa Devi. The marriage ceremony takes place at the bride's residence; and the consummation of marriage takes place at the groom's house. A feast is given by both the parties at their respective houses.

In case of Sikhs, marriage ceremony is performed by *anand karaj;* among Hindus by Vedic rites; and among Muslims by *nikah*. A few cases of inter-religious marriages in the community have taken place. An informant of the community reported having married his sisters by Vedic rites and the sons by *anand karaj*.

After death, pollution is observed for thirteen to seventeen days. *Pagri* and *bhog* ceremonies are held after that period. *Phul* are collected after three days, and these are disposed of in water at Kiratpur Sahib in case of some Sikhs and at Hardwar in case of Hindus. Rituals are being curtailed as these are becoming expensive.

Kambohs are engaged in business, trade, and private and government services; or they are self-employed in professions like law and medicine. They have many members in the teaching profession, both in schools and colleges. They also have their members in defence services. However, traditionally, it was a landowning community. Many relatives of this community own and cultivate land in their native villages. A traditional caste council known as Kamboj Sabha exists in the city, which is also its regional body. It is planning to construct a Kamboj Bhavan in the city of Chandigarh. It also brings out a magazine in Punjabi, called 'Jai Kamoj' for the community.

The Kambohs believe in Sikhism and Hinduism. The Hindu members of Manimajra worship the cow and Brahmdevta, and visit Mansa Devi temple. They also go to local Gurdwaras. The sacred specialists are from different communities; they perform worship, impart religious teachings and perform marriage and death rites.

The Kambohs celebrate Baisakhi, Lohri, Basant Panchami and other festivals common to the area. Festivals like Janmashtami, Dussehra, Diwali and Guruparab are also celebrated.

They have oral tradition. Folksongs are sung by both males and females in formal ceremonies. The community has a traditional liking for music. Only men participate in folk dances.

They have a very liberal attitude regarding other communities and exchange all types of food whether kachcha, pukka or *sidha* with the members of other communities. A few inter-caste marriages have also been reported. They share water resources, crematoria, religious shrines, fairs and festivals with other communities. Symbiotic relationship exists. They are well-represented in modern professions. Political leadership has emerged at the regional level.

The community has benefited a great deal from various developmental activities. Education is favoured for both boys and girls. They receive education up to college level or even higher. Attitudes to modern medicare and family planning are favourable. Married couples prefer two children. Dissemination of information is through political parties and mass media. Kerosene, cooking gas, solar energy are used as fuel.

Virinder Singh

# KAYASTHA

In Sanskrit Kayastha means 'one who resides in the body' (Rose 1919: 437). A different meaning has been suggested by Crooke, from the Sanskrit *kaya-sanstitch* which means staying at home (Crooke, 1896: 184). In Chandigarh, the community claims to have come from three places, Rajasthan and Uttar Pradesh, west Pakistan and Himachal Pradesh. Those from the latter settled there about four centuries ago from Uttar Pradesh through Maharashtra. In early ethnographic records it was noted that the community was not indigenous to this region, and that it was confined to commercial centres (Rose 1919: 437).

In this region, Kayastha was considered a 'well known writer class of Hindustan'; distributed only in administrative and commercial centres, claiming to be part of the north Indian Kayasth family which consists of 'Three regional communities, the Chitragupta Kayasth of north India, the Prabhu Kayasth of Maharashtra, and the Bengal Kayasth of Bengal, culturally and structurally, different communities, speaking Hindustani, Marathi and Bengali languages respectively', Leonard (1978: 10-13), all three being 'writing castes'.

'The *varna* status of the Kayastha has been a matter of controversy. They have been 'variously classified as Brahmans, Kshatriyas (rulers), or Sudras (peasants) thus ranking first, second or fourth in four-fold system, depending largely upon legal decisions in different areas of India' (Leonard 1978).

'But the difficulty of their placement has been overcome in the favourite Kayasth myth of origin. The ambiguity is resolved by postulating the creation of a fifth varna, the Kayasth, to keep records concerning the other four varnas. Brahma created the four varnas, then summoned the first Kayasth, with pen and inkpot already in hand, to record the activities of all other men. This first Kayasth was named Chitragupta, and he became revered as founder and patron deity of the community. Chitragupta's chief employment was as record-keeper for Yama, the god of death in Hindu mythology, for whom he recorded all the good and bad deeds of men' (Leonard 1978: 11-12).

The Kayastha community in Chandigarh perceives its distribution at the national level. The community uses the caste names Kayastha or sub-caste names, like Shrivastava, Mathur, Bhatnagar, Saxena, Sinha, etc. They take all types of food. Both men and women are regularly non-vegetarian. Rice and wheat are the most commonly used cereals. Those from Himachal Pradesh take maize as well. Although all types of pulses are taken, the use of *arhar* is maximum among the migrants from Uttar Pradesh and Bihar. It has moderate consumption of vegetables and fruits. The use of animal fat, *vanaspati*, mustard, sunflower and groundnut oils as cooking medium is reported. Male members of the community take alcoholic drinks.

The community has endogamous divisions at sub-caste level which are traced back to the time of Chitragupta. The twelve Kayasth endogamous divisions, are traced to his twelve sons by two wives, the Mathurs, Bhatnagars, Saxenas, and Srivastavas from the first wife; from the second wife the Gaurs, Nigams, Asthanas, Surajdwaj, Awasthas, Karans, Kulshreshtas, Balmiki. The Kayasths observed prohibitions and other restrictions for marriage, such as prohibited degrees of relationship. For example fifth cousins were not allowed to remarry (Leonard 1978: 113). According to Rose (1919: 437) all 12 groups had 84 *als*. It did not allow polygyny or *karewa*, somebody moving below social scale was excommunicated.

The Kayastha community at Chandigarh accepts the existence of the above divisions. In the opinion of some informants, the Mathurs consider themselves the highest in the community. Some sub-castes like Mathurs and Bhatnagars consider Saxenas and Kulshrestas as the inferior subcastes. However, divisions exist on the basis of the place of origin—Uttar Pradesh, Himachal Pradesh or Bihar. People from Bihar are considered of inferior social status. Although the community is well educated, it is differentiated at the occupational level. It is employed in all types of white-collar jobs, in public and private services. It has educationists, people in noble professions and administrative services. These differentiations help to regulate marriage alliances and indicate social status. Self-perception of the community is very high even if outsiders consider it of low status. It considers its status to be between Vaishya and Kshatriya. It considers itself as the fifth *varna*.

The community is endogamous at caste and even sub-caste levels. A few marriages have taken place with other castes and religious communities as well. However, these are exceptions. It is also exogamous at village level. In earlier times polygyny was tolerated, particularly in case of barrenness of a first wife but then, remarriage of widow was completely prohibited. The marriages take place by Vedic rites. It involves *kanyadan*, and seven *pheras* around the sacred fire.

Marriage alliances are negotiated. Marriage symbols like vermilion, bangles, *mangalsutra, bindi,* finger-ring, toe- and ear-rings are used. The practice of dowry exists and the parents of the girl are supposed to spend a lot on the marriage. However, it is reported that in the case of the Mathurs, the only consideration is the quality of women. After marriage the newly weds stay for a few days in the house of the groom's parents and then start living separately. Divorce is permissible for both the parties for various reasons with judicial approval. Divorce compensation and the custody of children are decided by the court. The community allows the marriage of divorced men and women, widows and widowers. There has been general liberalization in the rules of marriage. Age at marriage has risen and symbols of marriage are less strictly observed.

Avoidance relationship exists between mother-in-law and and son-in-law and also between father-in-law and daughter-in-law. Joking relationships exist between sister-in-law (*sali*) and brother-in-law (*jeeja*), and brother-in-law (*dewar*) and sister-in-law (*bhabi*) and between sister-in-laws (*nanand* and *bhabi*).

Despite the law to the contrary, the rules of inheritance in the community favour male equigeniture. Succession rules favour the eldest son. The community generally lives in nuclear families. Women have lower status than men. But the Kayastha women definitely enjoy higher status than women of other communities. Women participate in economic activities, contribute to family income and control family expenditure. They have decision-making powers and a role in social functions, rituals and social control. Among the various subcastes of the community, Mathur women have comparatively higher status. After birth, the mother is not allowed to work in the kitchen for a week. In some cases, purification ceremony is performed after forty days. The *mundan* ceremony of male children is performed in the odd years of age mostly before the sixth birthday either at the house or in a temple. A priest presides over the ceremony. When the child starts attending school a ceremoney of *takhti pujan* (worship of writing slates) is observed.

Marriage rituals take place at the bride's home. Feasts are organized by both parties at the time of marriage at their respective places. The consummation of marriage is at the groom's home.

The Kayastha deads are cremated and pollution is observed for ten days. After this a ceremony known as *daswan* (tenth day) is observed. The funeral pyre is lit by the eldest son of the deceased. The bones are disposed of in water at Hardwar. The rituals are now curtailed because these are becoming more expensive.

The Kayasthas have been traditionally working in private and public services. The service in the Mughal courts and other royal places had provided the community a good nexus with royal families. These days it is employed in various white-collar jobs, both in private and public sectors. It is also represented in educational, medical professions and in administrative and defence services. It claims to have about forty teachers in the faculties of Punjab University alone. In Chandigarh, it has one caste association known as the Kaistha Maha Sabha. This is a cultural body of the community, which celebrates various festivals. It publishes *Kaistha Samachar*, which carries news about history and matrimonial information about the community. They follow Sanatan Dharam. A few days after Diwali, the community also worships Chitragupta. The main festivals are Holi, Diwali, Dussehra,

Janmashtami. Folksongs of the places of origin are sung by women. The women have special liking for various types of music.

The community has a good social interaction with other communities. It exchanges all types of food, kachcha, pukka and *sidha,* with other communities. (The older generation has some hesitation in eating kachcha food from others.) This interaction is determined more by social status than by caste or community considerations. They are ready to have a good social relations with Scheduled Caste colleagues, but will hesitate to have it with a servant, even if he is of high caste origin. It is said that in the Mughal courts they had free interaction with the Muslims. They share water resources, crematoria, and shrines with other communities and also take part in regional and local festivals. The community is well represented in the modern professions.

Kayasthas enjoy all benefits of developmental programmes. The perception of the community about education is extremely favourable for both boys and girls. They generally get education up to college and university levels, and also technical and professional education. They favour modern medicare. Both men and women have accepted modern family planning.

Virinder Singh

# KHATIK

According to Rose (1919: 500), 'The Khatik are par excellence tanners and dyers of goat-skins. Brahma, is said to have assigned to them a goat's skin, the bark of trees and *lac*, so they graze cattle, dye the skins of goat and deer, and tan hides with bark and *lac*.'

The Khatiks of Chandigarh have two sub-groups, Chikbe and Chaudhary. According to Ibbetson (1916:296) 'The Khatik of the east is a pig-keeper and the Khatik of the west a tanner, the latter occupy a higher position than the former. The Khatik is said sometimes to keep sheep and goats and twist their hair into waistbands for sale, and even occasionally to act as butcher, but this last seems improbable from his low position, unless indeed it be as a pork-butcher. They appear to be closely allied to the Pasi, and indeed are sometimes classed as a tribe of that caste.' In Chandigarh, Khatiks have been staying for more than sixty years. They speak Punjabi and Hindi and use Gurmukhi and Devanagari scripts. They have been recognized as a Scheduled Caste and according to the 1981 Census of India, their total population is 1,170 individuals which includes 628 males and 542 females. They take non-vegetarian food occasionally. Cereals like, wheat, *jowar, bajra* and maize; pulses like, gram, *urad*, *moong*, *masur* and *moth* as well as a variety of vegetables are taken. The cooking medium is vegetable *ghee*. They take milk and milk products regularly but the alcoholic drinks and fruits are taken occasionally. They smoke *bidi*.

Khatiks have Bhambhaori, Kataria, Pawar, Paderia and Gorkhde as their *gotras*, which regulate their marriage alliances. They recognise their place in the *varna* order as Shudras and are considered of 'low' status by others. They are endogamous at community level, but observe exogamy at village and *gotra* levels. Boys and girls get married at eighteen to twenty years of age. Marriage is arranged by negotiation. Monogamy is practised. Married women use vermilion, glass bangles, *bindi*, finger-, ear- and nose-rings as symbols of marriage. Dowry in kind is allowed. Patrilocal residence is the norm. Divorce due to maladjustment is allowed with the approval of the Panchayat. Remarriage is also permissible. There is an increase in the age at marriage.

Khatik families are either joint or nuclear. Avoidance and joking relationships and conflicts occur in the family. All the sons equally inherit their father's property and the eldest son gets the succession. Increase in the number of nuclear families and resultant decline of the joint family are the major changes in the family system.

Women have a role in animal husbandry. Women attend to household jobs and their status is low. Post-delivery pollution is observed for eleven days and post-natal restrictions on mother continue for forty days. On the sixth day, *chhatti* is observed and the ceremony of *chouke charna* is performed. Khatiks observe *mundan* and visit Devi Balasundri or their *kuldevi* for this purpose. The first birthday of the male child is celebrated. Marriage rituals are performed according to the Hindu tradition of seven *pheras* between 4 and 6 a.m. at the bride's residence.

Khatiks cremate their dead and the bones are disposed of in the Ganges at Hardwar. Pollution period is observed for eleven to twenty-one days. Rituals have been curtrailed as they have become more expensive.

They have engaged themselves as butchers after 1947, when the Muslim butchers left India. Some of them are also engaged in agriculture on a share basis or as contract labour. They have their caste Panchayat. The *Pradhan* (*Nambardar*) is selected by voice vote. The Panchayat imposes cash fines (*dand laona*) and also excommunicates. On confession, a guilty person is often excused . They follow the Hindu religion. Lohri and Diwali are their main festivals. Some of them have also embraced Islam. According to Census of India (1911) 'Khatiks are both Hindu and Muslim (Sikh Khatiks are only 44 in number) and are found almost all over the province. The Hindu Khatiks are immigrant and are usually pig keepers, while the Muslim Khatiks are tanners. Total population is 23,081 individuals, which includes 12,855 males and 10,226 females.' Wall paintings, *sanji* and embroidery are some of their arts and crafts. Oral traditions are shared with other Punjabi communities. *Dhol* is the musical instrument used during the birth and marriage ceremonies. *Bhangra* is the dance performed by the boys.

The Khatiks are sometimes confused with the Chamrangs, but the latter tan buffalo and ox hides with lime and do not dye leather, so that they rank below the Khatik, who tan and dye only sheep and goat skins, using salt and the juice of the *madav* (*Calotropis procera*) but no lime. On the other hand, the Khatik is certainly below the Chamar because he will keep pigs and poultry, which a Chamar would not do; and he will even act as a butcher. About the relationship of Pasi and Khatik, Rose (1919: 204) observes, 'A Pasi is a low caste closely allied to the Khatik, who indeed are said by some to be nothing more than a Pasi tribe.'

According to Rose (1919: 501): 'He is, however, possibly a pork-butcher. He is also said to keep sheep and goats and twist their hair into waist bands for sale. The Khatiks appear to be by origin scavengers, who are rising in social scale by taking to dying and tanning, but have not yet attained the status of a worker in leather. They are closely akin to the Pasi and may even be a sub-group of that caste.'

They traditionally accept and exchange water and food with Brahmans, Rajputs, Banias, and Jat-Sikhs but not with Balmikis and Chamars. They share places of worship and crematoria with other communities and participate in regional festivals and festivities. The members of their communty are either in white-collar jobs, or teachers or in the defence services. Political leadership has emerged at the village level.

Boys and girls go for formal education; but due to economic or social reasons boys do not study beyond college and the girls study up to primary level. They avail themselves of the modern medicare, family planning methods and drinking water facilities in the form of piped water. Wood is used as fuel. Immunization of infant and mother is availed of. They get sugar, *atta*, kerosene from the ration shops.

Swaran Singh

# KUMHAR (HINDU)

The Kumhars are also known as Ghumars. The term Kumhar is derived from the Sanskrit *kumbha kara*, which means 'maker of jars' (Crooke 1896: 335). It is also claimed that the *kumhar* is derived from Hindi *kumbh*, which means earthen pot or vessel (Kainth 1961: 2). The community has two sub-groups, Gola and Mahar, which were until recently endogamous. A few members of the community claim that they can use Brahma and Prajpat as surnames, but this is denied by others. Ethnographic and historical accounts of the community exist. A few accounts of mythology were noted by Crooke (1896) about the origins of the community which continue to be narrated by Kumhars.

Crooke (1896: 335-6) states that 'According to the Brahmo *Vaivarta Purana* they are born of a Vaisya woman by Brahman father; the *Purana Sanhita* makes the father a Malakara or gardener and the mother a Chamar; while the Parasara Podhati holds that the ancestor of the caste was begotten of a Teli woman by a Pattikara or a weaver of silk cloth. Sir Monier Williams, again, describes them as the offspring of a Kshatriya woman by a Brahman. As a matter of fact, their respective lineage is claimed by only one subcaste the Chauhanuya Misr. According to a Bengal story, a water jar was wanted at the marriage of Siva, and no one knew how to make one. God took a bead from his necklace and created a potter out of it; while with a second he made a woman, who became the potter's wife. By a legend current in these provinces the progenitor of the caste was Kopa Bhagat, a Rishi who was ordered by Parameswar to make earthen vessels. ... Another account is that in old days people used to work up the clay for pots with their spittle; and Parameswar, deeming this unclean, revealed the secret of the wheel. That the trade is an ancient one is shown by the fact the earthen vessels are mentioned in the *Rig Veda*.'

The account of Shiva's marriage completely resembles the narration by the local community. A few members of the local community instead of Shiva, emphasize Brahma as central to this story, which on all other counts is the same. Ibbetson has described the Kumhar as 'potter and brick-burner of the country' and 'a true village menial, who also kept donkeys for carrying grain'. (Ibbetson 1916: 315).

Kumhars have migrated to the present place from various districts of Haryana, and their settlement in various colonies of the city dates back to the 1950s and 1960s. However, a few families in the town of Manimajra have lived there since early British times. These families had also originally migrated from the Patiala area.

In the family circle and within the kinship group the Harayanvi dialect is spoken, which is written in the Devanagari script. With other communities Kumhars converse in Hindi and Punjabi. A few members in white-collar jobs also know English. There has been change of dress in the community and young people especially have accepted the local Punjabi dress. Women of the older generation continue to wear Harayanvi dress, i.e. *lahnga, kurta/kurti.*

Kumhars eat meat and occasionally take alcoholic drinks. Members of the older generation smoke *bidi* and hookah, and younger people smoke cigarettes. Women working in brick-kilns also smoke *bidis* and chew tobacoo. They take all the pulses including gram, *urad, moong,* peas, *masur, moth,* etc. Wheat and maize are the most commonly used cereals, followed by rice. *Vanaspati* and mustard oil are the common cooking media. The community is changing from vegetarian to non-vegetarian diet.

The community is divided into two main groups, known as Gola and Mahar, which till recently were endogamous. It has eighty-four *gotras,* some of which are: Tedpuria, Jalandra, Kasania, Bariwaal, Khoal, Momodia, Bebarwal, Chauhan, Sambar, Sukhralia, Damewal, Gagodia, Rahodia, Jaolia, Jalwal, Dugal, Dhania, Rasania, Rajoria, Jajoria, Jajora, Rajora, Puwar, Simar, Bhadwal, Panchala, Katiwal, Jawalia, Pathadia, Marolia and Khadothia.

At Manimajra town, the community also pointed out a few more *gotras* like Nimshwana, Maurpankhi, Sundkarsia and Umbario for Gola; and Shalaria, Patharia, Badalia, Sakoha, Palpiha, Bambalia and Petmal for the Mahars. The latter group is settled in the place for a longer time than the earlier one. The origin of these *gotras* of Mahars was noted in early ethnographic records. According to this the forebearer of Mahars had four sons; the eldest of them was assigned the task of shifting the dust, he was called Sangroha; to the second was entrusted the wheel with its *kila,* so he was called Kilia; the third one shaped wet earth and brought out the ends (*nok*), whence he was called Nokal; and the fourth dried them, whence was called Sokkal. These later formed four *gotras* (Rose 1919: 564). But this does not explain the claim of eighty-four *gotras.* Rose has also noted that the Jalandhra *gotra* of Golas originated from Rupa, a Bhagat of the Devi, who was born in water.

The community at Manimajra also pointed out some divisions at other levels also, which included some occupational groups such as Shorgir, who make saltpetre. Such divisions were also noted earlier. These included Agria (who wear Janeu); Kundgars (members of Kunds); Kuzgars (makers of small vessels, *kuzes*); Nusigars (salt workers); Pajawars (kiln burners); Shorgirs (saltpetre maker) (Rose 1919: 565-6). However, these divisions do not exist here.

The community is also differentiated, at occupational level, into two main groups, those who work as potters and those who work in brick-kilns. In addition, a few also work in non-traditional white-collar jobs. Territorial division is manifested in the settlements of recent migrants in colonies of Chandigarh city and early settlers at Manimajra. The latter claim to have no relation with the former. All Hindu Kumhar can be distinguished from their Muslim brethren at Manimajra. Educational levels of the community vary. Some are illiterate, a few from younger generation are graduates. Social differentiations help in regulating marriage alliances. Kumhar self-perception is very high; but others consider the group to be of low status. The community recognizes the *varna* system, but is not clear as to its placing in the system.

Kumhar marriage practices favour endogamy at community and sub-group levels, exogamy at *gotra* and village levels. The recent migrants negotiate marriages in Haryana, while the community at Manimajra favours Patiala and Nabha area. Adult and monogamous marriages exist which are negotiated by parents. Vermilion, bangles, *mangalsutra, bindi,* and the finger-ring, toe-ring, ear-ring and nose-ring are symbols of marriage. However, Mahar women do not wear nose-ring or nose-pin. They practise *kanyadan.* Dowry is not demanded, yet the practice of dowry exists. On the day of marriage, the *chak* (potter's wheel) is worshipped.

Residence after marriage is patrilocal. There are cases of divorce by judicial approval. However, Kumhars accept the settlement at court about the responsibility for children. Remarriage of divorcees, widows and widowers is acceptable. Of late, marriage rules have become liberal and age at marriage has increased. The community lives in vertically extended families, but the number of nuclear families has increased.

Avoidance relationship exists between mother-in-law and son-in-law; daughter-in-law and father-in-law, and between sister-in-law and elder brother-in-law. Disputes in families arise due to property problems or challenge to the authority of elders. Rules of inheritance favour male equigeniture and succession goes to the eldest son. Women have lower status than men though they participate in production: they assist in pottery making and have decision-making powers and also control family expenditure. Their place in social functions, rituals and the religious sphere is also recognized. They have some role in animal husbandry in addition to pottery-making. They also work in the brick-kilns.

There are pre-natal and post-natal restrictions on the mother. Pollution is observed for a period that varies from area to area. Elder women of the family promise some offerings to the ancestors. The *mundan* ceremony is held at a place called Beri Wali Devi near Rothak. Marriage is arranged mostly by negotiation. The system of *vichola* prevails. Marriage ritual comprises the

Vedic seven *pheras*. At least one gold ornament is given at the time of marriage. The dead are cremated and bones are disposed of in the Ganges at Hardwar. A few families organize the *shradh* ceremony, but it is confined to first death anniversary. Death pollution is observed for twelve days.

The community is dependent on land as a source of clay for pot-making. The clay is bought from both individual proprietors as well as government agencies. In addition to its traditional occupation of pot-making and working in the brick-kiln, it is employed in various categories of jobs in the government offices. A few members are also self-employed. Some work as vegetable sellers. Some carry bricks from the brickfields with the help of donkeys. Since pot-making is of seasonal nature, Kumhars have to be engaged in other jobs, viz., vegetable selling, transporting bricks by donkeys during the winter, when pot-making and pot-selling go at a low key.

The technique of production involves cleaning and preparation of clay, modelling of *matka*, drying the product and firing it in the kiln. Articles produced include *matkia, matka, handi, jhanwala, pyala, koondi, karva, tau'a, diya, sakora, tastri, chilm*, etc. (Kainth 1961: 21-34). They manufacture only thirty-five pitchers, or a hundred *surahis* per day, with additional time required for finishing and firing. The activities of the community require large space to set up kilns and set out pots to dry in the sun. The administration of the Union Territory has not allowed Kumhars more than 10-12 sq. ft. per family in their resettlement plan for Ghumar Colony, Sector-25. The community needs more space for its activities, which has been recently promised by the administration. Child labour does exist in pot-making and payment is made in cash.

A traditional caste council or Prajpat Sabha protects the reservation rights of the community in government service. However, it does not interfere in other activities. It is intended to look after the petty local disputes in the locality.

Kumhars believe in the deities of the places of their origin, especially Beri Wali Devi in Rohtak district of Haryana. People go there to attend a fair every six months. The people also keep portraits of this Devi in their houses. The additional importance of the fair is the donkey fair, which is also organized by the community at the place. However, at Manimajra the Kumhars often go to Gurdwaras and also worship the local deity Mansa Devi. The community observes complete holiday on every *amavas*. Their sacred specialist comes from other communities. He performs worship and ceremonies at the time of birth, marriage and death and also imparts religious teachings. Economic transactions take place at the donkey fair, where Beri Wali Devi is also worshipped. The community also participates in other festivals like Diwali, Dussehra, Holi and Basant Panchmi. Pottery is their traditional craft, which is still continuing.

Kumhars have free interaction with other communities and exchange kachcha, pukka and *sidha* food with other communities. Even relations between Gola and Mahar have improved. The community shares religious places, water sources and crematoria with other communities. The community is aware of a few Kumhar leaders in Haryana.

The Kumhars have drawn only selective benefits from the developmental process. Education is partly favourable for both boys and girls, but both drop out to help the elders in pot-making. The girls also drop out due to social reasons. They generally study up to the eighth or tenth classes. However, one girl is at present studying in B.A. class. A few boys have completed graduation. Some have also passed diplomas in Junior Engineering (Civil). Their attitude to modern medicine is positive. They have also accepted modern methods of family planning. Couples prefer two children, but many have three. Drinking water facilities are very limited.

In Manimajra, all Mahar Kumhar families share a common tap. Electricity supply is available to them at Manimajra. In Sector-25, it has battery-operated TV sets. However, only a few houses have this facility. The younger generation also visits the cinema. Fire-wood, cow-dung cakes, kerosene and coal are the most commonly used fuels, both at home and for pottery-making.

Virinder Singh

# KUMHAR (MUSLIM)

Muslim Kumhars are also known as Ahitans, Ghamars, Ghumals, Ghumiars, Kurs, Langotras, Lehri Prajapats and Sohals. They identify and perceive their distribution at regional level. The community has migrated to its present habitat. They speak Punjabi, Urdu and Hindi and those who are literate use Devanagari and Gurmukhi or Perisan scripts. Males wear *lungi,* shirt and *pagri;* women's dress comprises *salwar, kameez* and *dupatta.*

In food habits, they are non-vegetarian. Their staple food is *dal* and *roti* though they occasionally take non-vegetarian food and eggs. They consume locally available vegetables, fruits and pulses in moderate degree. Food is cooked in *ghee* or musturd oil. Men drink alcohol especially on the occasion of festivals and festivities in the family. The intake of milk and milk products is plenty. They take tea, *lassi,* sweets prepared from milk and curd in varying quantities. Consumption of sweets increases during festive occasions . They smoke *bidi* and use hookah. They are changing from non-vegetarianism to vegetarianism. There is an increase in the use of vegetables, pulses and fruits. They prefer *roti* to rice.

Muslim Kumhars have two subgroups, Jatowali and Desawali. The community has various *gotras* such as Ahitan, Natal, Bagri, Baral, Khamb, Bhuae, Kals, Machro and Sang. These *gotras* regulate marriage alliances and indicate descent and ancestry. They are aware of the *varna* system. They consider themselves neither 'high' nor 'low' but other communities consider them to be of 'low' status. In marriage, they practise endogamy at the community level but exogamy at the *gotra* level. Parallel and cross-cousin marriages are practised. Marriage is settled by negotiations with the help of a *vichola.* Marriage is usually monogamous but polygamy is also allowed. Dowry in kind is allowed. *Mehr* is promised for future payment. Divorce and re-marriage are allowed. Maladjustment, impotency and cruelty may be reasons for divorce. Widow and widower may be allowed to remarry if they lose their spouse at an early age. Widower re-marriage with the wife's younger sister may be allowed if both families agree.

Both nuclear and vertically, or horizontally, extended family types are found among the Kumhars. Traditional interpersonal relations of respect, love and avoidance are observed in the family. Joking relations are rare. The elders are feared and respected, while younger members of the family get love and affection. Avoidance relationship is observed between daughter-in-law and father-in-law. Property matters may cause conflict and confrontation in the family. In a joint family, distribution of work is the most common cause of conflict. Inheritance is by male equigeniture, the eldest son being successor. There is a rise in the formation of nuclear families and resultant decline of extended ones.

Women have low status and are mainly confined to household jobs even as they contribute to animal husbandry and social functions and rituals. Some may add to family income. Women have limited say in the political sphere. But no social, religious ritual and festivity is complete without the active participation of women of the family. Their opinion is normally sought, especially of elderly women for settling a marriage and purchase of a house or other property.

Pre-delivery restrictions and post-delivery pollution are observed. On the third day, the ritual known as *tara dakhaona* (showing of stars) and after fifteen days the ceremony of *chauke charana* (to resume normal kitchen work) are observed. Post-delivery restrictions on the mother continue for forty days. When boys are around five to nine years old they are circumcised. They also perform *aqiqa* ceremony. Marriage rituals are performed at the bride's residence, according to Islamic tradition of *nikah* after consent of the bride is obtained. The amount of *mehar* is also announced and two advocates sign the document of marriage. A feast is given to the marriage party. Consummation of marriage is at the bridegroom's residence. The dead are buried, after which for three days, they do not use *haldi* (turmeric) in cooking. The family offer prayers on the third, tenth, twentieth and the fortieth day; this is known as *khatam*. They offer a feast to the members of the community. Rituals have been curtailed .

Muslim Kumhars are landless and make earthenware. They keep donkeys and work as petty carriers and also pull carts. Village Panchayats attend to their problems. They profess Islam and offer prayers according to their religious tradition. A *maulavi* from other Muslim communities performs various rites.

This group accepts food from and exchanges water and food with the members of other Muslim communities. They share sources of water, schools, places of worship, festivals and festivities such as Id-ul-Fitr, Id-ul-Zuha and Shab-e-Barat with members of other Muslim communities. Political leadership has emerged at village level.

Boys and girls do not stay at school beyond secondary level due to economic reasons. They have benefited by modern medicare and the family welfare programme. Piped water is used for drinking. Wood, cow-dung cakes and kerosene oil are used as fuel resources. Primary school children get bread at school. Immunization facilities are available for infants. They get kerosene, sugar, rice and *atta* through fair-price ration shops. Attitudes towards savings are favourable and whenever they need money they help one another instead of taking loans from shopkeepers.

V. Bhalla
Achla Sood

# LABANA

The term Labana appears to be derived from *lun* (salt) and *bana* (trade). The Lubana, Lobana, Labana was 'doubtless the great salt carrying and salt trading caste, as the Banjara was the general carrier, in former times' (Rose 1919). Rose (1919: 1-9) has given a very good ethnographic account of the Labana. There are various stories about their origin. The Labanas claim descent from the Rajputs.

The Labana group in Ludhiana reportedly hold seven small villages and share in three others. They disavowed all connections with the Muslim Labanas and *Dagnawat, Udaiana, Sukiana, Majrawat, Bartia* and *Balthia gots.* They had a fixed bride-price of Rupees one hundred and twenty in case of a child bridegroom, Rupees one hundred and forty, in case he was an adult to the father of the girl. They practised *karewa.* All were Sikhs (Rose 1919).

The Labanas today speak Bagri with members of their own community. With others they converse in Punjabi language. Their staple food includes wheat and maize as cereals and *urad, moong, masur* and *moth* as pulses. Vegetable oil and pure *ghee* are used as cooking medium. Non-vegetarians eat mutton, chicken and pork occasionally. Men drink on occasions like marriage, the birth of a male child and the arrival of a guest. Milk and milk products are consumed in large quantity. Seasonal fruits are consumed. A few among them smoke also.

The Labanas are today divided into different exogamous *gotras.* Some of their *gots* are Bhagtana, Ghara, Palea, Multani, Ghorewah, Patwalea, Khabreah, Khashrea. In their own perception and in the perception of others, they are placed in the middle ranks. They recognize their place in the *varna* system as Vaishyas. They marry within their community but observe exogamy at *got* and village levels.

The bride-price called *lehan* was prevalent. Now it has been replaced by dowry. At present, the boys are married when they are about twenty-five and girls between eighteen and twenty-five. Monogamy is the form of marriage, which is mostly arranged by negotiations with the help of a *vichola.* Marriages by exchange are also allowed. Married women use vermilion, glass bangles, *bindi* and finger-ring. However, the nose-stud or *koka,* and glass bangles are to be worn compulsorily. Dowry is paid in kind. Post-marital residence is patrilocal. All children equally share their father's property and the eldest son gets the succession. Increase in nuclear families and decline of joint families are some of the changes noticed in the family structure. Women enjoy equal status with men, have decision-making powers, contribute to family income and control family expenditure. Apart from this, they work in agricultural fields, look after domestic animals and attend to social functions and rituals. They observe pre-delivery restrictions, and post-delivery pollution.

Today the Labanas cremate their dead as *dag dena*. According to Rose (1919: 7) there was a curious mixture of Hindu and Muslim rites. In Ludhiana a dying Muslim person was laid on the ground, as in case of the Hindus, but after death the body was again put on a bed, a fire kindled at its right hand and the hand branded. Only after this was the body buried. The bones of the Sikh dead are disposed of at Kiratpur Sahib. On the seventeenth day, they offer prayers (*bog paona*) and feast the members of the community. They observe ancestor worship. Rituals have become quite expensive and hence have now been curtailed.

The Labanas are engaged in agriculture, animal husbandry and government service. They meet at *Labana Bhawan* every Sunday where they discuss the welfare and developmental programmes for the community. The village Panchayat elected by secret ballot also attends to various local problems related to property, theft, and marriage disputes.

About religion, Rose (1919) reported that the Labana had no caste religion. 'Some worship a *devi* or a deity, others a *sati*, while a good many observe the Sikh teaching. Isolated as they were from the Hindus in the beginning, they exhibit a total ignorance of their religious principles and though they have adopted several Hindu customs, they have as yet imbibed nothing of their religion. They fully believe in magic and charms such as the efficacy of mysterious characters written as a scrap of paper. In each village a raised platform serves as a *sthan*, a temple of the Devi. Here a disciple or hermit lives permanently and women constantly resort to this sacred spot with their hands which they present to him and ask about the future.

'The serpent is worshipped on the Gugga Naumi in Gujrat. Women take a *churi* and four *chapatis* and go to the hole of the serpent, The *churi* and *chapatis* are given and cow's milk is poured into the hole. This hole is called *gugga* or *bambia* and is a fixed place outside the village. The *pipal* is sacred tree. On the third day after marriage the bride and the bridegroom are taken to a pipal tree, whose stem is decorated with red colour and *mauli* thread. The married couple turn around the tree and after bowing their heads, come away' (Rose 1919).

Today the Labanas belong to the Sikh or Hindu religion. They celebrate Lohri, Diwali, Holi, Dussehra and Guruparab. The women observe *varat* (fast) during Nauratas and Karwa Chauth. Some of them have also become followers of Radha Swami. They visit Mansa Devi and Kapoori Mai. The priest can be from any community including Jats and Julahas. During Dussehra the girls worship *sanji*. The women do embroidery work and sing *geet* during marriage. They share Punjabi folklore and folktales. Women also take part in dancing.

Labanas accept and exchange water and food with Jats, Bania, Rajputs but not with Sansi, Lohar, Nai, Chamar and Chuhra. Today however the barriers are breaking down. They share crematoria, *dharamsalas*, places of worship, festivals and festivities with members of other communities. Some members are in the teaching profession, army and some hold white-collar jobs in government and private organizations. Political leadership has emerged at the village level only.

Even though facilities for higher education are available, Labana boys and girls do not study beyond secondary level because of their limited means and also for social reasons. They take advantage of modern medicare and family welfare facilities. The hand-pump is the source of drinking water. Though the attitude is favourable towards savings, they depend on the shopkeepers for loans to purchase various items of daily consumption or implements required for agriculture.

V. Bhalla
Kulwinder Kaur

# LOHAR

The term Lohar took its origin from the occupation of blacksmithy. To denote its synonyms and special branches a few names have been used which are Ahangar, Nalband and Koftgar. According to Crooke (1896: 372), the Lohar (Sanskrit *lauha-kara*), is 'a worker in iron', the blacksmith caste. The names for the smith have a three-fold origin. They are derived either from words designating metals or metal collectively (Hindi *lohar*) or from verbs that mean 'hewing'. Also substantives with the general meaning of 'worker', 'artificer', are specialised down to the narrower meaning of 'smith': thus Sanskrit *karmakara*, 'a blacksmith', which really means 'workman' par excellence. It has been suggested that the Lohar is ethnically connected with the Dravidian Agariya, or iron smelter.

All Lohars trace their origin to Visvakarma, the architect and handicraftsman of the gods, 'the fashioner of all ornaments, the most eminent of artisans, who formed the celestial chariots of the deities, on whom craftsmen subsist, and whom, a great and immortal god, they continually worship.' One tradition tells that Visvakarma was a Brahman and married the daughter of an Ahir, who was in her previous birth a dancing girl of the gods. By her, he had nine sons, who became the ancestors of various artisan castes, such as the Lohar, Barhai, Sunnar, Kasera, etc. By another tradition they are the offspring of a Brahman from a Sudra woman. However, the Lohar of Chandigarh do not know about these legends.

Lohars speak a language which is a mixture of Hindi and Punjabi amongst themselves as well as with the members of other communities. Those who are literate use Devanagari script, very few can use Gurmukhi. Normally the men wear *kurta, dhoti, pyjama* or trousers, whereas women wear *salwar, kameez* and *dupatta*. Men are usually non-vegetarian and are in the habit of taking eggs frequently, meat occasionally and fish rarely. The women in the community refrain from eating meat, although they do not mind cooking it. The Lohar prefer wheat to rice, and their staple food is *dal* and *roti*. They take seasonal vegetables like *simla-mirch, arbi, lauki, tinda*, beans, *ghia*, brinjals, lady's finger, etc. *Masur, rajma* and *urad* are their favourite pulses. Occasionally they take seasonal fruits like apples, oranges, bananas. Due to rising prices, the Lohar consume less *deshi ghee* than in the past. Mustard oil is the common cooking medium. Roots and tubers are also consumed. Alcoholic drinks are prohibited for women but most elderly men drink on occasions like marriage. *Lassi* and tea are the common non-alcoholic drinks. The Lohar smoke *bidis* or cigarettes.

The Lohars recognize the *varna* system and place themselves next to the Brahmans. Lohars definitely occupy a low rank in the regional caste hierarchy and were categorized as 'exterior caste', in the Census of India, 1931. Bimra, Nandra and Munda are the three prevalent *gotras*.

Marriage among the Lohars is within the community but not within the same *gotras*. At present the age at marriage for boys is twenty-one, whereas for girls it is eighteen. In the past, child marriage was quite common. They arrange marriage by negotiation with the help of a *vichola* who may be a relative also. Married girls use *sindoor, bindi*, ear-ring, finger-ring, toe-ring and nose-ring and glass and plastic bangles, as the symbols of their married status. According to the financial condition of the girl's parents, dowry is given in the form of furniture, clothes, fans, cycles, sewing machines, sofa-sets, etc. Previously there was a system of giving dowry comprising at least eleven items such as bicycle, chairs, bed, iron-chest, utensils, etc. Those who were economically better-off, used to give twenty-one or fifty-one items as dowry.

In the past, the health of the boy and proficiency of the girl in household work were the main factors on which stress was laid during the match-making. Today parents of the bride prefer a groom who has a job and an independent source of income. The bride usually stays with her in-laws after marriage. Divorce is not very common. Even in extreme cases of maladjustment they approach the community Panchayat first. They rarely go to the court for seeking divorce.

The Lohar usually maintain joint families though nowadays many nuclear families are coming up. Inter-personal relations of respect, love, avoidance or else joking and obligations are prevalent in the family. Joking relationship is observed between *dewar* and *bhabi*. Various avoidance relationships are maintained between mother-in-law and son-in-law, father-in-law and daughter-in-law, and between younger brother's wife and husband's elder brother. The daughter-in-law always keeps her head covered with a *dupatta* and avoids talking face to face with her father-in-law and other older male members of the family. Petty conflicts and confrontations arise in a family. All sons inherit the property of their father equally. The daughters get equal shares in the property if there is no son.

The status of women is low though they participate in important decisions. The primary duty of the women is to attend to the various household activities. In the community, the women look after the domestic animals, the cow and goat, collect fuel and collect drinking water from the tap.

After the birth of a child, the mother and child are confined to a room and are kept in seclusion. This restriction is for a period of ten days in the case of a male child but eight days or twenty in the case of a female child. A ritual is performed on the next day to purify the mother. A Brahman is invited for the purification, there is puja in the local temple or prayer at home. They give five or ten *rupees* to the Brahman who performs the puja. A feast is also offered to the Brahman and to a few other members of the community. The *mundan* ceremony is observed only in the case of a male child. The child is given a hair-cut within the first year without any elaborate ceremonies.

An engagement ceremony precedes the wedding. The *sagan* for the boy is performed by the parents of the girl with sweets like *laddu*, sugar-candy, coconut, dry fruits and nuts. They also send an engagement letter to the groom's side through a barber. The boy's parents offer *sagan* to the girl in the form of an engagement ring, sweets, cosmetics, and red garments, through a barber. The majority of Lohars are Hindu. Marriage rituals are performed partly at the bride's place and partly at the bridegroom's residence. A feast is given by bride's parents at the wedding.

The Lohars cremate their dead. A pollution period is observed for sixteen days in the case of a female and for seventeen days in the case of male. At the time of death, the body is placed on a sheet on the floor. Drops of Ganga water are poured into the mouth just before death. They cover the dead body with a sheet in the case of males and widows, but use a coloured cloth for a woman whose husband is alive. The dead are cremated in the morning. A Brahman recites *mantras* and performs death-rites. The dead body is taken to the cremation ground along a side-lane and not the main road. It is kept at five different places and offered *pinda* (food for the ancestor). Kinsmen break a *matka* (earthen pot) on the occasion. Finally they reach the cremation ground, carrying cow-dung and bamboo sticks for the fire. Brahmans utter *mantras* all along. During the pollution period only tea, water and fruit may be taken. During this period usually the male elders worship their ancestors.

The Lohars are traditionally blacksmiths. They make agricultural implements like hoe, sickle, *khurpa* and sharpen the plough. Previously they used to manufacture only agricultural implements but are gradually shifting from their traditional occupation. They have taken to carpentry along with iron work. Some also work as labourers. Generally agricultural implements are made for farmers who pay in agricultural produce at harvest. Poor families, mostly illiterate, send their children to work in the fields and factories as labourers. Their wages are paid in cash. Most of the Lohar have started their own business, dealing especially in woodwork, and keep direct links with the local market.

The Lohars have their traditional Panchayats which are delegated with powers to ex-communicate an individual or award punishment or fines as deemed fit. Instead of individually approaching the court of law to settle their disputes, the Panchayat sends for the police when the case is unmanageable. Besides, it is the duty of the village Panchayat to appeal to the government to keep the roads clean and look after the street lamps and for providing medical facilities to the people. In the community, there is a *chowkidar* who is paid one rupee per month by each house-owner of the village. The Panchayat or *sabha*, usually solves problems regarding the family disputes, marriage and land. Majority of the Lohar are Hindu and rest of them are Sikh.

Lohars have their family deities. Their traditional art includes wall and floor painting of the *sanji*, other deities and symbolic pictures. Women do embroidery on cloth and knit sweaters. They join to sing *geets* (songs) at the marriage ceremony. Occasionally men perform the *bhangra*.

Food and water are not accepted from Chamars and the Kasai. Untouchability is still practised at the village level to a certain extent and the individuals of castes like Brahman, Kshatriya, Vaishya, do not accept food and water from the Lohar. They can share a source of water and religious places with the members of other communities. They have their separate *maddia* (crematorium). The iron worker and cultivator relationship has been reported only at village level. Lohars are also employed in government offices and as industrial workers, but their number is very small.

Boys and girls attend school. Boys do not continue their studies after graduation. Due to the poor economic condition, the Lohar boys are not interested in pursuing higher education. Only a few girls study up to the secondary level.

Lohars' attitudes towards modern medicine are favourable; earlier they depended on traditional methods of treatment. They get facilities of immunization, etc., for children and their mothers through the *anganbari*. There is a marked awareness of various family planning methods. Couples prefer two or three children. Sterilization is accepted as a measure of birth control by men as well as women.

Community taps are the main source of drinking water which is available within the locality. Most Lohars take loans from banks for business, mostly as carpenters. There is a widespread use of electricity for domestic purposes and small-scale industries.

Wood is collected for use as fuel. Dry cakes made of cow-dung are an alternative. Children get bread from the *anganbari*. Ration cards are used to procure rice, *atta*, sugar, kerosene oil at subsidised rates. They have savings accounts in banks and maintain the system of monthly payment of cash to the shopkeepers from whom they regularly buy essential household commodities.

V. Bhalla
Nupur Pathak

# MAZHABI

The Mazhabi Sikhs are the Balmikis in towns and Chuhras in villages, who have embraced Sikhism and they do not touch the night soil. They are still considered of lower status. They identify themselves at the regional level.

According to the 1981 Census of India, the total Mazhabi population is 856 individuals, which includes 474 males and 382 females. They speak Punjabi and Hindi languages with Gurmukhi and Devanagari scripts. They have been recognized as a Scheduled Caste. Men wear mostly white turbans.

In food habits, they are vegetarian, but a few have started eating a non-vegetarian diet and eggs. Their staple food is wheat, rice and pulses, locally available vegetables are eaten; cooking medium is mustard oil; roots and tubers in the form of vegetables are also consumed. Alcoholic drinks are consumed by some Mazhabis; they take these in abundance on special occasions of festivals and festivities in the family, including marriage or birth of a male child. The intake of milk and milk products is moderate. Mazhabi consume tea, *lassi*, sweets prepared from milk and curd in varying quantities. The use of fruits, pulses, milk and other milk products depends upon economic conditions.

Mazhabis are divided into various *gotras* or clans. The main function of these is to regulate marriage alliances and indicate descent and ancestry. They have now started suffixing Singh to their names. These people are endogamous and observe exogamy at village and *gotra* levels. Self-perception of the community is low. They recognize the *varna* system and their position as Shudras. The age at marriage varies from eighteen years to twenty and from twenty to twenty-five years for boys. *Sindoor*, bangles, *bindi*, ear and nose-ring are used by a few, as symbols of marriage. Child marriage was practised earlier, but now marriages are solemnized when the boy and girl attain adulthood. Marriages are negotiated by elders, whereas relatives help in finding suitable matches. Various items like clothes, household articles and gold jewellery are given to the girl by her parents at the time. After marriage, the residence is patrilocal. Divorce is allowed on grounds of maladjustment, cruelty or adultery with judicial or social approval. Widow, widower and divorcee re-marriage is allowed. Increase in the age at marriage and the lack of strict observance of marriage symbols are some of the changes noted in recent days.

Both nuclear and joint families occur; nuclear families are becoming more common. Avoidance relationship is observed between father-in-law and daughter-in-law. Joking relationship is seen among *dewar* and *bhabi*. In property matters, sometimes conflicts arise. All the sons are allowed to share the property as per practice and succession goes to the eldest son. Status of women is considered equal to that of men and they play a role in household activities, looking after the animals, besides collecting fuel and arranging social functions and rituals. While they thus also contribute to family income Mazhabi women control expenditure. Pre-delivery restrictions are observed and *chilla,* a post delivery restriction on the mother, exists for forty days. *Namkaran* ceremony is also observed. The marriage ceremony is performed at the residence of the bride according to the tradition of *anand karaj.* A feast, called *roti,* is also offered by the bride's parents to the *barat* and close relatives. Consummation of marriage is at the groom's residence.

The Mazhabis cremate their dead and bones are disposed of at Hardwar, in the river Ganges. They also perform *shradh* ceremony or ancestor worship. Rituals are becoming fewer and less elaborate.

Mazhabis are landless and are engaged as sweepers, labourers, in animal husbandry, business, government service or as carpenters. They have their traditional caste Panchayats, and the *Pradhan,* or *Lambardar,* is elected by voice vote. The Panchayat looks after their interest and settles disputes relating to matters such as elopement and disrespect for traditional norms. The *granthi* who performs various rites associated with birth, marriage and death, may or may not be from the Mazhabi community. Festivals are of socio-economic and religious significance. Folksongs of neighbouring Punjab are prevalent; men and women both take part in folkdances like *bhangra* and *giddha.*

The Mazhabis accept and exchange water and food with members of other communities. However, due to their past association with the Chuhra, the Brahman, Jat and Bania avoid exchanging food and water with them There are no restrictions for sharing places of worship. Political leadership has emerged at village Panchayat level.

Formal education is favoured, but poverty prevents many of the boys and the girls studying beyond secondary level. The girls study usually up to primary level and start doing household jobs. Attitudes towards modern medicine are favourable and they take advantage of family welfare facilities. Drinking water is available within their locality. Hand-pumps are used for drinking water. Wood, cow-dung cakes, or kerosense oil, are used as fuel. They avail of mid-day meal scheme for the primary school children. Dependence on moneylenders or shopkeepers for loans still continues.

V. Bhalla
Sushil Kumari

# MIRASI

The Mirasis are traditional musicians and dancers. The meaning of the Arabic word *miras* is 'genealogist' (Ibbetson 1916), a person reciting the genealogies of his masters, the erstwhile rulers, similar to a Hindu Bhat. The Mirasis were treated as 'tenants-at-will' or attendants of the rulers who used to accompany their masters on important occasions or brought their daughters from their father-in-law's house. They used to sing and play the *tabla* and a string instrument known as *sarangi* and also used to beg in the country on ceremonial occasions. The name Mirasi is also derived from Mir Asa, the servant of prophet Mohammad (Rose 1919).

Thirteen subgroups of the Mirasis have been mentioned by Rose (1919), but in the study area the Mirasis belong to a Dom group. They claim the honorific title of the Mir or Meer. The community migrated from the neighbouring areas of Haryana and Punjab about two decades ago. They generally live in the outskirts of the city in the suburban areas, e.g. Manimajra in the west of the Himalayan foothills.

Mirasis generally speak Hindi but also Punjabi, both within and outside the community and usually write in Devanagari script. But Urdu is spoken in their religious gatherings when Persian script is used for communication with other Muslim communities. Men wear *kurta* and *pyjama* or trousers and sometimes a cap; women's dress comprises *kurta*, *salwar* and *dupatta*. Ear, nose, neck and wrist ornaments of silver and gold are worn.

Mirasis are usually vegetarian and occasionally take non-vegetarian food such as fish, eggs and *halal* meat. Sheep or goat's meat is a delicacy for Bakr-id (Id-ul-Zuha) fesival. The staple food is wheat and rice and occasionally maize. Various types of pulses like *urad*, *moong*, *kulth*, *masur*, peas, beans and grams are taken. The cooking medium is mustard oil or vegetable *ghee*. The fruit intake is occasional and various fruits available in the local market are eaten. Milk and its products are consumed, but intake is less and infrequent. The liquor is taken on festive occasions only.

Chombar, Halwa, Joiye, Dhammo, etc., are the *gotras* of the Mirasi which function as exogamous units to regulate marriage. In the regional Muslim hierarchy, however, the Mirasi are relatively low in rank. The community maintains endogamy. Exogamy at village and clan levels is maintained. Marriages occur through negotiation when both the boy and the girl are adult and monogamy is practised. Bigamy is only considered if there is no child from the first wife. Glass bangles and nose ornaments are the symbols of the wedded status. The traditional minimum of the *mehar* equivalent to thirty-two rupees and a quarter of silver coins is promised for future payment to the bride. It is given to her in case she is divorced as a maintenance amount. According to Islamic tenets both husband and wife have the right to divorce but at present, they also feel the necessity of a judicial approval and either spouse can divorce on grounds of maladjustment or cruelty. Both the divorcees can remarry after *iddat*. Widow remarriage in the form of junior levirate is permitted and a widower may also marry through junior sororate or any other girl. There is some trend of increase in the dowry. Residence is patrilocal.

The family pattern is predominantly nuclear among the city dwellers. The main reasons for the breaking of the joint families are economic compulsions and constraints of accommodation. Joking relationship may occur between *dewar* and *bhabi* and *jeeja–sali*. The rule of inheritance is male equigeniture, but unmarried daughters may claim some part in their father's property, which is however, a rare incidence. The eldest son succeeds his father. The status of women is low. They usually remain confined to the house and sometimes fetch potable water. They participate in the social and religious ceremonies but lack decision-making power though they sometimes regulate family expenditure. They usually do not seek any employment though one Mirasi woman works as a midwife.

Post-delivery restrictions and birth pollution are maintained for forty days. On the last day, a *maulvi* is invited to read the Quran, and also gives a name to the child. *Azan* is uttered in the ear of the male child at birth. The *khatna* is the only major childhood ritual and is performed before the fifth year by a Muslim *nai* (*abdal*). Recently, a doctor also did a circumcision. A feast is also given to the friends and relatives on this occasion and the *maulvi* is particularly entertained.

On the occasion of *mangni* or betrothal, sweets, some money and clothes are given to the boy and girl. *Nikah* is the major ceremony of marriage. In this, the *maulvi* along with another prominent person, takes the consent of the girl and the boy thrice and then the marriage is contracted by making an agreement. The amount of *mehar* is also specified in the agreement. Parents of the bride entertain the groom with a feast and the wedding ends with music and dance and a lunch is hosted by bridegroom's parents. The marriage is consummated on the following day.

The dead body is buried and death pollution is observed for forty days. Ancestor worship is observed on the third, tenth, twentieth and lastly on the fortieth day. On the last day called *chalia*, a feast (usually non-vegetarian) is given to friends and relatives and offerings are made to *fakirs* in the name of the dead person.

Members of the community are engaged as musicians, beggars and labourers. Many persons, however, work as luggage-carriers on the horse-carts. One person has retained the traditional occupation of musician for his livelihood. Child-labour does exist to some extent.

The community has its Panchayat which sometimes takes up matters concerning marriage and domestic problems. The issues pertaining to divorce are dealt by the Islamic committee elected by voice vote for about five years. This committee also punishes the guilty by social boycott. But at present, people ignore its dictates. Serious matters involving violence are taken to the police and courts.

The community believes in Islam and propitiates its *pirs* and Prophet. Some people have *silsila* affiliations to Baba Bandgi Sahib whose shrine is located at Sirhand (Punjab) and is visited every year. The sacred specialists are from other Muslim communities; usually a *maulvi* of the local mosque performs various life-cycle rituals. Some magic-cum-medicine men of other communities are also consulted. They celebrate various Muslim festivals, like Id-ul-Fitr, Id-ul-Zuha, Shab-e-Barat, etc., which are of socio-religious importance. They observe mourning on the eve of Muharram. Various local fairs are visited. They share various regional Punjabi and Haryanvi folk oral traditions, music and dances. *Qawali* is one of their folk song forms. The *sarangi* and *tabla* are traditional musical instruments now played by very few persons.

Mirasis traditionally exchange food and water with all Muslim communities, particularly with the Barhai and the Fakir. Earlier, Hindus did not accept water and food from the Mirasis, but now some of them do. But Mirasis accept food and water from the Hindus except from the Chamar and Chuhra.The water is taken from separate taps. Burial grounds are common for all Muslims. Mirasis had a specific role of greeting the people on marriage and child birth or other festive occasions, and played on their instruments to seek alms. They also visited people on death to seek offerings in the name of the dead. But, currently this tradition has almost died out among the younger generation. In modern inter-community linkages a few are in the defence services.

Modern development programmes have made some impact in certain areas. Mirasi children are receiving school edcuation, a few also go to college, but many still drop out from higher studies due to economic reasons. They favour both modern and traditional methods of health and medicare. Sacred or spiritual specialists are also consulted for certain diseases. The attitude towards family planning is becoming favourable these days because of economic compulsions and some women have also got sterilized.

They avail of the facility of tap-water and their houses are electrified. Fire-wood, coal and kerosene are used as fuel. The facilities of public distribution system through fair-price shops is available. Some people have got loans from banks for purchase of horse-carts. They usually favour savings in the post-office or bank though some depend on local moneylenders and shopkeepers for loans.

A.R. Sankhyan

# NAI

The Nai, according to Rose (1919: 140-50), 'form a highly organized occupational caste which performs several distinct functions. ... The word *nai* is unquestionably derived from the Sanskrit *napika*, (one who cleans nails). The Nai boast of many honorific titles. Among the Hindus, he is styled as Thakur or even Raja. Khwas is also a professional title of the Nai. Muslim Nais are called the Hajjam, honorifically styled Khalifa. The Nai are found in all the villages. They are also the hereditary bearers of formal messages such as news of auspicious events, formal congratualtions, letters, fixing of dates of weddings and the like from one village to another'. Folk-etymology derives Nai from 'who never refuses' because, once upon a time, 'Akbar bade Birbal to bring him an *an-mulla* slave, i.e. one who worked without wages. Birbal produced a Nai, whom the emperor sent with a message to Kabul. The Nai set out at once without asking for reward, wages or even provision for his journey, and thus earned the title of *an-mulla.*' (Rose 1919: 140-50).

The Nais in Chandigarh speak Punjabi, Haryanvi and Hindi. Those who are literate use Devanagari and Gurmukhi scripts. Men usually wear shirts, trousers, *pyjama* whereas their women generally wear *salwar*, *kameez* and *dupatta*. Traditionally they are vegetarian though recently the men have started eating eggs, meat and fish. Vegetarian food includes a variety of pulses and seasonal vegetables available in the market. The staple food of the Nais is *dal* and *roti*. They prefer wheat (*kanak*), *bajra*, gram, etc. Their cooking medium is mustard oil. Consumption of *desi ghee* is minimal because of its prohibitive cost. *Lassi* and tea are the common non-alcoholic drinks consumed by them. The men frequently take alcoholic drinks. Elderly persons smoke hookah but the younger generation prefers *bidis* or cigarettes.

The Nais recognize the *varna* system and consider themselves low in the regional social hierarchy. The other communities are also of the same opinion. Nais marry in their own community, but not within the same *gotra*. Marriage within the village is strictly prohibited. They generally observe the rule of exogamy which bars marriage in the *gotras* of paternal and maternal grandfather and grandmother.

Marriages are arranged through negotiation. The boys are generally married on attaining adulthood, but the age at marriage for girls varies from sixteen to eighteen and above. Usually negotiation is made through a *vichola*. They practise monogamy. Married girls use *sindoor*, *bindi*, big ear-rings, nose-rings, finger-rings, toe-rings as symbols of marriage. The married women use lipstick and wear bangles. Dowry is prevalent amongst the Nais. Before marriage, an engagement ceremony is performed and the bride's parents send a hundred and one rupees on the engagement day through the *vichola,* as a token of agreement. There is a custom of displaying the dowry at the time of marriage. A list of items to be given as dowry is prepared and shown by the bride's parents to the relatives and guests on the wedding day. The amount of money given in cash as dowry varies between five thousand and twenty thousand, depending on economic status. The articles given are utensils, almirah, radio, watch, television set, etc. The quantum of articles and money given is on the increase as it has become a status symbol. The customary practice of early marriage particularly of girls is declining. Liberalization of rules for remarriage is reported. Parents of the bride prefer a groom who is employed and has an independent source of income. Residence after marriage is patrilocal and divorce is rare among Nais. In case of maladjustment, the *Sarpanch* or the Panchayat is approached at the community level for a settlement. Widow re-marriage is permitted.

The Nais usually maintain joint families though many nuclear families are coming up. Traditional interpersonal relations of respect, love, avoidance, joking and obligation are common in the family. Joking relationship exists between *dewar* and *bhabi*. Avoidance relationship is main-tained between the mother-in-law and son-in-law and the father-in-law and daughter-in-law. All sons inherit property equally. Daughters get equal shares in the property in case there are no sons. The status of women is low and their activities are generally restricted to routine household chores, looking after the domestic animals like cows, buffaloes, etc., and collecting fuel.

After the birth of a child, post-delivery pollution is observed for seven days in the case of a boy and forty days in the case of a girl. During this pollution period mother and child are confined to a room where only women are allowed. The mother does not bathe, brush her teeth or change her clothes during this period. A ritual is practised to purify the mother and child on the completion of this pollution period when they bathe for the first time after delivery and wear new clothes. Guests are received on this occasion. It is customary for the maternal uncle of the new-born to bring new clothes for his sister and her child on this occasion. *Mundan* is done in the case of male children. At the age of four or five, the child is given the first haircut by another Nai or a close relative. On that day, parents of the child go to the local temple and offer the child's hair in the temple and perform puja, and sweets are distributed among neighbours and relatives.

The marriage ceremony is held at the residence of the bride. A feast is given by the bride's parents at the marriage. Marriage rituals are performed according to Hindu tradition. The Muslim Nais follow Muslim rituals. For the wedding, a Brahman is called to perform the appropriate rituals. The Nais cremate their dead and immerse the ashes in the holy Ganga at Hardwar. The children of the deceased observe pollution period of eleven days for their parents. During this period, a Brahman is invited to perform the rituals. The male members worship their ancestors. According to a convention they tie a *matka* (earthen pot), which has a hole at its bottom, to a *pipal* tree and pour water in it everyday.

The ritual of offering *pinda* is performed under a *pipal* tree. On the twelfth day, a ceremony called *pagri* is performed for the ancestors. The maternal uncle bears the expenditure of the ceremony. Twelve Brahmans and also relatives are invited on the occasion and are served a meal of *roti* and *sabzi*. Death rituals are now being curtailed because of economic constraints and growing social awareness.

Hair-cutting is the main Nai occupation. Some Nais are also employed in beauty parlours as hair dressers. Besides, they have agricultural land and are engaged in animal husbandry. They worship Shiva and Durga. Holi, Diwali, Dussehra, Lohri are their celebrated festivals. Majority of them in Chandigarh are Hindu and a few are Muslim. They traditionally accept food and water from the Brahmans, Rajputs, Khatris, Banias, Jat, but not from the Chamar, Chuhra, Sansi, Bazigar, Deha, Mochi, etc. They share roads, schools, places of worship, crematoria with other communities. They also participate in various festivals and festivities of other communities.

Boys and girls attend school. The girls usually give up at the secondary stage but boys may continue, depending on performance and inclination toward studies. The Nais take advantage of both traditional and modern medicare. Their attitude towards family welfare is positive. They have a general awareness of various family planning methods. It is mostly the women who go in for sterilisation.

Many Nais are employed in government service and engaged in other professions like business, administration, teaching, etc. Most of them take loans from banks for purchasing livestock and also for their own business such as hair-dressing parlours. Cow-dung cakes and kerosene oil are used as fuel.

V. Bhalla
Nupur Pathak

# NOONGAR

The Noongars derive their name from *noon,* 'salt' and they are manufacturers of salt. The Noongar of Chandigarh claim Rajput descent. During the Muslim regime, they claim to have drifted away from the mainstream. The legend about their origin is that two Rajput brothers were invited for marriage and one of them was married to a widow without his knowledge and this fact was discovered later on. Once this fact was known to the community, he was declared an outcaste and he took up the occupation of salt-making and thus got the name of Noongar. They claim that they differ from Rajputs in terms of only one ritual, i.e. *karewa* (widow remarriage) which is being practised by the Noongars. Synonyms like Nunia, Lunia, Nunari, described by Ibbetson (1916: 317) are not in vogue in our area. Noongars identify at the regional level and speak Punjabi with kin and Punjabi and Hindustani with others. The scripts in use are Devanagari and Gurmukhi.

Wheat is the staple cereal and *urad*, *moong*, *kulthi*, beans, *masur* and *moth* are pulses that are taken. *Vanaspati* (hydrogenated vegetable oil) is their cooking medium. Vegetable consumption is high though men are occasionally non-vegetarian; women are strictly vegetarian. The menfolk also consume country liquor occasionally which is purchased from the local market. Fruit consumption is moderate. They smoke *bidis* and cigarettes and also use snuff. In recent days, non-vegetarians are becoming vegetarian. Increase in consumption of pulses has been reported.

The community has social divisions. Out of thirty-six *gotras* reported, in Chandigarh only a few could be located. These are Jundwan, Thonwan, Jetowadiya and Chundwan. All these *gotras* are equal in status and their function is to regulate marriage alliances. Noongars self perception, as well as other's perception, places them at medium level. They recognize the *varna* system and identify themselves as Kshatriya. Village and *gotra* exogamy are the rules of marriage. Junior levirate and sororate are permissible for widow and widower remarriage. The boys marry around the age of twenty-two to twenty-four and girls around twenty to twenty-two. Marriage alliances are arranged through mutual negotiations between parents. Monogamy is the prevalent type of marriage. Vermilion, glass bangles, *bindi* and nosepins are the symbols of married women. *Kanyadan* is an important ceremony during marriage rituals, when the father hands his daughter over to the groom. Dowry is given in both cash and kind. After marriage, the newly-wed couple stay with the groom's parents. Divorce is sought with judicial approval in some cases. The quantum of compensation and responsibility for children are decided by the court. Widow remarriage (*karewa*—where no *phera* are taken) and widower remarriage are permissible. Changes reported in the institution of marriage are increase in the age at marriage of boys and girls and strict observance of the marriage symbols.

Nuclear and vertically extended types of families are common. Avoidance and joking relationships have almost disappeared. Check on the freedom of youngsters and challenge to the authority of elders lead to conflict and confrontation within the family. Male equigeniture with an additional share to the widow is the rule of inheritance; succession goes to the eldest son. There is a rise in nuclear families, as the newly-wed couples set up a separate home after a few months. Invariably, the root cause is conflict between the mother-in-law and daughter-in-law. This trend has resulted in decline in the extended family. Women are given equal status as they control family expenditure. They perform household chores, besides helping in agricultural operations and animal husbandry, thus indirectly contributing to family income. They have a definite role in rituals and religious spheres.

*Sootak* restriction is observed. On the sixth day, the woman takes a bath, known as *chauke charana,* and only after this are restrictions withdrawn. A naming ceremony is conducted for boys when a *pandit* is called to give the name to the child. If a *pandit* is not available, this is done by the child's paternal aunt. The *pandit* also performs puja for the welfare of the child and the family. The *mundan* ceremony is observed in the case of male child only. For this, they go to Mansa Devi or Naina Devi. This ceremony is performed between the age of one to three years. *Janeu* ceremony is performed before the age of twenty or at the time of marriage, but its importance and practice is disappearing very fast. *Shagun* precedes the wedding. Marriage rituals are performaed at the bride's residence. *Bedi* (a specially arranged place) is prepared for the wedding. The *barat* is given a feast by the girl's parents. The consummation of marriage is at the groom's residence.

Death pollution is observed for four days (*chautha*) and all types of rituals and pollution observance are over on the thirteenth day, called *terahvin.* The dead are cremated and the bones are disposed of in Ganga water at Hardwar. The *shradh* is observed annually. Changes in life-cycle rituals include curtailment of rituals and increase in expenses.

Land is the main natural resource and is controlled by individual proprietors. Agriculture is the traditional occupation, but due to fragmentation of landholding Noongars are now marginal farmers, most of them having taken to vegetable and fruit selling. A sizeable number of Noongars are working as agricultural labourers. Their increased landlessness has resulted in their shifting from their traditional occupation. Their traditional caste Panchayat is in the Majoli village, distt. Patiala (Punjab) about fifty km from

Chandigarh. The statutory Panchayats exist and their function is to look after the welfare of the area.

The Hindu Noongars propitiate regional deities like Mansa Devi, Naina Devi and Vaishno Devi. Their sacred specialists are the Brahmans. These specialists perform worship, impart religious teachings and officiate at life-cycle rites. The festivals are of socio-economic and socio-religious importance. Folksongs and folklore are the forms of oral tradition. The *dholki* (percussion instrument) is used as accompaniment for light music and folksongs.

Noongars accept from, and exchange water and food with castes like Brahman, Khatri, Bania, but they do not exchange the same with castes like the Chamar, Chuhra and Muslims. The Brahmans are given *sidha* and kuchcha food on certain occasions and festivals. Noongars share their crematorium with other communities. Landlord-tenant and cultivator-labour relationships exist with other communities.

Boys and girls study up to secondary and primary levels respectively. The main reasons for dropping out is lack of interest in studies and economic constraints. The boys have to supplement family income, whereas girls have to help in the household chores, and so primary-level education is considered adequate. The attitude to both modern and traditional medicare is positive and they are also in favour of family welfare programmes and prefer two to three children. Sterilization is accepted and either spouse get sterilized.

Drinking water is available in the locality. Each household has either a hand-pump or piped water source or both. Fire-wood, cow-dung cakes, kerosene oil are the fuel they use. The mid-day meal scheme operates and ICDS facilities are fully utilised. They avail of the public distribution system. Their attitude to savings is favourable and they avail themselves of loan facilities through banks.

R. Malhotra

# PENJA

The Penja, according to Ibbetson (1916: 324), 'often called Pumba or Dhunia, and in cities Naddaf, is the cotton scutcher who, striking a bow with a heavy wooden plectrum, uses the vibrations of bow string to separate the fibres of the cotton, to arrange them side by side and to part them from dirt and other impurities'. In the Union Territory of Chandigarh, the Penjas are distributed in Burail, Manimajra village, Manimajra town, Dhanas, Khudasher-Ali, Kansal, etc. Men wear shirt, *lungi*, cap; the women, *salwar, kameez* and *dupatta* and also use the *burqa* (veil). The Penjas migrated to Burail from Uttar Pradesh, and the adjoining state of Punjab. They speak Hindi, Urdu and Punjabi; but use the Persian script only. They are non-vegetarian but their staple food is *roti*, *chawal* (rice) and *dal*. Fruits and vegetables are taken seasonally. Milk and milk products are not very important. Some take alcoholic drinks on the occasions of birth, marriage, festivities and festivals. They also smoke.

The Penjas had *gotras* in the past which were used to regulate marriage alliances. They practise endogamy at community level. Consanguineous marriages are allowed; these include parallel as well as cross-cousin marriages. Real uncle-niece marriages are prohibited. Child marriage is in vogue, but *gauna* takes place after the bride attains puberty. They practise polygyny. According to Crooke (1896: 297), 'To the west of the province the Hindu Dhuniyas claim to be of Rajput origin. They are divided into five endogamous sub-castes: Chouhan and Bargujar, which are well known Rajput septs; and the Dhakeri, Bargali and Chunkari, which take their names from *dhak* (Butea frondosa), and *bar* (Ficus Indica) and the *chankar* (Prosopis spicigera) all of which are sacred trees and regarded with special respect by those Dhuniyas who take their names from them.'

Married girls wear bangles, toe-, ear- and nose-rings as marriage symbols. Dowry includes household articles such as utensils, clothes and jewellery. Residence is patrilocal. The child marriage practised in the past has now been replaced by adult marriage. The age at marriage is between twenty and twenty-two years. Marriage is performed by the *maulavi*. The girl repeats the word *qabool* (acceptance) thrice in the presence of one witness and one advocate. The minimum amount of *mehar* is Rupees thirty-two and six *annas*. In case man and wife are incompatible, or if the boy is a drunkard, divorce is permissible with the approval of the Village Panchayat. Remarriage is allowed. Divorce compensation is given to the wife. Nuclear and joint family types are common. Elder members of the family are respected and the younger ones of the family get love and affection. Inheritance is by male equigeniture and succession is by the eldest son. Women have low status and attend to various household jobs. They have a role in social, religious and ritual activities.

The Penjas are Muslims and follow various life-cycle rituals, associated with birth, marriage and death according to the Islamic tradition. When the boy is six to ten years of age, the *sunnat* is performed. Those who can afford, offer a feast to the members of their community at a simple ceremony. At death, according to Crooke (1896: 298), 'If there is an educated Mohammadan present he reads the *fatiha*; but this is not indispensable. They are usally worshippers of the Panchonpir, and they have one special usage, known as the Piyala or "cup", when on Tuesday in the month of Aghan the men and women go to the river-side and offer sweet to Sahjamai, this is consumed by the Dafali who acts as priest. They spend the whole night by the river listening to the songs sung by the Dafali in honour of the goddess.' Penjas bury their dead. The dead body is bathed with warm water and the clothes changed. *Namaz* is offered before burial. After forty days, they offer prayers and recite the Koran.

According to Crooke (1896: 298-9), 'The primary business of the Dhuniya is the carding or rather scutching of cotton. This is done by subjecting it to vibration produced by a bow string (*dhanuhi*, Sanskrit, *dhanus*).' Now apart from cotton ginning they also are engaged as labourers or rickhaw-pullers. They are a landless community. The village Panchayat settles their disputes. Election of the village Panchayat is done by secret ballot. Penjas go to the mosque and offer *namaz* and celebrate festivals such as Id, and Bakr-id. They share folksongs, folk-tales with other communities of the area.

Penjas traditionally accept from, and exchange water and food with, the Balmikis (Chuhra), Chamars and Ramdasias. Very few of their members hold white-collar jobs or serve in the defence services. Boys study up to college or secondary level, but girls up to primary level only. Health and modern medical facilities are availed of. They are aware of the family planning programmes. They listen to radio and watch television in the neighbourhood. Electricity is available for domestic and business purposes. Wood, kerosene oil and cow-dung cakes are the fuel sources. The mid-day meal scheme for nursery children is availed of. They use ration shop facilities. Attitudes towards saving are positive. At Manimajra, they approach the Bania for loans if they need money to defray the expenses of marriage or to purchase livestock.

V. Bhalla
Achla Sood

# RAJPUT

The name 'Rajput' is derived from Sanskrit '*rajputra*' (*raja* - king; *putra* - son) meaning son of a ruler. The term *rajanaya,* implies a warrior or Kshatriya. There was, however, a distinction between Rajputras and Kshatriyas. The former were deemed to be superior. The Kshatriyas were entrusted with the administration and military duties of a kingdom, while Rajputras were the sons of the royal household or members of the nobility. The history of Rajputs in India can be traced back to the time when the Sakas and Hunas entered India from the north. In the third century AD, the resurgent tribes in Punjab freed this land from the Kushanas. In the fourth century AD, the Gupta empire took shape with Chandragupta as founder. According to Jat folklore he is said to have belonged to Jat tribe of Sakls (Sialkot) area. Persians invaded the Punjab in AD 456, but Skanda Gupta drove them away. In AD 477 the White Huns under the Laelih, expelled the Kushanas from Gandhara.

The Huns were a nomadic tribe from Central Asia. Some migrated to Europe and some to India. They ruled Punjab and Kathiawar, and went as far as Bihar. They were very good at fighting, which eventually led to the establishment of Huna pockets in north-west India. These pockets are believed to have been represented by some of the present day Rajputs. Toraman who belonged to the Jaula clan of the White Huns advanced up to the Chenab and attacked east Punjab (Sanghol, Dist. Ropar). He captured Malwa (in Central India) and fought battles in Saugar in AD 510. His son Mihirakula ruled over north India from AD 515. The Rajputs today are known as Raghubansi, with a number of clans such as the Rathor, Sisodia, Pundir, Chauhan, Rangar, Mandhar, Palwar, Parihar, Janwar, Rawats, Bargujar, Barwar, Bhadauria. The migrations of Rajputs from Rajasthan took them to Punjab, Uttar Pradesh, Haryana and Himachal over the past four hundred to thousand years. The reasons due to which Rajputs migrated to other areas, are numerous. Some of the people from various clans migrated in the wake of the invasions of various invaders. A number of famines also compelled such migrations. The Rajput community perceives its distribution at the national level.

The Rajputs are distributed throughout the Union Territory. They are Hindus and speak Punjabi and Hindi and use Gurmukhi or Devanagari scripts respectively. Men's dress includes turban, *achkan* and *pyjama* and women wear *jumur* at their forehead. There was *pardah* in the past.

In food habits, Rajputs used to be pure vegetarians, but now some have started taking occasionally non-vegetarian diet and eggs. Some Rajput men eat non-vegetarian food, while they are in the military services. Their staple diet is *roti*, *dal*, and rice. They eat vegetables and groundnut oil is used as cooking medium. They eat locally available vegetables, fruits and pulses in varying degree. Roots and tubers in the form of vegetables are eaten. Alcoholic drinks were prohibited earlier but the younger people, now occasionally take alcoholic drinks especially on the occasion of festivals and festivities in the family. Cosumption of milk and milk products is in plenty. They take tea, *lassi*, and sweets prepared from milk and curd in varying quantity. The intake of sweets increases during festive occasions whereas consumption of fruits, pulses, milk and other food items vary depending on economic conditions.

The Rajputs have various *gotras* which regulate marriage alliances and indicate descent and ancestry. They follow a system of marriage in which consanguineous marriages are proscribed. Marriages are largely regulated on the principle of community endogamy and clan exogamy. Marriage within the *gotras* is impossible and in fact would be regarded as incest. Besides this, although a Rajput boy may accept a bride from a family inferior in status to its own, a similar privilege is denied to the Rajput girl, whose husband must be equal, and if possible, her superior. The regulation of *sapinda* further prohibits marriages between kin, descended from a common male ancestor up to the seventh generation on father's side, and up to the fifth generation on the mother's side. When a boy is eleven his father deputes a *ghataka* or professional match-maker, to negotiate with the parents of a girl, belonging to a suitable clan. The symbol of consent is the coconut sent by the father of the girl to the father of the boy and signifies that the former makes an offer of his daughter's hand. If the proposal is accepted, the coconut is retained; but if alliance is declined, it is returned. Then a *pundit* is engaged to scrutinise the boy's *janampatri* and the constellations are consulted to decide whether the lunar position in which boy and girl were born indicates a good match. On receiving a favourable reply, a *tilak* or *tika* is affixed to the boy's forehead and the question of dowry is then discussed. As soon as this matter is disposed of, relations and friends are informed of the engagement, and the betrothal called *sagai* (or *barricha*) is complete. The next step is to select an auspicious date for the *becah* (marriage) ceremony. Marriage symbols are vermilion, bangles, *bindi* and finger-ring.

The practice of *kanyadan* prevails. Dowry is given in both cash and kind. It consists of clothes, household articles and jewellery of gold. After marriage the residence is patrilocal. Divorce is permissible and is usually carried out with judicial approval. Reasons for divorce may be adultery, maladjustment, or cruelty. Both parties can sue for divorce. Divorce compensation is given to the wife. Status of children is decided in the court.

Rajputs, aware of the *varna* system, recognize their position as Kshatriyas.

One who becomes a widow or widower at a very early age, is allowed to remarry. Divorcees are also allowed to remarry. Widower remarriage with wife's younger sister may be allowed if both families agree. An increase in the age at marriage, liberalization of rules for remarriage, non-observance of some of the marriage symbols are the changes in marriage rules.

Both nuclear as well as joint family types are found among the Rajputs. Traditional interpersonal relations of love, respect, avoidance, joking and obligations are observed in the family. The elders are feared and respected, while younger members get love and affection. Avoidance relationship exists between father-in-law and daughter-in-law, younger brother's wife and husband's elder brother, and between women and elder male community members. Joking relationships are between *bhabi* and *dewar* ; *sali* and *jeeja*. Conflicts arise due to property disputes and equitable sharing of jobs in the household. Only male members of the family have a share in the property. In the past, male primogeniture was in practice, and it was called *tikka* and youngest son was paid *kharcha* (compensation). However, at present, succession is by the eldest son. Among Rajputs, the women do not join the company of men and are not admitted to equality with them. The household jobs of the Rajput woman are the same as those of women of other castes. She grinds the corn, cooks food, spins, and brings in wood (fuel) and water. But owing to her being secluded like Muslim ladies, she is not like the women of the economically weaker communities available for agricultural labour, and unlike the Jatni, can take no part in outdoor work in fields.

Pre-delivery as well as post-delivery rituals are observed strictly. Post-natal restrictions are observed. On the birth of a male child, the father or a relative at once summons the *purohit* (family priest) and enquires of him whether the infant was born at the propitious moment. The *purohit* consults the stars, keeping a note of every statement in the *janampatri*. After a week of feasting and rejoicing, the *purohit* is asked to fix a propitious day for naming of the child. This is done after the consultation of *janampatri* and other formalities. Forty days after birth, the infant is taken outside the house and *mantras* and sacred hymns are repeated to Surya, the Sun god. The *mundan* ceremony is performed in two phases. When the child is two years old, an auspicious day is selected for the ceremony of tonsure which is performed twice. On the first occasion the hair is entirely cut and a tuft called *churti* or *choti* is left on the head. On the birth of a daughter all feasting and rejoicing is dispensed with, and only the bare rites are observed. Among some Rajput clans, birth of a daughter is regarded as a misfortune. *Annaprashan* and the thread wearing ceremony are observed among Rajputs. The *janeu* or sacred thread, is the emblem worn by the three highest castes of Hindus to symbolize their second or spiritual birth, and as a mark of distinction. It consists of three strings of spun cotton, varying in length according to the caste.

On the morning of the bridegroom's departure for the bride's house, he is dressed in yellow adorned with jewels. Marriage rituals are performed at the bride's residence. A feast is given by the bride's parents.

Rajput dead are cremated. The funeral rites are always conducted by Maha Brahmans. The period of mourning is ten days, during which members of the family are not allowed to shave, wear shoes or eat cooked food. On the first day, all near relatives should have their heads shaved. On the third day after cremation, bones and ashes called *phul*, are collected and placed in a vessel, which is immersed into the Ganges at Hardwar or some other sacred river. On the eleventh day after death, the *shradh* ceremonies commence. These are reverential offerings to ancestral spirits. The *shradh* ceremonies are repeated, in a simple form, every month for a year.

The primary occupation of the Rajputs is settled cultivation. They also engage in animal husbandry and are also found in government or private service. In addition to their traditional Panchayat, they have an All India Rajput Student Aid Society in order to provide educational facilities not only to Rajputs, but also to students of other communities. The first step in this direction is to construct a hostel for students and they are doing so by constructing Maharana Partap Bhavan with about 200 rooms, at Chandigarh. Punishment is imposed by the Panchayat in the form of social boycott or excommunication. Generally, they try to arrive at an agreement in most of the cases. They follow Hindu religion, visit temples and celebrate Holi, Diwali, Baisakhi, Basant Panchami, Makar Sakranti, Amavasa, Ram Naumi, Raksha Bandhan and Dussehra. They have folksongs and folktales as prevalent in the area. Family deities also exists. Worship of Ganesh and village household deities also exists. Ganpati or Ganesa is the god of good luck and remover of difficulties. Surya, or Suraj Narain, and Lord Visnu are worshipped.

Rajputs do not accept and exchange water and food or *sukka atta* (dry flour), oil or dry food with lower communities, but do share food and water with the Banias, Saini, Khatri, Brahman and Jat. They have the same crematorium and visit the same religious places. Their members are scholars, creative artists, engineers, doctors, defence personnel, etc. Political leadership has been found at the regional level.

Boys and the girls study up to college level. They take advantage of modern medicare and family planning facilities and prefer two or three children. Dissemination of information is mainly through voluntary agencies. Facilities of food and ration distribution through fair-price shops are availed of.

V. Bhalla
Swaran Singh
Achla Sood

# SAINI

The Sainis are also known as Shursaini and Mali. According to Ibbetson (1916) 'they appear to be only a sub-division of the Mali, while the Mali appear to be more of an occupational category of gardeners, whose women work in the field. Sainis are expert agriculturists whose women do not work in others' field'. Chaudhary is the title used by them. They are divided broadly into two sub-groups, Hindu and Sikh. They claim to have served in the *sena* (army) of Lord Krishna and having fought the great war of the Mahabharata, they believe they got their name from *sena*.

Ibbetson describes further, 'The Mali and the Saini, like all vegetable growers, occupy a very inferior position among the agricultural castes; but of the two the Saini are probably the higher, as they more often own land of even whole villages, and are less generally mere market gardeners than are the Mali.' They claim to be originally Yadavs, from whom originated the Shursaini. They are spread all along the Shivalik foothills, especially in Ropar, Hoshiarpur and Jalandhar districts in Punjab. They converse in Punjabi and use Devanagari and Gurmukhi scripts.

Both vegetarian and non-vegetarian food is eaten. The staple food is *dal* and *roti*. Locally available pulses, vegetables and fruits are taken. Alcoholic drinks were a taboo earlier, but at present no such attitude, especially in the new generation is seen. The intake of milk, milk products and tea is common. Smoking is seen among the Hindu Sainis only.

According to Ibbetson (1916: 189), the Sainis do not appear to have had any large clans except in Hoshiarpur, where some of the largest clans are Boli, Pawan, Gaddi, Hamarti, Badwal, Alangi, Mangar, Badyal, Barayat and in Gurdaspur many of the Sainis showed their clans Salahri. Some of the clans of Arains and of Sainis in Jalandhar today bear the same names. They are further divided into a number of *gotras* like Hare, Bhere, Dhur, Vaid, Lambe, Gegyan, Badwal, Daule, Togar, Benwets, Masute, Bange, Dhamrhait, Pablay, Giru, Chepru, Kapoor, Dheak, Chauhan and Chinde. The *gotras* regulate marriage alliances. They claim to be Kshatriya in *varna* order.

The Sainis are endogamous at community and sub-group levels and exogamous at *gotra* and village levels. Monogamy is the rule of marriage and is arranged by negotiation, when the boys and girls attain adulthood. Marriage by exchange was practised earlier and was known as *batta-satta*. *Kanyadan* exists and dowry is in cash and kind. Divorce is very rare and may be allowed with judicial approval for reasons of extreme incompatibility. Widow and divorcee remarriages are allowed. Junior sororate and levirate remarriages are also permissible. Both nuclear and joint family types are prevalent. Inheritance is by the male equigeniture and succession is by the eldest son. Women have low status and are mostly confined to the home but help in agriculture, animal husbandry, collection of fuel, fetching water and in ritual, religious and social spheres. Pre-delivery and post-delivery restrictions are imposed. Post-delivery pollution, called *sootak,* is observed for thirteen days. There is a naming ceremony and *mundan* is confined to the Hindu Saini boys. Marriage rituals consist of seven *pheras* in case of the Hindu Saini and four *pheras* around the *Guru Granth Sahib* in the case of Sikh Saini. The dead are cremated and the bones are disposed of in water. Death pollution is observed for thirteen days.

Traditionally, the Sainis are agriculturists. With education and decreasing landholdings they have diversified into trade, industry and private and government jobs. The *biradari* system is prevalent at local, district and higher levels, and is functionally important for social control and for the welfare activities. It is slowly losing its effectiveness. Some Sainis have joined the Arya Samaj, Radha Swami or Nirankari, while others belong to the Vaishnav sects. The traditional Hindu deities are worshipped by the Hindu Sainis and Sikh Sainis revere the ten Gurus. Major fairs and festivals include the Diwali, Dussehra, Holi, Baisakhi, Lohri and Guruparab. Oral traditions are the same as in other Punjabi communities. Inter-community linkages are seen with other communities except those belonging to Scheduled Castes and castes like Dhobi and Nai and groups dealing with leather. They traditionally do not accept or exchange water and food with the Chuhra, Chamar, Deha, Dom, Dhobi, Nai and the Muslims. With other communities they accept and exchange water and food in any form kachcha, pukka or *sidha.* The Sainis share water sources, roads, crematorium, *panchayat-ghar* and religious places with other communities. Putative kinship exists on personal level. In modern intercommunity linkages, they have businessmen, scholars, teachers, doctors and in white-collar workers.

Formal education is favoured for both boys and girls. Both traditional and modern medicare is made use of. Family planning norms are accepted. Dissemination of information is through extension agencies, political parties and voluntary organizations. Rain water, tube-wells, and canals are used for irrigation. They use organic manure, chemical fertilizer, insecticides and pesticides to improve their yield.

A.K. Bhatia

# SANSI

The Sansis were described by Ibbetson (1916: 277) as 'a wandering group, seldom or never settling for long in any one place'. The Sansis in Chandigarh are however a settled people with little indications of their earlier nomadic life. Some derive the name Sansi from the Sanskrit *svasa* 'breathing', or *srasta*, 'separated', others from *svaganika*, 'one who has to do with dogs', or *savapaka*, 'dog-cooking' (Crook 1896: 2,7). They trace their origin from Marwar and Ajmer where they are numerous (Ibbetson 1916: 277). According to Crooke (1896), 'Some of them hold that they are a sub-caste of Nats; but the Nat do not acknowledge kinship with them. By one account when the Agnikula or fire-born races were created, the Chauhan Rajputs created the Sansiyas to act as their bards and sing their praises. Their first ancestor was, it is said, one Sans Mal or Sahasman, who has given his name to the tribe.'

Bhedkut and Manesh are two synonyms of Sansi. Their total population is 1,344 which includes 701 males and 643 females, according to the Census of Chandigarh, 1981. Most of the Sansis in Chandigarh have migrated from Rajasthan and only a few are from Punjab. The Sansis have a peculiar dialect; the Sansis in Chandigarh claim it to be closer to Rajasthani. They converse in Hindi and in Punjabi with members of other communities.

Ibbetson (1916: 277) states that they were once 'great hunters, catching and eating all sorts of wild animals, both clean and unclean'. The Sansis in Chandigarh are non-vegetarian but they eat eggs and goat's meat only. However, because of poverty they cannot afford to eat non-vegetarian food regularly. Their staple food is *roti* and *dal*. They prefer maize and *bajra* as cereals. They purchase seasonal vegetables and fruits when they are reasonably cheap. Primarily they were known to distil illicit liquor. But the Sansis in Chandigarh have given up these practices and buy their alcohol, *deshi sharab*, from the market. The men drink and their womenfolk also join them occasionally.

The Sansis recognize the *varna* system. They consider themselves to be of low rank in the social hierarchy. The other communities are also of the same opinion. In Chandigarh, they are categorized as a Scheduled Caste. The *gotras* of the Sansis in Chandigarh are Adlan, Badvan, Gajwan, Advan, Mattwan, Diran, Kirhan and Balan. The Sansis marry in their own community, but not within the same *gotra*. They avoid the *gotra* of paternal as well as maternal grandfather and grandmother in the selection of partners. Usually marriages are arranged through negotiations. Generally, the mediator is the *phupha* or father's sister's husband of the bride or bridegroom. Boys generally marry on attaining adulthood but the age at marriage for girls varies from sixteen to eighteen years. Vermilion, *bindi*, ear-ring, finger-ring, toe-ring, nose-ring, glass or plastic bangles are symbols of marriage.

The parents give clothes and jewellery as gifts at the time of marriage of their daughters. It is a patrilocal society and the bride stays with her in-laws, after the marriage. They do not go to court for seeking divorce. Even in extreme cases of maladjustment they approach the Panchayat at the community level. Widow remarriage is permitted. The Sansis maintain joint families mainly for socio-economic reasons. Avoidance relationships are maintained between the father-in-law and daughter-in-law. Joking relationship is observed between *dewar* and *bhabi*. Property is equally divided among the sons. The status of women is superior to that of men. The women look after their children, do the various household activities, collect fuel, bring drinking water from the tap. Women take important decisions in the family and contribute to family income.

After the birth of a child, post-delivery pollution is observed for one month and fifteen days. During this period the mother is not supposed to touch utensils in the kitchen. Usually, food is prepared by the mother-in-law or sister-in-law for the mother. The mother does not eat with other members of the family during these days. After the completion of this post-delivery pollution period, the rooms are cleaned and the mother starts her normal activity. On the sixth day of the birth, *chhatti* is observed. On that day they distribute sweets to the neighbours.

The *sagan* for the bride is sent by the parents of the bridegroom: send dress, engagement ring, jewellery and sweets are sent through the relatives and they celebrate the day with a feast and drinks. The marriage ceremony, according to Ibbetson (1916: 277), is peculiar, 'the bride being covered by a basket on which the bridegroom sits while the nuptial rites are being performed'. In Chandigarh, the wedding is at the residence of the bride's parents who host the feast. The marriage rituals are performed by the women of the community. They do not invite a Brahman for these rituals.

According to Crooke (1896: 277), 'The real vagrant Sansiyas often merely expose their dead in the jungle, where they bury their dead.' In Chandigarh, the Sansis cremate their dead. They do not light their oven until the dead body is cremated. The pollution period is observed only by the male members (sons) for eleven days. During this period the male members (sons) worship their ancestors. They take boiled rice and milk only in the meals. At every meal they keep some food aside for the spirit of the deceased. The rest of the family eats rice and boiled *dal* during these eleven days. Usually, the eldest son of the deceased person invites the relatives and on the twelfth day distributes a minimum of 250 grams sugar to each member of the invited families and offers them a mid-day meal which includes rice, *dal* and *sabzi*.

They call it *kriya*. They do not invite a Brahman for the death rites.

Earlier the Sansis did not mention anything about their traditional occupation. They are now, by and large, settled people engaged in different professions. Men attend to various types of jobs such as polishing shoes, wage labour at construction sites, etc. Women go out for work early in the morning after finishing their household chores. They earn money by selling different kind of lace in open places, weigh people on weighing machines, or with their children collect waste paper, plastic bottles, small tin cans, etc., from the roads and lanes. They have a Panchayat to deal with various types of offence which deserve punishment or fines. The Panchayat (*sabha*) usually solves family disputes.

The Sansis are mainly Hindus. They worship Hindu gods and goddesses. Local gods and goddesses like Guggi Mai, Santoshi Ma are also worshipped. They celebrate festivals such as Holi, Diwali, Dussehra, and Lohri. The Sansis have special folkdances and songs of their own. At the marriage ceremony, women dance and sing together.

The Brahman, Kshatriya and Vaishya traditionally did not accept food and water from Sansis and food and water are accepted by them from the Chamar, Chuhra, Bazigar, Mochi, etc. Now the situation is changing. Due to poverty their boys and girls do not avail of the educational facilities provided by the government. The attitude towards modern medicine is positive. They get the facilities of immunization for the children and mothers through the *anganbadi*. Each family has more than five children who are an economic asset to them. The community taps are their source of drinking water. Some of them have battery-operated radio sets. They use wood and dry cow-dung cakes as fuel. Children get bread from the *anganbadi*. They have ration cards to procure rice, *atta* and sugar at subsidised rates.

V. Bhalla
Nupur Pathak

# SIKLIGAR

The word *sikligar* is of comparatively recent origin and derived from the Arabic *siqal*, a polisher or furbisher of metals. The Sikligars have descended from their blacksmith ancestors who were the descendants of Khimad, the third son of Thida. They used to make weapons in the service of Muslim invaders and rulers of India and acquired a great skill in this art. They used to sharpen and shine weapons by rubbing and using their own indigenous mixtures. The work of sharpening and imparting luster to weapons was called *saiqal* and persons who used to do it were *sikligars* or *saiqalgars*. According to some scholars, however, the Sikligars are an offshoot of the Banjaras.

Sikligars are identified at the regional level. They migrated from Rajasthan and perceive their distribution at the regional level. In Chandigarh, Sikligars are found at Manimajra (Sanjay Colony) and there are about 20 families who have migrated from Rajasthan (Jaipur) about 10 years back. Sikligars have some concentration at Randhawa Colony (Manimajra). There are about 25 families of the Sikligars at Maloya village. The Sikligar settlement from Attawa has been sifted to Dadumajra and Maloya colonies. According to the 1981 Census of India their total concentration in the Union Territory is 312 individuals with 163 males and 149 females. The dialect is a mixture of Punjabi, Marwari and Hindi. Scripts used are Gurmukhi and Devanagari. About a century back women used to wear a typical Marwari dress, which included a *ghagra* (skirt) and an *angi* (blouse) and silver ornaments around the neck and wrists. But at present they wear the outfits of the people of the province in which they live. The community has been recognized as a Scheduled Caste.

According to Sher (1966), their food is very poor in quality and standard. They cook all the vegetables and pulses in water though they put in them a lot of spices, salt and chillies. The Sikligars are especially fond of meat; *salteer khichri* is a favourite dish. They prepare *karah* (pudding) and *kheer* on auspicious occasions. *Sewian* is also a favourite dish prepared specially during the celebration of Gugga festival.

Both men and women are non-vegetarian and consume pork and eggs. Vegetable consumption is moderate. Cereals used are wheat, rice, *jowar* and maize. Mustard oil or vegetable *ghee* is the medium for cooking. They drink alcohol and take milk and milk products. They are changing from non-vegetarianism to vegetarianism.

The Sikligars have a number of *gotras* which regulate marriage alliances, indicate social status and ancestry. They are aware of the *varna* system and recognize their position in the *varna* order as Sudras. They are endogamous but follow exogamy at *gotra* and village levels. Acquiring of mates is done mainly by mutual consent, exchange or negotiation. Any violation of rules results in the excommunication or heavy cash fine. The age at marriage is twenty for girls and twenty-five for boys. Monogamy is the rule but polyandry is also observed. According to Sher (1966: 205-8) the marriage rites of the Sikligars are as follows.

The father does not demand any bride-price for his daughter from the parents of the proposed bridegroom. But the parents of the boy approach the father of the girl for paying him five to ten rupees as a *thaka* or *rokna* to affirm the engagement of the girl with their son. Marriage by service is called *kaul-parose.* All the members of the family of the boy go to the house of the parents of the girl and serve them. The marriage is considered to be finalised only when the parents of the girl agree to the proposal, satisfied with the service rendered by the family of the boy. The girl's father offers two rupees for purchase of a coconut and this indicates his approval. In doing so the Panchayat is taken into consideration. If the father of the girl keeps quiet for a long time the father of the boy takes the initiative of making the request through the Panchayat in the most humble way (*gal wich palla paa ke*). During the service period the prospective bridegroom has to observe certain rules. He cannot speak to his mother-in-law but he does so only if the father-in-law permits him to do so. Sometimes though quite rarely, the boy and the girl elope during the period of *kaul-parose.* For this however the father of the boy is heavily fined by the Panchayat.

In case of betrothal by *vatta* the *kurms* (respective fathers of the boy and girl) do not go to each other's house. They convey their intentions to the Panchayat which approaches each on behalf of the other and on getting their mutual consent, the members of the Panchayat get some money from either party for distributing sweets as celebration of the betrothal.

In all social activities the Panchayat of the Sikligars plays the most prominent and leading role. The Panchayat goes to the house of the girl's father, who welcomes them and seats them respectfully. Then after consultations with other members of his family he tells them the date of the wedding of his daughter. After this members of the Panchayat go to the house of the boy's father and inform him about the date, for which he thanks them. On the day of *gauna* the wrist-cord is to be tied to the boy and the body of the boy is rubbed with the *vatna.* At the time of bathing the womenfolk invoke blessings for him by placing coins under his feet. These coins are later given to the sisters of the boy. A similar ceremony of *gauna* is performed for the bride and songs suiting the occasion are sung. *Mehandi* is applied to the hands of both boy and girl on this day. It may be noted that the members of Kheechi sub-caste of Sikligars use myrtle only once in life and that is on the occasion of their marriage.

Three days after the *gauna* ceremony, the marriage party is to go to the house of the bride. The marriage party usually does not go to a distant place because mostly the marriage alliances of the Sikligars are made within the same encampment, or *dera*. Both men and women can go along with the *barat*. They will go beating a *dholki* and singing auspicious songs. The boy has a sword or *chhuri* or any other weapon made of iron in his hand. This is done to dispel the evil spirit. Such a weapon is constantly kept by the boy from the day of the *gauna* until the marriage ceremonies are completed. A *vedi* is erected before the house of the bride. The mother of the bride performs *arti*.

The rite of *phere* is performed on the very first day. In all seven *pheras* are performed. The bridegroom leads the bride in the first four *pheras*, whereas the bride leads the bridegroom in the last three *pheras*. The bridegroom passes four days living in the *vedi*. Food and other necessaries are supplied to him by his in-laws. On the fifth day the marriage party again comes. The bride is dressed in the best new clothes which her parents can afford. She is taken to the *vedi* and in the presence of all, she is seated on a cloth spread on the ground. The bride and the bridegroom are seated face to face and their *ganas* are united. Then a *chhala* or a rupee is thrown in a *praat* (platter) full of water and the bride and bridegroom are asked to catch it. It is thrown seven times and the one who catches it more often wins. This competitive game is great fun for all present there. In reality it is done to create some familiarity between the bride and the bridegroom.

Sikligars observe the Sikh functions, festivals, guruparabs and anniversaries and read and listen to the recitation of the *Guru Granth Sahib* with great devotion and respect, but in their social customs and manners they do not care much to observe Sikh ceremonies. Before partition, there was hardly any case in which the marriage rites were performed according to the Sikh religion, but now some of them have begun to ignore the marriage rites of their community and have been performing marriages according to the rules of Sikh religion.

The symbols of marriage include vermilion, bangles, *bindi*, toe-ring, ear-ring and nose-ring. Dowry in cash and kind includes utensils, clothes, but dowry is given according to economic status. Residence is patrilocal. Remarriages of widow and widower, male and female divorcee are permitted. According to Sher (1966: 215), 'divorce is practised among the Sikligars but neither the husband nor the wife can effect divorce without proper sanction of the Panchayat. The divorced woman cannot take any property of the husband, from whom she has been divorced, to her new husband or anywhere else. The children, if any, belong to her first husband and they are retained by him. The infants are allowed to be kept with their divorced mother till they become somewhat independent to live without her and are taken back by their real father. In some cases the mother is allowed to retain her children from her first husband, but they retain the caste name of their real father, irrespective of the caste of the new husband of their mother.'

Families are mainly nuclear or vertically extended. Avoidance and joking relationships and conflict and confrontation all exist in a family. Points of conflict and confrontation are usually property. All the sons inherit the property of their father equally. Succession is by the eldest son. Women have a low status, but they contribute to the family income. They have a role in the rituals and social functions and assist their husbands in their traditional occupation and make *taslas* (bowls) and other iron baskets. The life-cycle rituals, associated with the birth, naming, marriage or death are observed according to Sikh traditions. Those who are Hindu perform life-cycle rituals according to prescribed Hindu rituals.

The period of pregnancy is not considered unclean by the Sikligars and pregnant women perform all the household duties as long as their health allows them to do so. The woman is provided with especially nutritious food which she eats before the birth of the child. In some cases where a woman can not afford to remain in confinement for a long time, she begins her normal life of a housewife thirteen days after delivery. During this period they prohibit entry of all pregnant women into the house so that their voice may not reach the ears of the mother. The naming ceremony according to Sher (1966) is as follows:

> In naming the child, the child is never given the exact name of its father or the mother depending on its sex. The dead ancestors are also avoided as they believe that the child dies if he or she is given the name of some ancestor. Usually, the name of father's sister or *maama* (mother's brother) is preferred. The Hindu Sikligars offer a feast on the occasion of *nam* ceremony of their male children. When the child is about one year or one year and three months old, they shave the head of the child at the temple of any goddess at Seekar, Indergarh, or at Gurgaon.

The death ceremonies, according to Sher (1966: 226), have many aspects: An infant who is suckled on the breasts of the mother is buried. It does not matter whether the *kafan* (shroud for wrapping the dead) is old or new. At the time of death, the infant is embraced by the mother and she says, 'I forgive you all that you are or drank from me.' They do it in the belief that the soul of the dead may not remain indebted in the next world. Usually, they bathe the dead infant before wrapping it with the *kafan*, but if water is not available on the spot and the *dera* is on the move, the dead baby is buried without bathing. The infant is buried and the group resumes its journey onward. If the infant dies when the wandering group has already encamped somewhere, the following ceremonies are performed:

> The dead body of the infant is carried to the grave by the father, guardian or any other close relative. After burying him the men return to the encampment. Women do not accompany the dead body to the grave. Reaching the encampment, the person who lifts and carries the dead infant goes ahead of the other persons of the funeral procession and draws a line (*kaar*) crossing the path. By this they symbolically banish the soul of the dead. All the persons stop for a while after crossing the line and say,

'O, the soul of the dead one, do not cross this line and never come to our encampment.' They also throw water backward from above their heads and shoulders (*puthe hath da paani sutna*). Then they bathe themselves somewhere and return to the encampment. The father, mother or any guardian of the dead draws a line by sprinkling water with a green branch of some tree. All the persons who have joined the funeral procession cross over this line and enter the house of the deceased. The owner of the house gives one pinch of dry flour to each of them, which they put into their mouths and go to their respective houses. The father or the mother of the deceased infant goes to the grave on three consecutive days after the burial and places a *kauli* or cup full of milk at the grave and returns home. This milk is consumed by birds or animals. The milk cup is never taken back to anybody's house as it contains the ghost of the dead which may cause great harm.

In the case of the death an adult the following rituals are performed. They believe that one should die or resign from life in the lap of *dharti mata*. A dying person is laid down on the ground when he or she breathes his or her last. The dead body is very much dreaded by the Sikligars and is never left alone. So several persons remain awake to watch it so that the ghost of the deceased may not kill or harm anyone. The ghosts of the persons who die of dreaded diseases like small pox are feared much and several magical measures are adopted to control them. Similarly it is believed that the soul of the person who dies of an accident, becomes a ghost and is harmful for the tribe as well as for the family concerned, if not controlled with the help of incantations. The adult members are cremated. If a person dies after sunset, his body is not burnt in the night as the cremation always takes place in the day time, because the Sikligars believe that in the dark of the night the ghost of the dead may come to the house and may do some harm to somebody.

The dead body of the adult is bathed and wrapped in a new cloth sheet. Then some butter and a coin are put into the mouth of the dead, believing that the soul of the dead may not face difficulty on way to heaven.

The bier is prepared in a very simple way and the dead body is carried by four close relatives of the deceased to the cremation spot, *marhi*. Only men may accompany the dead to the cremation place. On the way the bier is placed on the ground and some small pots, *kujji,* are broken by close relatives of the deceased near his head. Again the bier is lifted by the closest relatives of the dead to carry to the cremation spot and the dead body is placed on the pyre which is set on fire by these relatives. All the persons keep standing around the burning pyre and when it is fully ablaze the eldest son, or any other close relative of the dead, gives *choke* (breaking the skull) with the help of a long stick. After this all the people depart . In the past the Sikligars did not have a permanent or particular place of burning their dead because they kept on wandering. However, in case of the nomadic Sikligars, they encamp for three or four days near the pyre because after three days the bone-picking (*phul chugne*) ceremony is performed. Three days after the cremation of the dead body the close relatives of the dead go to the *marhi*, taking a new empty pot and a vessel containing *kachi lassi* (a mixture of milk and water). The *kachi lassi* is sprinkled on the ashes of the dead body. So that the thirst of the soul of the dead is quenched.

The ashes are thoroughly searched and all the pieces of burnt bones are put into the empty new pot. Those who can afford, go to Hardwar to throw these ashes into the sacred Ganges. The poor ones throw them in any stream or river or in a canal's running water. The elderly Sikligars say that this ceremony of throwing the ashes in water has developed in the recent times.

The Sikligars' primary occupation is metalwork, such as metal polishing, making baskets of iron wire (*tokri*), making *tasla, chimta* (tongs), *khurchna* (scraper), *kadukas,* etc. Some also work in government offices and in private institutions. The males and the females visit neighbouring villages to sell their iron implements. Payment is made either in cash or in kind. Child labour exists. They have traditional caste council or Panchayat. Election to such bodies is by voice-vote. Their traditional Panchayat has a Pradhan who is elected by voice-vote for life. Social boycott, ex-communication, physical punishment, cash fine are the forms of punishment awarded by the Panchayat. Generally they try to arrive at an agreement in most cases.

The Sikligars who belong to Hindu religion worship according to their own religious traditions. They visit temples and celebrate festivals such as the Holi, Diwali, Baisakhi, Dussehra, etc. The Sikh Sikligars visit the Gurdwara and celebrate Guru Gobind Singh's birthday, besides other festivals. They have folksongs and folktales.

They traditionally accept water and food from the Sansi, Balmiki, Chuhra, Bania, Brahman, and Jat. They share the crematorium and religious shrines with other communities. Political leadership has emerged at the village level.

Formal education is favoured for the boys but partly favoured for the girls. Boys study up to the primary level. Their attitude towards indigenous and modern medicare is favourable. Couples prefer three to four children and family planning is acceptable. Drinking water is available within the locality in the form of hand-pumps. They use electricity, listen to the radio and occasionally visit cinema. Kerosene and *gobar* gas are the fuel, but some of them use only wood. The facility of ration distribution through fair-price shops is available and they get sugar, *atta*, rice through these shops. Their attitude towards saving is positive.

V. Bhalla
Achala Sood

# SOOD

The term Sood has been ascribed different meanings. In Persian *sood* means *beaj* or interest. According to Sud (1976: 6) the Persian word has nothing to do with the naming of the community. He thinks *sood* is of Sanskrit origin meaning a courageous and brave person, or a victor. It also means a man who can easily make progress. According to Ram Kashyap, a Sanskrit scholar, *sood* has been mentioned twenty-three times in the *Rig Veda*, the *Yajur Veda* and the *Atharva Veda*. Each time it has been used in the same sense and carries the same meaning.

The forms 'Sood' and 'Sud' both are used by the community. The Sud according to Ibbetson (1916 : 245-6) is a Punjabi caste, apparently an ancient one and almost entirely confined to the lower hills of erstwhile Punjab and the districts that lie immediately under them as far west as Amristar. The major places of concentration are Ludhiana and the neighbouring town of Machhiwara. Sud (1976) further states that there are references to 'Sood' in the *Bhavishya Puran, Upsarg, Ardhang Adhyaya.*

Tracing the history of the community, Sud (1976) writes that the capital of the kingdom of the Sood dynasty for eight generations was Pattan in Sind, and later it was shifted to Alwar. Finally Jai Singh, son of king Dahar, shifted his capital to Amarkot. On leaving Amarkot, Soods migrated to Sirhind, in 1316, under their Raja Rai Mehta Sood. After settling in Sirhind, the first difficulty the Soods had to face was that there were no other royal Rajput families in the area and it became a problem to marry their sons and daughters. They then divided themselves into sub-castes and started inter-marriages. According to Sud (1976: 48) their 52 *gotras* are as follows:

1. Dosaj, 2. Phakka, 3. Phassi, 4. Bourie, 5. Teji, 6. Sulhan, 7. Balagan, 8. Beri, 9. Varanwal, 10. Gopal, 11. Vgal, 12. Law, 13. Makaura, 14.Tagala, 15. Kajla, 16. Behal, 17. Dhanda, 18. Dhalli, 19. Gajri, 20. Jari, 21. Mahidhar, 22. Dhiri, 23. Moman, 24. Baddhu, 25. Poora, 26. Mohni, 27. Nehra, 28. Bharak, 29. Vassan, 30. Rohri, 31. Bodhi, 32. Dhookhi, 33. Bhokaha, 34. Mukandi, 35. Nandu, 36. Dadan, 37. Dhaunchak, 38. Dauli, 39. Gondal, 40. Sanwal, 41. Jandpaul, 42. Rudher, 43. Paul, 44. Dhoop, 45. Rara, 46. Gajja, 47. Udher, 48. Bhola, 49. Pharwaha, 50. Brahmi, 51. Mandal, 52. Mahiyer.

There are 96 Sood *gotras* according to the *Souvenir* (1984)

| | | |
|---|---|---|
| 1. Maria | 4. Gach | 7. Boury |
| 2. Karol | 5. Dhoop | 8. Bowry |
| 3. Bahu | 6. Gajri | 9. Chojar |

10. Bhagra
11. Mohindra
12. Phassi
13. Dosaj
14. Phakey
15. Gopal
16. Nehra
17. Kuthiala
18. Chuppa
19. Gondal
20. Langa
21. Kashyap
22. Myare
23. Chabb
24. Dhanda
25. Doegar
26. Goyal
27. Dhup
28. Bhakaya
29. Beri
30. Mayor
31. Udheir
32. Mehdoodia
33. Balagan
34. Dhuki
35. Moman
36. Mandal
37. Mahindra
38. Makara
39. Didi
40. Duli
41. Gajree
42. Chiamra
43. Dogar
44. Badoo
45. Ogal
46. Didian
47. Baghla
48. Madhudia
49. Medhdudya
50. Tokhey
51. Baboo
52. Fakay
53. Tezzy
54. Dhokhi
55. Meyaman
56. Beny
57. Ugal
58. Saluria
59. Bouri
60. Uder
61. Dadan
62. Dosajh
63. Bajwaria
64. Thokhi
65. Lashiaria
66. Cheerma
67. Jari
68. Chupe
69. Phake
70. Chimra
71. Balagan
72. Dhiri
73. Bharak
74. Banta
75. Phaka
76. Togal
77. Tagala
78. Facha
79. Salhuria
80. Chumra
81. Luseria
82. Mohindera
83. Parhak
84. Chimade
85. Udhair
86. Kalender
87. Mithoo
88. Kashap
89. Chali
90. Goel
91. Bhagre
92. Madudia
93. Casiva
94. Berri
95. Tugal
96. Tagale

Soods today speak Punjabi and Hindi. Literate persons use Devanagari and Gurmukhi scripts. Men dress in shirt, trousers, *pyjama*, and women in *salwar*, *kameez* and *dupatta*. Traditionally they are vegetarian though men have started eating eggs, meat and fish regularly. The Soods eat a variety of pulses and seasonal vegetables available in the market. The staple food of the Sood is *dal* and *roti*. They also eat rice. Groundnut oil is the cooking medium. They eat seasonal fruits like apple, orange, banana; milk and tea are the common non-alcoholic drinks consumed. The men occasionally drink especially on occasions like marriage. Elderly persons smoke hookah but the younger people prefer cigarettes. The Soods place themselves in *varna* order between Kshatriya and Vaishya, and their social position according to Ibbetson and Crooke (1896: 331-2) is 'very close to the Kayasths'.

Soods marry in their own community. They observe the rule of exogamy which bars marriage in the *gotras* of the paternal and maternal grandfathers. The *gotra* and the subcastes were named after the name of the ancestor or the name of the village they first settled in. Usually, marriages are arranged through negotiations by the parents. The married girls use *sindoor, bindi*, ear-rings, finger-rings, glass or gold bangles as symbols of wedded status. Earlier, child marriage was common but today the age at which a boy is married is twenty-one to twenty-five years and for girls eighteen to twenty-two years.

The parents give clothes, utensils, etc., as gifts at the time of marriage to their daughters. The bride usually stays with her in-laws after marriage. They rarely go to court for seeking divorce. Widow remarriage is permissible. Among the Soods, after the death of a wife, one can marry the younger sister of the deceased. They usually maintain joint families although today nuclear families are coming up. Joking relationship exists between *dewar* and *bhabi*. Avoidance relationship is maintained between father-in-law and daughter-in-law. All sons inherit property equally. The status of women is equal to that of men. Besides the routine household chores, the women take important decisions in the family and contribute to family income.

After the birth of a child, post-delivery pollution is observed for thirteen days in the case of a male and for forty days in the case of a female child. During this pollution period both the mother and the child are confined in a room where only women are allowed. The mother does not bathe during this period. On completion of this period the mother and the child take a bath for the first time after delivery. In the case of the birth of a boy Soods offer *laddus* to their neighbours. *Mundan* of boys is performed in a temple. On that day, parents of the child go to a temple to offer the child's hair and perform puja and *havan* when sweets are distributed among neighbours and relatives. The marriage ceremony is held at the residence of the bride and a feast is given by the bride's parents. A Brahman is called to perform the marriage rituals.

The Soods cremate their dead. During the pollution period, men (sons) worship their ancestors. On the fourth, a ritual called *uthala* is arranged. On that day all the relatives come and the male members (sons) take permission from their relatives to resume work from the next day. On the thirteenth day, a ceremony called *terhavin* is performed. The maternal uncle bears the expenditure of this ceremony. They invite a Brahman to recite *mantras* and perform death rites. Relatives are invited on the occasion and are served a meal consisting of *poori* and *sabzi*.

According to Ibbetson and Crooke (1896, 331-2), the Soods were 'today proverbially acute and prosperous men of business'. Many of them are educated and occupy high positions in the government service, in teaching, legal profession, administration, engineering and industry.

The Soods were both Hindu and Sikh. According to Ibbetson, the Hindu Sood 'wear a sacred thread made of three instead of six strands, and many of them practise widow marriage. With the exception of a few, who are Sikhs, they are almost all Hindus, but are, in comparison with the other mercantile classes, very lax in the observance of their religion.'

Today in Chandigarh, majority of the Soods are Hindu and only a few of them are Sikh. The Hindus worship Hindu gods and goddesses such as Durga, Siva, etc. They visit temples or Gurdwaras on religious occasions to offer prayers. The Holi, Diwali, Dussehra and Lohri are the festivals celebrated.

They traditionally accept food and water from the Brahman, Khatri, and the Bania but not from the Chamar, Chuhra, Sansi, Bazigar or Mochi.

They have access to modern medical facilities and education. Both boys as well as girls go for higher studies depending upon their means and performance. There is a marked awareness of various family planning methods. Couples prefer two or three children. Most of them have LPG as fuel source. Sarvdeshik Sood Sabhas are organized by the Soods in Chandigarh. To reunite and promote their community interests, they arrange conferences and collect funds, out of which scholarships are given to the needy students to pursue their studies. Widows and disabled members of the community are also helped by this Sarvdeshik Sood Sabha.

V. Bhalla
Nupur Pathak

# SUNAR

The Sunar, also known as Suniara, Zargar, Sawarnkar, Soni and Verma, are goldsmiths and silversmiths and also moneylenders lending money against gold and silver ornaments. Ibbetson (1916: 316) mentioned two sub-groups of Sunars, the Dase and Deswale. The former practise *karewa*. But the local community distinguishes the two sub-groups as Mad and Tank Sunar. Rose (1919: 442) stated that Bari Tank were originally Khatris but had changed the name of their section after taking to the profession of goldsmithy. The Mad Sunars were of pure ancestry and Tank Sunar were those who intermarried with other castes and were not pure. The Sunar today claim their origin from Vishwakarma and find mention in the *Valmiki Ramayan*.

Sunars migrated to the present habitat in this century from Uttar Pradesh, Bombay, Calcutta and erstwhile west Punjab. The common languages spoken by them are Hindi, Punjabi and Hindustani and the scripts used are Hindi and Arabic. The male members of the community can be identified by the *murki* (gold ear-rings) which they start wearing from childhood. The piercing of the ears is done for wearing the *murki*, at the time of the *mundan* ceremony of the children.

Sunars are occasional non-vegetarians. The womenfolk cook but do not eat meat. The quantum of vegetable consumption is on the higher side, but fruits are eaten occasionally. Wheat, rice and maize are the principal cereals. Among the pulses gram, *urad*, *moong*, *kulthi*, peas, beans, *masur* and *moth* are in common use. Groundnut and mustard oil are used as cooking medium. Consumption of roots and tubers is in plenty. The menfolk drink occasionally, mainly country liquor. They feel that liquor at least once a week is good for them, as it neutralizes the poisonous acidic smoke inhaled during the making of ornaments. They take milk and milk products like curd, *ghee*, butter, etc. Smoking of *bidi* and hookah, chewing of *khaini* (tobacco) and betel and the use of snuff are quite common. The changes in food habits include non-vegetarian to vegetarian food, decrease in the consumption of pulses and fruits. They now prefer *roti* to rice.

The Mad Sunar consider themselves higher than Tanks and trace their origin to the Rajputs. The function of these social divisions is to regulate marriage alliances. They are aware of and recognize the *varna* system and consider themselves Kshatriyas. The community's self perception and others' perception place them at the middle of the hierarchy.

Marriage is exogamous at the *gotra* level among the Mad Sunar but endogamous at all levels among the Tank with instances of cross-cousin marriage. Marriage after attaining adulthood and monogamy are the norm. Marriages are settled through negotiations by parents. Vermilion, glass bangles and nose rings are the symbols of marriage for women. Levirate (junior) and sororate (junior) are permissible. *Kanyadan* at the time of marriage is an important ceremony, performed by the girl's father. In the absence of the father, the elder brother, or one of the uncles performs *kanyadan*. Dowry is quite common and is paid both in cash and kind.

Rule of patrilocal residence is prevalent. Vertically extended families are quite common, followed by the nuclear type. Male equigeniture is the rule of inheritance and succession goes to the eldest son. Changes in the institution of marriage include observance of marriage symbols strictly and liberalization of the rules of re-marriage. Further, a reduction in the marriage rituals and minimization of their duration has been reported. Women are treated on an equal footing with men and they have a specific role in social, ritual and religious spheres.

*Reetan* is the pre-delivery ritual performed in the seventh month of pregnancy. Post-natal pollution and restrictions are observed. *Mundan* and *janeu* ceremonies are observed. *Janeu* and *murkian* for boys are given by the maternal grandparents. *Shagun,* a pre-marriage ritual, is observed. The girl's father along with the male relatives and friends visit the bridegroom's house and offer some cash and gifts to him. Marriage rituals are performed at the bride's residence. A feast is given by the bride's parents to the bridegroom's party. Consummation of marriage is at the bridegroom's residence.

The dead are cremated and three to thirteen days' pollution is observed. The bones are immersed in the water at Hardwar or Pehowa (near Kaithal), Haryana. Ancestor worship is observed during the *shradhs*. The rituals are becoming more and more expensive.

The traditional and primary occupation is jewellery-making. The secondary occupations are tailoring, and automobile repairing. The community is mainly involved in the craft of jewellery-making. The traditional caste council, elected through voice-vote, has a strong role in maintaining social norms. They can impose cash fines or boycott the members for flouting norms. Punishment can be imposed for offences like adultery and elopement. The statutory Panchayats exist and their function is to look after the welfare of the area. At the national level they have the All-India Sawarnkar Sangh, to fight for the rights of the Sunar.

The Sunar profess Hinduism and have family, clan and regional deities. They worship Jawala Devi, Mansa Devi, Vaishno Devi and other Hindu deities. For *mundan* they go to Tirlokpur. Durga Puja is the most important festival and is celebrated twice a year. During Navratri (the nine days period before Durga Puja) liquor and meat consumption is taboo. The Brahmans are the ritual specialists and perform birth, marriage and death rites beside worshipping the deities during festivals most of which have socio-economic significance. The folksongs sung by the women are the oral tradition. *Dholki* is in common use as a musical instrument and is often used by women for singing at the time of *mundan*, marriage, etc. Modern light music, viz., Hindi film songs are popular among the young.

The Sunars traditionally accept from and exchange water and food with all communities in the area except the Balmiki, Muslim, Chamar, etc. They give *sidha* food to the Brahmans on Ekadashi. Putative kinship in the form of *dharm bhai* or *bahin* exists. Inter-community marriages are prohibited for Mad but among Tank some cases have been reported. They share the water sources, religious shrines and their crematorium with other communities. Modern inter-community linkages are well-reflected as Sunars are also teachers, engineers, doctors, in the defence services and businessmen. Political leadership has emerged at local, regional and national level.

The attitude of the boys and girls towards education is positive. They normally study up to secondary level and drop out due to the lack of interest in their studies and also due to economic reasons. The girls have the additional reason as they have to help in the household chores also. They make full use of modern medicare and have a favourable attitude to family welfare programmes and prefer two to three children. They use modern methods of family welfare and these are preferred over sterilization. Fire-wood, coal, kerosene and LPG are the fuels in use. The mid-day meal scheme is availed of.

R. Malhotra

# TELI (HINDU)

The Telis derive their name from their occupation of extraction of *tel* (oil). Crooke (1896), Russell and Hira Lal (1916) and Ibbetson (1916) have given ethnographic accounts of the Telis. They are described as a functional group and most individuals who took up this profession might have been from different Hindu castes at the initial stages. During the Mughal period a large number of the Telis were converted to Islam. However, a few Hindu Telis survived. Mustard oil has a very significant role at various auspicious occasions especially birth and marriage. So the purity of the caste engaged in the pressing of oil was considered very important. The Telis of Chandigarh migrated from western Uttar Pradesh and Rajasthan along with their Rajput patrons and settled here for the last six to eight generations. The Hindu Telis are further sub-divided into Byahut (those who do not allow widow remarriage), Jaiswar (who derive their name from a town Jais in the Rae-Bareli district), Jaunpuri (who trace their origin from Jaunpur, Kanauria) and so on. The Umare derive their name from the Bania sub-caste. All the sub-castes of the Telis were endogamous. The Hindu Telis of Chandigarh have marriage alliances with those of Haryana and Punjab.

Earlier Telis, *kohlu* (oil press) was driven by a blind-folded ox round the oil mill. Some *kohlus* were driven by a single ox, others by two. However, some of the traditional *kohlus* have been replaced in Chandigarh by electrically operated oil mills.

The Hindu Telis speak both Hindi and Punjabi and use Devanagari and Gurmukhi scripts. The older generation can also read Arabic. Men's dress includes trousers, shirt and in some cases *pagri*, while women wear *salwar, kameez* and *dupatta.* They take vegetarian food which includes pulses such as *moong, moth, masur, channa* (grams), *urad*, peas and beans. Wheat and maize *rotis* are eaten during the summer and winter seasons respectively. The common seasonal vegetables such as peas, cabbage, cauliflower, brinjals, lady's finger are consumed by them. Diet includes onion, potato, tomato. The consumption of non-vegetarian food is limited to festival seasons, marriage ceremonies or the arrival of a special guest in the family. Non-vegetarian food includes eggs, mutton and chicken only. Cooking medium is mainly mustard oil. Milk and milk products including curd are eaten. Telis smoke *bidis* and cigarettes. Alcoholic drinks are generally avoided except on special occasions or the arrival of a guest. They are changing from non-vegetarian to vegetarian diet due to the high cost of meat. There is an increase in the consumption of vegetables. Telis can afford a limited intake of fruit.

The Telis are an endogamous community and are divided into exogamous *gots*. Some of the common *gots* are Jaqah, Bhetla, Arbi, Sohal, Lohar, Landra, etc. The names of the *gots* are derived from the village of origin or titles or nicknames. The various *gots* help to regulate their marriage alliances. Telis practise village and *got* exogamy. They avoid the *got* of the father, mother, *dadi* (paternal grandmother) and *nani* (maternal grandmother). The marriages of boys and girls are arranged when they are around twenty to twnety-five and eighteen to twenty-two years of age respectively. *Rokna, sagan, kurmai* and *byah* are arranged according to the convenience of both parties. The *sagan* which includes a rupee, clothes (trousers, shirt) and sweets is offered by the girl's father to the boy. The *kurmai* (engagement ceremony) is performed after the *rokna* or a day before the marriage ceremony and the *chunni charana* is performed at the residence of the girl. The boy's parents and his close relatives, especially the women, visit the girl and offer her clothes (*salwar, kameez* and *chunni*) and *sagan* in the form of eleven or fifty-one rupees, sweets and fruits. The date of marriage is fixed according to the convenience of both the parties. The paste of *baisan* (gram flour), *haldi* (turmeric powder) is prepared which is called as *batna* and is applied to the bodies of the boy and the girl in their respective houses two days before the actual date of marriage. The hair is washed with *dahi* (curd), for the ceremonial bath. All the ladies including sisters of the boy and girl join on this occasion and sing folksongs. Separate feasts called *roti* are offered by the parents to their close relatives and friends a day before the actual date of marriage. The *barat* including the members of the family, close relatives and friends arrives at the residence of the girl. The marriage party is offered a ceremonial reception and the *milni* of the close relatives of the couple takes place. The marriage ceremony consists of seven *pheras* according to the Hindu tradition. Dowry in the form of gifts of cloth, furniture, ornaments, is offered to the girl's parents at the time of the marriage. The married women use vermilion, bangles, finger and ear-rings and nose-studs as the symbols of marriage. The girl after marriage goes to the house of her husband and pays a visit the next day to her parent's house which is called the *phera pauna*. The girl then returns along with her husband and the nuptial ceremony takes place at the residence of her husband. Divorce with judicial approval due to maladjustment, lack of a male child or barrenness is allowed. Compensation (*kharcha*) is offered to the aggrieved party. Both husband and wife can approach the court of law for divorce. Widow and widower, male and female divorcee remarriages are allowed. Junior levirate and junior sororate remarriages are permitted.

The nuclear family is prevalent. Avoidance relationships between the *bahu* and *sauhra*, *jeth* and *bahu*, *sas* and *jamai* are observed. Joking relationship between *dewar* and *bhabi* is reported. Property, challenge to the authority of the elders are reasons for conflicts. The age at marriage has increased, and the rules of remarriage have become more liberal. Male equigeniture is the rule of inheritance. The eldest son gets the succession. Nuclear families are on the rise and extended families, though present, are on the decline.

Women attend to various household jobs apart from their role in rituals on special functions, such as the birth, engagement and marriage ceremonies. They look after the children. Yet their status is low.

The first delivery takes place at the residence of the girl's parents. Post-delivery restrictions and post-delivery pollution are observed for forty days. After this, the mother offers prayers to the Sun (*bahar badhana*) and after this she can enter the kitchen. Sweets and clothes (*salwar, kameez* and *dupatta*) are offered to the fatherand his mother by the maternal grandparents.

The Telis cremate their dead. The bones of the dead called *phul* are collected on the third day and are immersed in the Ganges at Hardwar. A pollution period of ten days is observed. On the eleventh day, the prayers for the peace of the dead are offered by the priest. Close relatives and friends are offered a feast. Rituals associated with birth, marriage and death ceremonies have become more expensive.

The Telis have their own traditional caste Panchayat/councils specially at Manimajra, Borail and Maloaya. The *Pradhan* of the caste council is elected by voice vote and is assisted by members, who help him to arrive at mutually acceptable decisions. They impose cash fines depending on the deed which includes theft or divorce. The statutory village Panchayat looks after the welfare of various communities. The members of the statutory Panchayat are elected by secret ballot.

As Hindus the Telis worship Rama, Krishna, Shiva, Ganesh, Vishwakarma and celebrate Holi, Diwali, Dussehra and Lohri. They visit the Mansa Devi temple at Manimajra. The men and women perform *bhangra* and *giddha* respectively on special occasions like wedding and use the *dhol/dholki* as the musical instrument.

The Telis accept and exchange water and food with Julahas, Lohars, Tarkhans, Ramdasias, etc., but not Sansis, Gandhiles, Dheas, or Bangales. The attitude to education is positive. The boys and girls study up to matric and primary levels respectively. They drop out from school due to economic reasons. They have benefited from the modern medicine. They prefer more than three children. Hand-pumps/piped water as the source of drinking water are available in their residence. Agricultural, industrial labour, animal husbandry are their mode of self-employment. Cow-dung cakes, wood and coal are the fuels. ICDS and immunization facilities are availed of.

Swaran Singh

# TELI (MUSLIM)

These Telis call themselves Malik. According to Rose (1919), 'The Muhammadan Teli claim descent from Baba Hassu, who invented the *Kohlu* or oil press and whose shrines are at Chauk Jhanda at Lahore and at Sialkot.' The Telis of Chandigarh maintain that they migrated to their present place from western Uttar Pradesh six or eight generations back. Their forefathers migrated along with Rajput patrons, whom they were serving in their original niche.

They speak Punjabi and Hindustani dialects with their kin group and use the Devanagari script. The men and women are occasional non-vegetarians. Their staple food consists of wheat, rice and maize. Gram, *urad*, *moong*, peas, beans and *masur* are the pulses used by them. Vegetable *ghee* is the cooking medium. Milk and milk products are consumed regularly. Smoking of *bidis*, cigarettes, hookah and indigenous cheroot is common among men. Use of roots and tubers is also common. Men consume alcoholic drinks occasionally. The increasing cost of non-vegetarian food has resulted in a change in food habits from non-vegetarianism to vegetarianism. Consequently, consumption of vegetables has increased. Consumption of fruit has also been adversely affected.

The *gotras* are the only form of social division. Rose (1919: 463) has listed 53 *gotras* in Gurgaon. However in Chandigarh, the informants could name only seven *gotras*, Nagah, Khetla, Arbi, Sehal, Hira, Lohar and Mandru. The function of these *gotras* is to regulate marriage alliances. Only one's own and one's mother's *gotras* are excluded for contracting marriage alliances. The community's self perception and others' perception place them at the medium level. Ibbetson (1916: 324) places them at low social standing almost at the level of Julaha. They are aware of the *varna* system.

Marriages are exogamous at village and *gotra* level. Telis approve sororate and levirate at junior as well as senior levels for widowers and widows. Adult marriage is the norm. Men marry at the age of twenty-two to twenty-five, women between nineteen and twenty-two. Parents settle the marriage of their children through negotiations. Monogamy is the normal form of marriage and the rule of residence is patrilocal. Bangles and the finger-ring, ear-ring and nose-stud are the symbols of marriage. *Mehar* is promised for future payment and is normally fixed at a minimum of rupees thirty-two and six *annas*. Dowry is given in cash as well as kind. Divorce is permissible with social approval. However, if the settlement made by the elders is not acceptable, people go to the courts. The reasons for divorce are adultery, maladjustment with the husband's family or between spouses. The latter factor is quite common as the cause of divorce. Compensation is given to the wife or her parents, whereby the *mehar* promised is paid, and gifts received at the time of marriage and other occasions are returned by the husband.

Traditionally only men could divorce but now under judicial recourse either party can divorce. The children are the liability of the father. Widow and widower remarriages are permissible. Similarly they can opt for sororate and levirate marriages. Increase in the age at marriage, observance of rules for remarriage, right of divorce to the women under judicial approval are some of the changes reported in the institution of marriage.

The nuclear family is the most common type. Avoidance relationship between the daughter-in-law and father-in-law and with husband's elder brother is reported. Similarly joking relationship has been reported with the husband's younger brother and wife's younger sister. Normally, conflicts in the household arise when the authority of elders is challenged or the freedom of youngsters is checked. Male equigeniture is the rule of inheritance and the succession goes to the eldest son. Changes in family structure include a rise in the formation of nuclear families at the cost of extended ones.

The status of women is low and the role of women is generally restricted to social, ritual and religious functions and attending to household work. They control family expenditure.

Only post-delivery pollution and restrictions are observed. Women are allowed in the kitchen only forty days after the birth of a child. Maternal grandparents give clothes and other presents (*tiyor*) to the mother and child. The *maulvi* is called for the naming ceremony of the male child generally. Circumcision is performed on the male children and a Nai (Muslim barber) does the job, or else a medical practitioner. Circumcision is normally done during March and May so that the wound is quickly healed. The *aqiqua* ceremony is performed; the community members are invited to feast and one or two goats are also slaughtered on this occasion. Marriage rituals are performed at the bride's residence where a feast is given by the bride's parents. A *walima* may be arranged by the boy's parents a day after marriage, depending on the financial position. Consummation of marriage is at the groom's residence.

The dead are buried and pollution period of eleven days is observed.

The Telis' traditional occupation was extraction of oil from oil seeds. But at present their main occupation is field, construction and factory labour in and around Chandigarh.

The traditional caste councils are quite strong among the Telis. There are many councils in the area known as *chauntras,* located in Burail, Malala, Manali, etc. The election to these *chauntras* is through voice-vote and the function of these caste Panchayats is to maintain the social norms of Teli society. Punishment includes social boycott and cash fines for violating social norms. Fines thus collected are utilized for the welfare of the community, in giving monetary help to the needy of the community or for repair of religious shrines, etc. Statutory Panchayats exist, but their role is restricted to the village welfare.

Professing Islam. they have family affiliation to a *pir*. The major pilgrim centres are Roje Sharif near Sirhand-Bassi (Punjab), Ajmer Sharif (Rajasthan), Sadhora Sharif (Naraingarh, Haryana), Manik Sharif (Ropar, Punjab) and Kaliyar near Roorkie (Uttar Pradesh). The sacred specialists are *maulvi* and *kazi*, whose function and role is to worship, perform life-cycle rituals, offer religious teachings, cure diseases and protect the people from the evil spirits. The festivals have great socio-religious significance. The major festivals are Shab-e-Barat, Id-ul-Zuha, Id-ul-Fitr, Jamat-ul-Vida.

Folksongs are sung only by women. *Dhol* (percussion instrument) and *been* (wind instruments) are the musical instruments in use. The effect of modern cinema music is quite strong on the new generation.

The Telis accept water from all other Muslims and caste Hindus. The communities with whom the food and water is neither exchanged nor accepted are the Chuhra, Chamar, Sansi, Gandhile, Dhea, Bangale, etc. Putative kinship exists. They share water sources with other communities. Landlord-tenant relationship exists in only a few cases.

Of late, the attitude of the boys and girls towards education is becoming positive. But they are educated up to secondary and primary levels respectively. This is because the boys help their father in economic pursuits and the girls have to render help to their mother in domestic chores. The attitude to modern medicare is positive and they make full use of the available facilities. Married couples generally prefer three children and mostly the women come forward for sterilization.

Drinking water through hand-pumps and pipes is available in every Teli household. Animal husbandry and petty contractorship are the only means of self-employment. Cow-dung cakes, kerosene oil and cooking gas are the fuel sources. ICDS scheme is availed of and immunization programmes are fully utilized. Public distribution system is well utilized and the attitude to saving is positive.

R. Malhotra

# BIO-ANTHROPOLOGICAL INFORMATION

The Union Territory of Chandigarh formed one of the nodal points in the All India Bio-anthropological Survey (AIBAS), conducted by the Anthropological Survey of India from 1972 to 1980 (Ghosh 1988). The demographic data revealed greater number of males (112 for every 100 females). Child-women ratio showed around 44 children per 100 females, which when compared with all India figures revealed the lowest fertility rate in the country, with the exception of Delhi. There are more unmarried males (56 per cent) than unmarried females (48 per cent). However the incidence of divorced/widowed females (4 per cent) is greater than those of males (2 per cent). The people of Chandigarh prefer small households (i.e. 1-6 members per family) as is shown by the high percentage (69 per cent) of small households. Only 31 per cent of males and 24 per cent of females are non-literate. Chandigarh has one of the highest rates of literacy both among males (69 per cent) and females (75 per cent). Chandigarh has returned the highest incidence of males with higher education (i.e. above matriculation) (19.33 per cent). Even among females (9 per cent) the incidence of higher education is high besides Punjab, Haryana, Delhi and Goa.

Kaul (1988) reported dermatoglyphic investigation of Bania, Brahman, Jat Sikh and Khatri. Incidence of loops is greater (52-7 per cent) in all communities studied than whorls (36-41 per cent). Pattern intensity index varies between 13-14.

Around a dozen studies are available on colour blindness. It is completely absent among Scheduled Caste communities like Balmiki and Ramdasiya (Sushil Kumari 1987); Bazigars and Sikligars (Sood 1988; Balgir 1982). The highest incidence of colour blindness has been reported by Agarwal and Bhalla (1981) among Brahmans (5.06 per cent) and the lowest among Jat Sikhs (3 per cent). Non taster gene (t) (PTC) has the lowest occurrence in Balmikis (31 per cent) (Sushil Kumari 1987), whereas the highest incidence is reported among Banias (57 per cent) studied by Agarwal and Bhalla (1981). The frequency of t gene is relatively low in Scheduled Castes (31-44 per cent) except Bazigars where Achla Sood reported values as high as 54 per cent. In caste communities it varies from 44 per cent to 57 per cent.

The Balmiki community has the highest occurrence of non secretor gene (ABH) (73 per cent) (Sushil Kumari 1987). Generally Scheduled Caste populations show higher incidence of non secretor gene (48-73 per cent) than caste communities (38-43 per cent). Agarwal and Bhalla (1981) reported the lowest values of non secretor gene in Brahmans (38.29 per cent).

G6PD deficiency is relatively high in the caste population of Chandigarh. It varies from 5 per cent found in Banias to 10 per cent among Jat Sikhs (Agarwal and Bhalla 1981). Sikligars, the only Scheduled Caste population studied for G6PD deficiency, have low incidence (3 per cent) (Balgir 1986).

ABO blood group system presents high gene B frequency (22-31 per cent) than gene A (13-19 per cent) in caste communities and Scheduled Castes. Interestingly in Scheduled Castes Balmiki and Ramdasiya, studied by Sushil Kumari (1987), have relatively high A gene frequency (30 per cent and 24 per cent respectively) than B gene (27 per cent and 24 per cent). Both the communities also show a high incidence of A gene (4 to 8 per cent).

M gene shows a wide range of occurrence (52-88 per cent), which is invariably above 50 per cent. Highest values of M are recorded in Jat Sikhs (88 per cent) by Bhatnagar (1967), though Agarwal and Bhalla (1981) reported only in 65 per cent of individuals studied by them. Lowest incidence of M gene is returned from Sikligars (53 per cent) studied by Balgir, 1986. Populations of Chandigarh have high frequency of $R_1$ haplotype. Maximum values have been recorded among Bazigars and Sikligars (69-70 per cent) studied by Achla Sood (1988). The frequency of r haplotype varies from 15 per cent (Bazigars) to 27 per cent (Sikligars). However Rh negative values show high frequency of d gene in Jat Sikhs (45 per cent) (Bhatnagar 1967), whereas, Sood (1988) reported lowest values of d gene (14 per cent) in Bazigars.

In serum proteins, Haptoglobins and transferrins have been studied by Sunderland *et al.* (1976) on Banias, Brahmans, Jats and Khatris. The Sikligars have been studied by Balgir (1986). $Hp^1$ gene occurs in 18-27 per cent of the populations studied. Sunderland *et al.*, (1976) have reported presence of $Tf^b$ gene in Khatri (1.39 per cent) only.

V. Kaul
N.K. Bagchi

## REFERENCES


Agarwal, S. and V. Bhalla, 'Serological differences among three North Indian Caste groups', *Indian Journal of Physical Anthropology and Human Genetics*, 7 (3), 1981, pp. 135-46.

Balgir, R.S., 'Etude de quelques traits morpho-genetiques chez les Sikligars de Chandigarh', L' Anthropologie, 85, 1982, pp. 313-20.

——— 'Serological studies in Gypsy Sikligars of north western India', *Human Biology*, 58 (2), 1986, pp. 171-86.

Bhatnagar, D.P., 'A study of blood groups and secretor factor among the Jat and Khatri Sikhs of Chandigarh (Punjab), M.Sc. dissertation (unpublished), Chandigarh: Panjab University, 1967.

Ghosh, G.C., 'All India Bio-Anthropological Survey', Calcutta, Anthropological Survey of India, 1988.

Kaul, J., 'A study of finger and palmar prints among Panjabi girls of Panjab', M.Sc. dissertation (unpublished), Chandigarh: Panjabi University, 1988.

Kumari, Sushil, 'Analysis of gene frequencies at six loci in Brahmins and Ramdasiya of village Burail (Chandigarh, U.T.)', M.Sc. dissertation (unpublished), Chandigarh: Panjab University, 1987.

Sharma, J.C., 'Blood and P.T.C. studies in Panjabis and the effect of age and certain eating habits on taste threshold, *The Anthropologist*, 6 and 7, 1959-60, pp. 40-66.

Singh, K.S., V. Bhalla and V. Kaul, 'The Biological Variation in Indian populations', National Series Volume X, Delhi: Oxford University Press, 1994.

Sood, A., 'A genetic profile of two endogamous communities of village Attawa (Chandigarh, U.T.)—Bazigars and Sikligars', M.Sc. dissertation (unpublished), Chandigarh: Panjab University, 1988.

Sunderland, E., K.S. Sahwney, R.A. Cartwright and J.G. Jolly, 'Studies of hapto-globin and transferrin types in four centres of Punjab, North India', *Human Heredity*, 26, 1976, pp. 16-24.

# GLOSSARY

| | |
|---|---|
| *abotava* | first feeding of cereals |
| *amrit chakhana* | baptism as per Sikh tradition |
| *anand karaj* | circumambulation round the holy *Guru Granth Sahib* during the marriage |
| *arjava* | candour |
| *akhand path* | non-stop recitation of *Guru Granth Sahib* |
| *arti* | prayer |
| *artia* | commission agent |
| *bachola/bichola/vichola* | mediator |
| *bahu/bahuti/nuh* | daughter-in-law |
| *bahin* | sister |
| *bakrid* | muslim festival of Id-ul-Zuha |
| *bara dolna* | death ritual |
| *barat* | marriage party |
| *bart* | fast |
| *barebadere* | ancestors |
| *barha* | death ritual performed on the twelfth day |
| *batna* | applying mixture of gram, flour, oil and turmeric as premarriage ritual |
| *bazi* | acrobatics |
| *beaj* | interest in terms of cash |
| *bedi* | a specially prepared place where marriage ceremony is held |
| *beeah* | marriage |
| *been* | wind instrument |
| *bhabi* | elder brother's wife |
| *bhagat* | devotee, follower of a sect |
| *bhai* | brother |
| *bhaijee* | Sikh sacred specialist |
| *bhalle* | fried cakes of pulses |
| *bhangra* | Punjabi folk dance performed by men |
| *bhiksha* | alms |
| *bhog* | completion of a religious ceremony |
| *bhooa/bhua* | father's sister |
| *bichoo* | toe-ring |
| *bindi* | forehead mark used as marriage symbol by women |
| *biradri* | endogamous unit/caste council |

| | |
|---|---|
| *chacha* | paternal uncle |
| *chaddra* | sheet of cloth used as coverlet |
| *chak* | potter's wheel |
| *chakreti* | stick used in moving the potter's wheel |
| *chalia* | a non-vegetarian feast, held on the last day of death rites |
| *challe* | finger ring |
| *chhatti* | ceremony observed on the sixth day of birth |
| *chauke charana* | after eleventh day of child birth, the mother starts normal kitchen work signifying end of birth pollution |
| *chauntras* | traditional caste council |
| *chawal* | rice |
| *chhaj* | winnowing fan |
| *chhamachhri* | the holiest day of the Jains |
| *chhuri* | knife |
| *chimta* | tongs |
| *chittron ki bochar* | shoe beating as a form of traditional punishment |
| *choli* | short blouse |
| *chunni* | head cover of ladies |
| *chutki/choti* | tuft hair, kept after head shaving |
| *chhilla* | post-natal confinemant till the completion of pollution period |
| *churian* | bangles |
| *dag dena* | to creamate the dead |
| *dada* | paternal grandfather |
| *dadi* | paternal grandmother |
| *dahi* | curd |
| *dai* | midwife |
| *dal* | pulse |
| *danda bhatti* | kiln |
| *dari* | a thick bed-spread |
| *dasai/daswan* | purificatory rite observed on the tenth day of death |
| *dastarbandi* | ceremony associated with the wearing of turban |
| *deor/dewar* | husband's younger brother |
| *desi ghee* | clarified butter |
| *dhol* | drum |
| *dholki* | percussion instrument |
| *dhona* | to wash |
| *dhotar* | piece of cloth to cover head |
| *diya* | earthen lamp |

| | |
|---|---|
| *dhoti* | coverlet |
| *dupatta* | head cover of ladies |
| *doli* | wedding procession of bride |
| *gauna* | consummation of marriage |
| *geet* | song |
| *ghagri* | loose skirt |
| *ghat* | river bank |
| *ghia* | gourd |
| *ghorian* | folk-songs sung by women on the occasion of boy's marriage |
| *ghund* | parda, veil |
| *giddha* | folk dance of Punjab performed by women |
| *gotra/got* | clan |
| *granthi* | Sikh priest |
| *gunti* | taking of cow's urine |
| *halal* | slaughtering of animals by Muslim butcher |
| *handi* | wide mouthed earthen vessel used for cooking |
| *hansli* | necklace |
| *har* | month of June |
| *havan* | fire sacrifice |
| *howkli* | anklet |
| *hookah* | hubble-bubble |
| *hukkapani band karna* | ex-communication |
| *iddat* | period from the date of divorce or death of husband among Muslims |
| *jamai* | son-in-law |
| *janeu* | sacred thread |
| *jantri* | astrological diary of the Hindus |
| *jeth* | husband's elder brother |
| *jeeja* | sister's husband |
| *jhapa* | wooden topper |
| *jharna* | iron sieve |
| *jotri jharanam* | post-birth ritual performed in Jains when child is three months old |
| *kabari* | one who collects and sells rags or waste materials |
| *karanvedh* | ear-piercing |
| *karva* | earthen container |
| *koonchi* | brush |
| *kabrisatan* | burial ground |
| *kabool* | agree |
| *kachcha* | food prepared in water |
| *kalabazi* | acrobatics |

| | |
|---|---|
| *kameez* | shirt |
| *kaj* | death ritual |
| *kanku* | turmeric |
| *kanyadan* | the ritual of giving away of girl in marriage |
| *kan bindhana* | piercing of ear |
| *karah* | sugar, ghee and flour mixed and cooked together into pudding |
| *kareva/karao* | widow remarriage |
| *karwachauth* | fast observed by women for the long life of their husbands |
| *keela* | pivot |
| *khadi* | handloom |
| *khatam* | Muslim death rituals |
| *khurpa* | a soil scraping implement |
| *kheer* | pudding prepared from milk and rice |
| *khurchna* | scraper |
| *kiria/kriya* | ritual signifying end of death pollution |
| *koka* | nose stud |
| *koodal* | digging instrument |
| *kohlu* | oil press |
| *koonda* | stone morter |
| *kashama* | forgiveness |
| *kuldevi* | family deity |
| *kundli* | horoscope |
| *kurm* | the respective fathers of the boy and the girl |
| *kurta* | long shirt |
| *laddu* | sweet balls prepared from gram flour, ghee and sugar |
| *lauki* | gourd |
| *lassi* | butter milk |
| *matkia* | big earthen pitcher with wide mouth |
| *maddia/marhi* | crematorium |
| *mahurat* | auspicious time, inauguration |
| *mama* | maternal uncle |
| *mandir* | temple |
| *mangni* | engagement |
| *mangal sutra* | marriage symbol for women—necklace |
| *mantra* | hymns |
| *mata dian bhetan* | religious songs sung in honour of Goddess |
| *matka* | earthen pot |
| *maulavi* | Muslim priest |
| *mehndi* | myrtle |

| | |
|---|---|
| *mehr* | bride price promised in case of divorce |
| *moorha* | sitting cushion/seat with cushion |
| *mundan* | tonsure ceremony |
| *muniari* | general merchandise |
| *murki* | ear-ring |
| *nai* | barber |
| *namaj* | prayer by the Muslim |
| *namkaran* | naming ceremony |
| *nani* | maternal grandmother |
| *nata* | widow remarriage |
| *nautanki* | a folk drama |
| *nikah* | Muslim marriage ceremony |
| *navaratra* | first nine days of Chaitra and Kartik |
| *pagri* | head-gear/turban |
| *pazeb* | anklet |
| *parda* | veil |
| *parwana* | notification |
| *pathis* | cakes of cow dung |
| *patti* | a piece of cloth placed over the lips during speaking or reading |
| *phul* | charred bones of the dead |
| *phul chugna* | collection of charred bones of the dead |
| *pir* | Muslim saints |
| *pinda* | ball of kneaded flour of wheat offered after the death of a person |
| *puja* | worship |
| *pukka* | food prepared in ghee |
| *pyala* | small cup used for drinking purpose |
| *pyjama* | trouser |
| *qalmi* | men of pen—writers |
| *rabri* | gram or jowar fermented in butter milk |
| *rajgiri* | masonry |
| *rajma* | beans |
| *rajoharma* | a kind of brushing stick |
| *rasm pagri* | wearing of new turban by the chief mourner during death purificatory rite |
| *raaslila* | Stage presentation of Lord Krishna's love life |
| *reetan* | pre-delivery ritual observed in the seventh month of pregnancy |
| *roti* | feast/staple food made of wheat |
| *sakora* | earthen pot |

| | |
|---|---|
| *sava maheena* | birth purificatory rite held after fortieth day of child birth |
| *safa* | turban |
| *sag* | spinach |
| *sali* | wife's sister |
| *salwar* | ladies' trouser |
| *samyana* | self restraint |
| *sanji* | image of goddess Durga |
| *sankalpa* | vow taken before any religious ceremony |
| *sas* | mother-in-law |
| *sarangi* | musical string instrument |
| *satarwan* | a post birth ritual held on the seventeenth day of death |
| *satsang* | religious congregation |
| *satta-batta* | marriage by exchange |
| *satwan* | a post death ritual held on the seventh day of death |
| *satya* | truthfulness |
| *saura* | father-in-law |
| *sevian* | vermicelli |
| *shagun/sagan* | marriage gift to a girl or a boy |
| *sharatnama* | contract in marriage |
| *sharbat* | lemonade, sweetened water |
| *shradh* | ancestor worship |
| *sidha* | raw food offered during rituals |
| *simla-mirch* | capsicum |
| *sindoor* | vermilion, a marriage symbol |
| *sootak/sutak* | post-delivery pollution period |
| *sota* | wooden rod used in rotating a potter's wheel |
| *sucha* | purity |
| *suhagrat* | consummation of marriage |
| *sunnat/khatna* | male circumcision |
| *surahi* | earthen pitcher with long neck, used for keeping drinking water |
| *swastika* | sacred mark used in Hindu rituals |
| *tastri chilm* | smoking pipe |
| *tabla* | percussion musical intrument |
| *thaka* | betrothal |
| *takhti pujan* | worship of wooden slates, used for writing by the children, initiation of education |
| *talaq* | divorce |

| | |
|---|---|
| *tamba* | a sheet of cloth used as a leg cover |
| *tara dakhaona* | to show the stars |
| *tasla* | iron bowl |
| *taula* | wide mouthed earthen pitcher |
| *taya* | father's elder brother |
| *teej* | festival of ladies held in the month of July-August |
| *tehrvin* | purificatory rite held on the thirteenth day of death |
| *tilak* | forehead markings |
| *tirni* | taxation |
| *tiyor* | cloth and other presentation given to woman by her parents in purificatory rite on child birth |
| *vanaspati ghee/dalda* | hydrogenated vegetable oil |
| *vartan bhaji* | gift exchange |
| *walima* | post-marriage feast arranged by the groom's parents |

# BIBLIOGRAPHY


Census of India 1951 *An Ethnographic Study*, Vol. XIII, *Punjab*, Part V (B) (ii) 25, Delhi, Manager of Publication.

Census of India 1961 'Special Tables on Scheduled Caste and Schedule Tribes', *Punjab*, Vol. XIII, Part V (A), Delhi, Manager of Publication.

Census of India 1971 Series I, *India*, Paper 2, Delhi, Manager of Publication.

Census of India 1981 Series 26, *Chandigarh*, Chandigarh, Directorate of Census Operation.

Chib, Sukhdev Singh 1977 *This Beautiful India: Union Territories of India*, New Delhi, Light and Life Publishers.

Clarenceo, Mc 1982 'Christianity in the Punjab', in *St. Thomas Christian Encyclopaedia of India*, George Manachery (ed), Vol. I, pp. 140-3.

Crooke, W. 1896 *The Native Races of India*, Delhi, Cosmo Publications (rpt 1975).

——— 1925 *Religion and Folklore of Northern India*, New Delhi, S. Chand & Co.

——— 1950 *Statistical Abstract Punjab*, Research and Reprint Division Public Relations Dept Punjab: 1947-50.

——— 1974 *The Tribes and Castes of the North-Western India*, Delhi, Cosmo Publications.

——— 1975 *The Castes and Tribes of North India*, Delhi, Cosmo Publications.

Fox, R.G. 1967 'Resiliency and Change in Indian Caste System: The Chamar of U.P.', *Journal of Asian Studies*, 16 (4): 575-87.

Gayor, W.A. 1985 'Notes on Bhatras', in *The Criminal Classes in India*. M. Kennedy (ed), Delhi, Mittal Publications.

Gould, Herold 1971 'Some Aspects of Kinship among Business and Professional Elite In Lucknow', *Contributions to Indian Sociology*, 5: 116-30.

Gupta, H.R. 1984 *History of the Sikhs*, New Delhi, Munshiram Manoharlal.

Ibbetson, D. 1916 *Punjab Castes*, (rpt. 1981), Delhi, Cosmo Publications.

Kainth, P.K. 1961 'Village Pattern Field Investigation', First and Final Draft. *Census of India, 1961*, Vol. XIX, Part 8-2 (ed), Baldev Raj, Delhi, Census Commissioner.

Kamboj, Bishan Singh 1980 *Kamboj Parkash*, Patiala, R.M.S. Azad Prakashan (in Punjabi).

Kaur, Jatinder 1977 'Marriage among the Christians of Chandigarh: Field work Monograph', M.A. 1977, Department of Sociology, Punjab University, Chandigarh (unpublished).

Kethkar, S.V. 1909 *The History of Caste in India*, Vol. I, New York Publications.

Latif, S.M. 1964 *History of Punjab: from the remotest antiquity to the present time*, New Delhi, Eurasia Publications.

Leonard, K.I. 1978 *Social History of an Indian Caste: The Kayasths of Hyderabad*, Delhi, Oxford University Press.

Mundanan, A.M. 1982 'Origins of Christianity in India First Centuries', in *St.*

*Thomas Christian Encyclopaedia of India*, George Manachery (ed), Vol. I, *Trid*, pp. 4-9.

Randhawa, Indira 1969 'Caste system among Sikhs', in *Illustrated Weekly of India*, 47:27.

Randhawa, M.S. 1968 *Chandigarh*, Chandigarh Government Press.

Rao, N.J. Usha 1981 *Deprived Castes in India*, Allahabad, Chugh Publications.

Risley, H. 1909 *People of India* (rpt 1969), Delhi, Oriental Books Corporation.

Rose, H.A. 1919 *A Glossary of the Tribes and Castes of the Punjab and North-West Frontier Province*, Lahore, Printed at the Civil and Military Gazette Press.

Russel, R.V. and Hira Lal 1916 'The Tribes and Castes of the Cultural Province of India' (rpt. 1975), Delhi, Cosmo Publications.

Shastri, Pandit Raghovara Mithulal 1931 'A comprehensive study into the origin and status of Kayasth', *Man in India* 11(2) 1931, pp. 116-59.

Singh, I.P. 1961 'The Study of ABO blood groups of Sainis of Punjab', in *Amer. Jr. Phys. Anthrop.* 19: 223-5.

Singh, Inder Paul 1977 'Castes in Sikh Village', in *Caste Among Non-Hindus in India*, Harjinder Singh (ed), New Delhi, National.

Singh, Khushwant 1977 *A History of the Sikhs*, Vol. I, 1469-1839. Delhi, Oxford University Press.

Singh, Soran 1987 *Scheduled Castes of India: Dimensions of Social Change*, New Delhi, Gian Publications.

Sher, Singh Sher 1966 *The Sikligars of Punjab* (Gypsy Tribe), Delhi, Sterling Publishers (P) Ltd.

*Souvenir* 1984 'Sood Mela-cum-Sammelan', Chandigarh, Sood Bhawan Trust (Regd), Sector: 44-A.

Stewart, A.C. 1905 'Notes on Bhatras', in *The Criminal Classes in India*, M.Kennedy (ed), Delhi, Mittal Publications.

Sud, Madan Mohan 1976 *Origin and History of Soods*, Chandigarh, Chandigarh Sood Sabha.

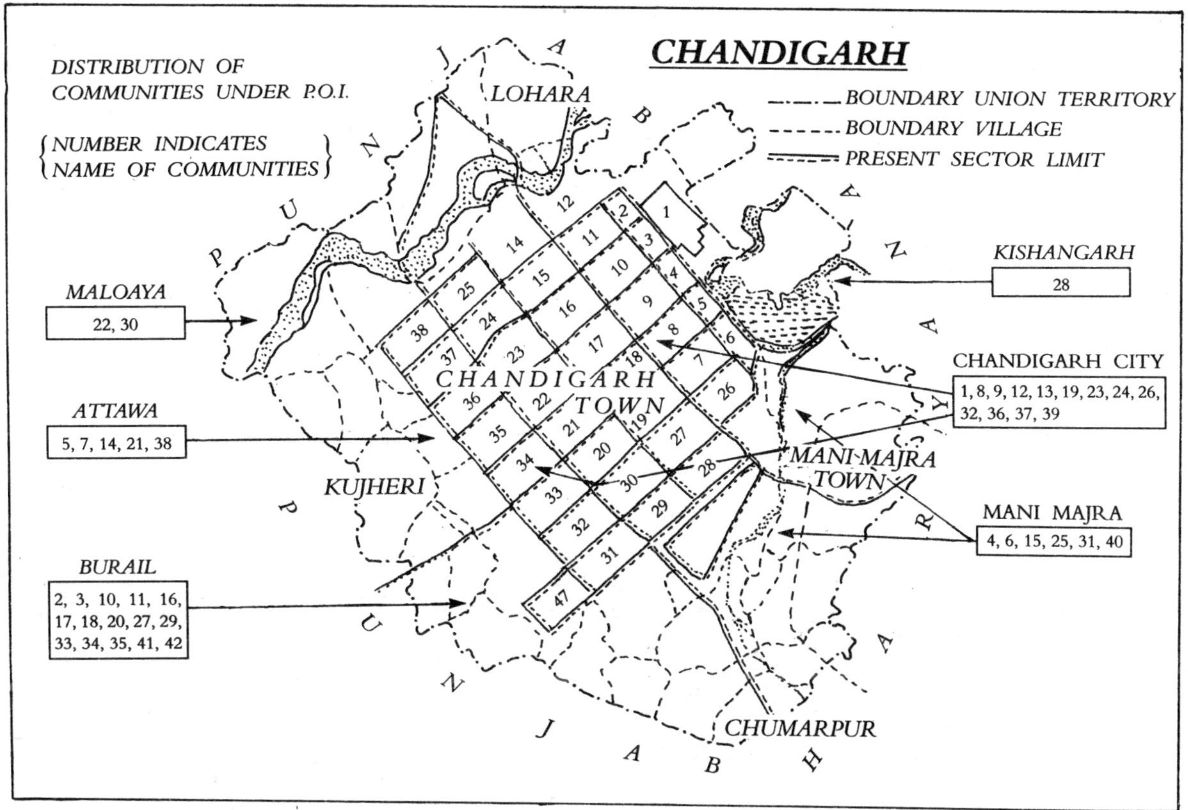


| | | | | | | |
|---|---|---|---|---|---|---|
| 1. Ahluwalia | 2. Balmiki | 3. Bania (Aggarwal) | 4. Barhai | 5. Bazigar | 6. Bharai | 7. Bharbhunja |
| 8. Bhatia | 9. Bhatra | 10. Brahman | 11. Chamar | 12. Chhimba | 13. Christians | 14. Dhanak |
| 15. Dhea | 16. Dhobi (Muslim) | 17. Gaderia | 18. Gujjar | 19. Jain | 20. Jat | 21. Jheewar |
| 22. Julaha | 23. Kamboh | 24. Kayastha | 25. Khatik | 26. Kumhar (Hindu) | 27. Kumhar (Muslim) | 28. Labana |
| 29. Lohar | 30. Mazhabi | 31. Mirasi | 32. Nai | 33. Noongar | 34. Penja | 35. Rajput |
| 36. Saini | 37. Sansi | 38. Sikligar | 39. Sood | 40. Sunar | 41. Teli (Hindu) | 42. Teli (Muslim) |

# INDEX